# A DEATH IN ZAMORA
Third Edition

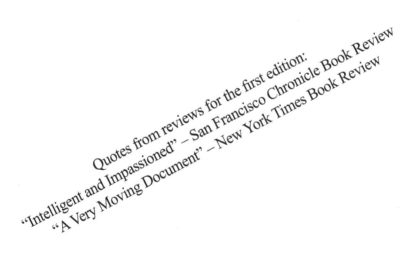

Quotes from reviews for the first edition:

"Intelligent and Impassioned" – San Francisco Chronicle Book Review

"A Very Moving Document" – New York Times Book Review

# A DEATH IN ZAMORA

## by
## Ramón Sender Barayón

Introduction by Mercedes Esteban Maes-Kemp
Prologue by Paul Preston
Essays by Helen Graham &
Francisco Espinosa Maestre

A third English edition with new materials from
the Spanish Edition published by
Post-Metropolis Editorial, Madrid (2017).
Spanish translation by Mercedes Esteban-Maes Kemp
Royalties donated to the Recuperación de la Memoria Republicana

Calm Unity Press
Third Edition
ISBN 978-1-882260-30-0
© 2018 Ramón Sender
First Edition 1989 University of New Mexico Press
Second Edition 2003 Calm Unity Press

# CONTENTS

I dedicate this book with love and admiration to me sister Andrea (Sister Benedicta OSH) who has carried Amparo's image faithfully all her life.  Her pilgrimage to Spain proved to me that it was possible to re-enter the land of our dreams, and her confrontation of our childhood nightmare set me an example of emotional and moral courage.  This story is as much hers as mine.  Without her love, her tender concern and prayers, I would not have been gifted with the invulnerability to disaster that I seem to enjoy.

*Judith Levy- Sender, the author's American stepmother Florence Hall Sender, and the author.*

I also dedicate this third edition to my beloved wife Judith Levy-Sender, whose skills as translator during interviews in Spain, and her ongoing emotional support, made this book possible.
She fulfills all my dreams.
Also, in loving memory of my stepmother, Florence Hall Sender. Without her total devotion to my father (despite his divorcing her twice), he would not have lived long enough to return to Spain in triumph.

## Spain, July 1936

Nationalist lines
Republican lines

PROLOGUE
by Paul Preston

One of the least well-known aspects of the repression against civilians carried out by the partisans of the military coup of 17-18 July, 1936, is the scale of their deliberate and systematic persecution of women. Throughout the rebel zone, many women were murdered, and thousands of the wives, sisters and mothers of executed leftists were subjected to rape and other sexual abuses, the humiliation of head shaving and public soiling after the forced ingestion of castor oil. Murder, torture and rape were generalized punishments for the gender liberation embraced by most liberal and left-wing women during the Republican period. Moreover, for Republican women, there were also the terrible economic and psychological problems of having their husbands, fathers, brothers and sons murdered or forced to flee into exile, which often saw the wives themselves arrested in efforts to get them to reveal the whereabouts of their men folk.

They and the many women who had been politically active faced appalling conditions in overcrowded, unhygienic prisons in addition to being subjected to sexual abuse. Those who came out of prison alive suffered deep life-long physical and psychological problems. After the war, the cruelty visited upon women was justified by a Catholic rhetoric of 'redemption.' As well as confiscation of goods and imprisonment as retribution for the behavior of a son or husband, the widows and the wives of prisoners were raped. Many were forced to live in total poverty and often, out of desperation, to sell themselves on the streets. The consequent increase in prostitution both benefited Francoist men who thereby slaked their lust cheaply and had the satisfaction of being reassured that 'red' women were whores, a fount of dirt and corruption.

For a variety of reasons, more is known about the sexual violence carried out in the areas of Andalucía and Extremadura than the experiences of the relative minority of Republican women in the north of the country. The extent to which the abuse of women was official policy can be deduced from the speeches of General Queipo de Llano who was effectively the viceroy of southern Spain. His daily broadcasts were larded with sexual references, describing scenes of rape with a coarse relish that encouraged his militias to repeat such scenes. In one notorious speech, Queipo de Llano declared: "Our brave Legionaries and *Regulares* have shown the red cowards what it means to be a man. And incidentally the wives of the Reds too. These Communist and Anarchist women, after all, have made themselves fair game by their doctrine of free love. And now they have at least made the acquaintance of real men, and not milksops of militiamen. Kicking their legs about and squealing won't save them."

Comparable atrocities were committed in the north, albeit on a lesser scale and without the kind of publicity generated by Queipo de Llano. For instance, the conquest of Catalonia by Franco's forces throughout the second half of 1938 witnessed horrific scenes of sexual violence. Similar abuse occurred in the deeply Catholic areas of Castille and León. One of the most extreme examples of the impact on innocent women of the repression was what happened in the town of Zamora to Amparo Barayón, the wife of Ramón J. Sender, world-famous novelist and anarchist sympathizer. Sender and his wife and their two children were on holiday in San Rafael in Segovia at the beginning of the war. He decided to return to Madrid and told Amparo to take the children to her native city of Zamora where he was sure they would be safe. In fact, on 28 August, despite being a Catholic, she was imprisoned along with her seven month-old daughter, Andrea, after protesting to the military governor that her brother Antonio had been murdered earlier the same day. This thirty-two year-old mother, who had committed no crime and was barely active in politics, was mistreated and eventually executed on 11 October 1936. Her crime was to be a modern, independent woman, loathed because she had escaped the stultifying bigotry of Zamora and had children with a man to whom she was married only in a civil ceremony.

Amparo was not alone in her suffering. Kept in below-zero temperatures, without bedding, other mothers saw their babies die because, themselves deprived of food and medicines, they had no milk to breastfeed them. One of the policemen who arrested Amparo told her that 'red women have no rights' and 'you should have thought of this before having children.' Another prisoner, Pilar Fidalgo Carasa, had been arrested in the nearby town of Benavente because her husband, José Almoína, was secretary of the local branch of the Socialist Party. Only eight hours before her detention and transport to Zamora, she had given birth to a baby girl. In the prison, she was forced to climb a steep staircase many times each day in order to be interrogated. This provoked a life-threatening hemorrhage. In her account of her treatment published in exile, "A Young Mother in Franco's Prisons," she wrote: 'Because I continued hemorrhaging, I constantly begged the warden for help. Finally she brought the prison doctor Pedro

Almendral who came merely as a matter of form. Upon seeing my suffering, he commented that "the best cure for the wife of that scoundrel Almoína is death." He prescribed nothing – neither for myself or my baby.' Numerous young women in the prison were raped before being murdered.

Pilar Fidalgo's horrifying memoir is not the only evidence of what happened to women in Zamora. The investigation into what happened to Amparo, *A Death in Zamora,* is a deeply moving, indeed deeply upsetting book, which has much to say to several different audiences. The central narrative relates the quest by a man brought up in the United States to discover the fate of his mother in Spain during the Civil War of the 1930s. The author, Ramón Sender Barayón, is the son of Amparo and Ramón J. Sender. His mother was a target for the military rebels simply because of her husband's fame as a left-wing novelist. He had told her to flee to Zamora on the assumption that she would be safe there with her Catholic family. In his book, the painful and painstaking research of Ramón Sender Barayón finally managed to reveal the truth of how she was imprisoned, tortured and eventually executed – her horrendous fate typical of what happened to many innocent women at the hands of the supporters of General Franco.

In that sense, the book is a major contribution to the history of right-wing atrocities during the Spanish War. In addition, however, the subsequent story of how Ramón J. Sender took his two children to the United States and then virtually abandoned them is also harrowing in its way and makes for a tragic psychological drama that will be of interest to many people not concerned with Spanish history. The story of Ramón Sender Barayón's quest also happens to be a riveting detective story. I read the first edition of this book nearly twenty years ago and immediately bought several copies to give to friends, and their reaction confirmed my own. One of the people to whom I sent a copy was my great friend and mentor, Herbert Southworth, who worked in Washington during the Spanish Civil War for the last Republican Prime Minister, Dr Juan Negrín. Herbert was very excited when he read the book and told me that he remembered going with his friend, the great journalist Jay Allen, to meet Ramón and his sister, Andrea, at the docks in New York when they arrived.

*A Death in Zamora* is a unique contribution to the quest for the memory of what happened to innocent civilians during the Spanish Civil War. It is an important and neglected masterpiece that I am delighted to see republished in Spain.

*The only surviving photograph of the author's parents together,*
*taken by a street phototrapher in Madrid, circa 1935.*
*Courtesy of Doña Concha Sender.*

# THE GHOSTS OF CHANGE
## Helen Graham

In 1989, the North-American-raised son of the renowned writer, Ramón J. Sender, published in English an account of his own and his sister's search for the remains of their mother Amparo Barayón, and for the truth about her imprisonment and extrajudicial murder. She was killed at the age of thirty two, in Zamora, in the early months of the Civil War. The book, called simply *A Death in Zamora*, charts an extraordinary odyssey in time, space and memory. On his return to Spain in the 1980s, the son (also called Ramón) discovers he has a whole extended Spanish family, which emerges like a lost continent, bearing with it the history, the traces, the unquiet ghost of his mother Amparo. This book can, then, be read as a detective story in which the protagonist, Ramón *hijo*, struggles to assemble and make meaning from the many fragments and shards of knowledge, which he holds dear – and which have come down to him from the – literally shattering – experience of Civil War: of family decimation, and his own refugeedom and exile. When he starts his journey of discovery, he lacks – precisely because of what has happened – much of the interconnective, granular detail of past events. And because he left Spain as a small child, nor does he fully understand the society and culture in which the life-changing events occurred. But what he does not lack is a larger knowledge – conscious and subconscious – of what happened, and of the damage done.

Amparo Barayón's story is a harrowing story – in some of its dimensions almost Gothic in its horror, and striking even among the many tens of thousands of wrenching personal and family tragedies the civil war produced. In historical terms, one can, nevertheless, put it straightforwardly: Amparo was a victim of the extrajudicial killing triggered by the military coup of 17-18 July, 1936.

The history of that violence across Spain has now been researched and its broad parameters are well established. A great deal of its detail is also known, so for readers who want to learn more, they may refer to the specialist works of history. Ramón's book offers something else, something crucial, which is not so easily gleaned from the history books: his is a testimony of the devastating psychological impact of past violence on one family, and of its lasting toll on the peace of mind, and memory, of all those caught up in it but who remained alive. For this reason above all *A Death in Zamora* is an extraordinary book. It deserves to be more widely read and known, whose full and devastating meaning lies as much in how it is told as in what it relates.

But the historical events themselves also bear further consideration, in particular because they tell us something crucial about the nature of that 'war,' something that is still often occluded and that we would do well to understand in present times too. Zamora was a place where the military rebels were in control from the outset of the coup, where there was no armed resistance, and no real political resistance to speak of either – in short, one would be hard-pressed to find a 'war-situation' at all – at least not according to a conventional definition of 'war.' Nor was there any collapse of public order: the Falangist, Carlist and other volunteers of the right could at any time have been disciplined by the military authorities who underwrote public order in Zamora from the beginning. Not only did this not happen, but instead, as the historical research of the 1990s and 2000s has shown, the military actively recruited thousands of civilian vigilantes to carry out a dirty war behind the lines. It was in this 'war' that Amparo Barayón was killed. Those targeted by the rightist vigilantes tended to be people associated with the reforming Second Republic against which the military rebels had risen.

But this connection was not always, or even mostly, about the party politics or the organizational affiliations of those targeted. Many, such as Amparo, had none – but they were nevertheless associated, almost symbolically, in the case of progressive, or 'new' women such as Amparo, with the broad process of change then in course in Spain, as across Europe, and of which the Republic itself was as much a symptom as a cause. In this process of change, social hierarchies across Europe were becoming more fluid, sometimes even undergoing a degree of leveling. For those who supported the military coup in Spain they did so because they were fearful of what all this might mean for themselves – not only loss of wealth and status, but also the loss of a familiar world, or of other certainties, whether religious or gendered.

Out of this there emerged a fear-saturated desire to 'put things back' in what was perceived as their rightful place. This became one very powerful dynamic of the vigilante violence, as it was of the orchestrated Francoist repression, which came after. Precisely because of this psychological dimension, the violence also engulfed many relatively affluent and propertied people, middle class professionals, such as the

Barayón family in which three siblings, including Amparo, were extra-judicially murdered. These included Amparo's much-loved younger brother, Antonio, who was an engineer by profession and 'disappeared' by vigilantes because he was perceived as 'having ideas' and thus was insufficiently bound by the rules and strictures of conservative provincial small town life. The military rebels and their civilian supporters were redefining 'the enemy' as entire sectors of society, which were perceived as 'out of control' because they were already beyond the control of traditional forms of discipline and 'order.'

Emancipated women in particular became a target of this fear and loathing. Amparo Barayón wasn't just killed in lieu of her husband the famous, Republican-identified journalist and writer, Ramón Sender, as some commentators have previously claimed. She was killed, as it were, in her own right, as a modern woman. In 1930, as Spain's monarchy crumbled, Amparo had, aged 26, left the conservative provincial backwater of Zamora and gone to Madrid, the 'big city' to become independent. She found work as a telephone switchboard operator - a new employment opportunity that was itself an indicator of Spain's burgeoning modernity. In Madrid she supported herself, she lived independently, educating herself both politically and culturally, and there she met Sender and began living with him without marrying – which was quite something for those times, even in urban metropolitan Spain, for Madrid was not Berlin or Paris.

Although back in Zamora they would not have known about Sender, nevertheless the very fact that Amparo had spread her wings inspired horror among the pillars of provincial society and also among conservative members of her own family who saw her as on the road to damnation. It would be some of Amparo's own extended family members, determined to ensure fulfillment of their own bigotry masquerading as prophecy, who it seems became implicated in denouncing her to the military authorities in Zamora in late summer 1936. It was the existence of many similar conservative social worlds, which allowed the emerging Francoist order to speak of their victims as 'impure' or 'diseased,' an 'anti-nation' – all of which echoed the lethal social Darwinist thinking then causing havoc across Europe as a whole. Highly charged echoes of this unreconstructed social Darwinism also emerge in the early twenty-first century Zamora press polemic over Amparo, which Francisco Espinosa documents here in the Appendix, and that perfectly demonstrates how the time of Franco has, in crucial ways, not passed in conservative, small-town Castile·

Even though these extrajudicial murders of the Civil War happened a long time ago in chronological terms, for many of the relatives of the unquiet dead, Amparo's included, it seems like only yesterday: for all the years that have elapsed, they are still *'muertes recientes'*. 'Recent' because there is still an awkwardness and unresolved quality attaching to them: as Ramón the writer and protagonist puts it at one point, it is as if Amparo were still 'unshriven.' In part, the answer to why this is so lies in the four decades of Franco's dictatorship that came after, and in the dictatorship's toxic distortions of the Civil War, which it disseminated for its own political purposes, supported in this by substantial sections of society, for political reasons, as well as self-interest. Even so, that forty year dictatorship now lies a further forty years in the past. Yet still the Republican dead remain 'unquiet,' indeed awkward. Mention of them causes unease, even embarrassment, as if the victims – which is to say those who speak for them or commemorate them in the civic memory movement today – were somehow themselves to blame for 'disturbing the peace' of the present.

It is an odd situation, which inevitably leads observers – including many historians – to ask what this strangeness is actually about. Put simply (though resolving it will not be simple at all) it has to do with the fact that, in raising/commemorating the Republican dead so they can be recognized as victims of a Civil War's internecine violence, they implicitly call into question the definition of another category of Civil War dead. These are the people – both civilians and military personnel – who were killed extrajudicially in Republican territory during the war and that the Francoist state declared at the outset to be the 'pure' victims, enshrined and mythologized as the 'martyrs' of its 'new Spain.' As victims like Amparo now pass from *el olvido* to History, so too must those other, Franco-commandeered dead make a journey – to pass back from myth to the terrain of History; to become not martyrs, but simply other victims of the internecine violence of a Civil War. This is the 'problem' raised implicitly by the civic memory movement, and that remains unresolved in Spain today. The logjam on the road from myth to History is not only, or even principally, about the 'awkward' dead like Amparo, excoriated by Francoism, but about those other dead, cemented at the foundations of the Francoist order and whose 'disinterment' as such remains blocked by something powerful, even today, in 2017. Ramón has now laid his mother Amparo to rest, in the knowledge of History; but the 'martyrs' too need to return to History before today's society in Spain can be said to have reckoned with its difficult past and be ready to move on.

Helen Graham
Professor of Contemporary History
Royal Holloway, University of London

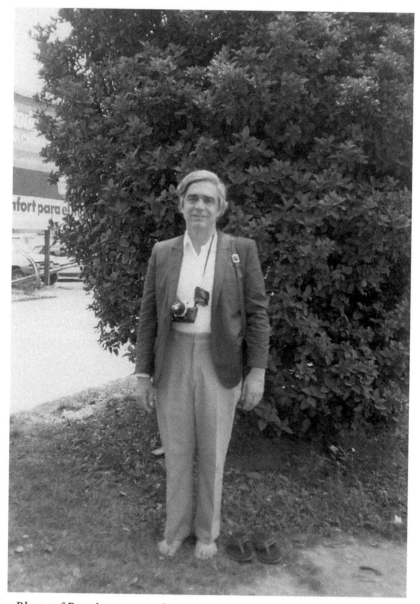

*Photo of Ramón stepping barefoot on Spanish soil in San Sebastián.*
*photo by Elizabeta Sauzon*

## AGAINST OBLIVION
### Mercedes Esteban-Maes Kemp

There is a photograph of my cousin Ramón that captures an eloquent gesture. He appears smiling, in travel attire, camera hung around his neck, relaxed. His feet are bare, stepping on Spanish soil for the first time in 45 years.

It is the moment of his return, and the beginning of his search for the memory of his mother, Amparo. He had to wait for the death of his father, Ramón J. Sender, to undertake his journey into the past. I like to imagine that in his jacket pocket he carries his father's list of his Spanish family's addresses that he had refused to reveal. There is no doubt that Ramón padre was a strong-headed man, an Aragonese, but it is hard to believe that he kept his children in ignorance throughout his whole life. He also forbid my mother, Magdalena, Amparo's niece, with whom he kept a copious correspondence, from revealing the tiniest detail of the fate that overcame their mother. The story that Ramón tells in this book is, for me, the story of my family; fundamentally a story of women remembered by women. Ramón met many family members during his search, but it is notable that primarily it was the women who helped him recover the memory of his mother, and his wife Judith's fluent Spanish that translated conversations with them.

I grew up in Spain during the years of the dictatorship. In my house there was no silence. My mother spoke of Amparo assassinated, of her orphaned children escaping to France, of great-uncles Antonio and Saturnino also assassinated, their bodies abandoned no one knows where, of her own years in jail after the war. At home, we spoke of everything, but we knew, without anyone saying it, that these things were not talked about in public. She also told us of Amparo, a marvelous pianist, adored aunt, modern woman, independent, who went to Madrid to make her own life and marry a great author. Amparo, who promised her favorite niece, my mother, to bring her to Madrid with her so that her uncle Ramón could teach her journalism, who was a lively woman, who was courageous, laying down guidelines for a better future for women within the framework of the Republic.

It was not to be. The horrendous dictatorship reserved the hardest repression for women. We passed from the jurisdiction of our fathers to that of our husbands. We did not have any rights, no possibility for economic independence. We were indoctrinated into a demure and submissive model of femininity. In the midst of this dark panorama, Amparo's memory shone as an example of another way of being a woman. The act of her vile assassination, like that of so many other women victims of the violence of the war, clamored for restitution.

Ramón, barefoot, setting foot on Spanish soil in 1983 for the first time in forty-five years, is the catalyst for the recovery of Amparo, both in his personal memory and for Historical Memory. His journey through the memories of the women in his family gave back to him both his mother and his Spanish lineage. But things did not stop there. Years later, in 2004, Dr. Ana Isabel Almendral, granddaughter of doctor Almendral, whose performance in Zamora's women's prison is cited in *A Death in Zamora*, published slanderous statements in the local press about Amparo. Ramón, his sister Andrea and their Spanish family responded with indignation. We do not know even today if the slander was by mistake or malice, because the slanderer never replied. Maybe it's true that 'whoever remains silent, admits guilt.' But this time we were not alone.

Two distinguished historians, Paul Preston and Helen Graham, joined us in our campaign to maintain the dignity of Amparo's memory. They have already written about Amparo in their books about the Civil War, and the great value of her son Ramón's testimony, which they repeat in this book. They lent us their unconditional support, writing letters to the press and advising us. Another great historian of the War and the Repression, Francisco Espinosa Maestre, documented the case in his book, *Silencing the Messenger.* The full text of the chapter, 'Amparo Barayon: History of a Slander,' is republished as an appendix to this edition. The author of the slander never took back her words. We did not win, but we convinced.

Amparo is always present in our family's memory, but she has also become a part of our Historical Memory. This book forms a part of the process of recovery, as necessary and current today as in the moment it was written.

Mercedes Esteban-Maes Kemp
Cornwall, August 2017

*The only photograph of our mother Amparo Barayón that my sister*
*Andrea and I ever saw as children, a passport photo taken in 1936 with*
*a dedication to Ramón Sr. on the back.*

"You have with you," a voice replied, "the melancholy of the crimes you did not commit, and of the deaths you will not know how to face."
from *The Affable Hangman,* Ramón J. Sender

When a person is totally lost, all directions seem equally possible.  To find my way home, I found it necessary to fall into my true self.  As I fell, I found myself regressing backwards through my life towards the blinding moment of conception.  At a certain point, I encountered an unknown woman, my mother Amparo.
"I loved you, and then you were gone," I told her, and began a twenty-year pilgrimage to her side.
This pilgrimage, also one of self-discovery, has brought me to where I now address all beings, starting with myself, with kind regard and compassion.

Ramón Sender Barayón

# Chapter 1
# Beginning the Search

When my father Ramón J. Sender died, I thought all the horrible secrets of his life and my own would be buried forever. What really happened to his first wife, my mother? How had she died? Why had she been taken away? Who killed her? My father, the obvious person to ask, always refused to divulge any details. He was considered the greatest Spanish novelist of his generation, winner of the National Prize in literature in 1936, the Critics Prize in 1967, the Planeta Prize in 1969 and nominated for the Nobel Prize in literature in 1970.

My father died of a heart attack on January 15, 1982, just two weeks before his eighty-second birthday. Sorrow, relief, anger – awash in conflicting emotions I prepared to fly to his last home in San Diego. How could he die with so many unresolved questions hanging between us? And shouldn't I alert the Spanish family? I telephoned cousin Magdalena in Málaga with whom I had spoken for the first time only a month earlier. When her distant voice came on the line, I struggled to explain what had happened in my long-forgotten native tongue.

"*Papá es muerte*," I said.

My fiancée Judy, in fluent Spanish, quickly corrected me. "*Papá se murió.*"

I had said, "Papá is death."

Yet in a sense I had spoken the truth. Throughout my life, my main contact with my father had been through his translated novels: *Pro Patria, Seven Red Sundays, Counterattack in Spain, Chronicle of Dawn, The Sphere, Dark Wedding*, and *The Affable Hangman*. They all contained a macabre element, a fascination with death that struck an alien tone within the "happily-ever-after" American culture that absorbed me as a four-year-old refugee from the Spanish Civil War.

Throughout Franco's reign, my father refused to return to Spain. For thirty-five years his books went unpublished in his native land. In 1974, when the dictator lay more dead than alive in a final lingering illness, Papá allowed two visiting Spanish novelists to coax him home for a series of literary conferences. He was greeted in Barcelona by enthusiastic crowds. "Sender Returns!" shouted the newspaper headlines. His life work, comprising more than eighty books, finally overcame the years of censorship and a new generation of Spaniards began to read them.

On his return to California that year, he told me that wherever he went, two bodyguards took the hotel rooms on either side of his. He had received death threats from both the far right and far left, and he warned me not to visit Spain under my own name. Yet I knew I had to go back. The thread through my particular labyrinth led across the Atlantic to Zamora, a provincial town in Old Castile. Must I risk my life to find it? To find her?

Time and again I begged my father for details about the death of my mother Amparo Barayón, but all my efforts proved fruitless. I even turned to hypnosis in the hopes of retrieving my earliest memories. One night a phrase in Spanish floated up from the depths: "*No quiero ir*" – "I don't want to go." I repeated it over and over. During the next hours I seemed to experience an event that had occurred forty years before, Amparo's arrest and my abandonment for what seemed a whole night.

The few definite facts I knew could be summarized simply: My mother Amparo had trained as a concert pianist, and my father had established a reputation as a novelist and radical journalist. They had met in Madrid, where I was born during "Red October" 1934. According to my father, machine-gun fire from outside the clinic doors greeted my birth. Meanwhile, in the northern province of Asturias, General Franco's foreign legionnaires and Moroccan mercenaries were slaughtering the striking miners and their families.

One year later, my father had won the National Prize for literature for his novel *Mr. Witt among the Rebels*. The announcement had been made just before my sister Andrea was born and the February 1936 elections swept the Popular Front coalition into power. In July, army garrisons rebelled all over Spain. We were trapped in San Rafael, a resort that suddenly became the front lines. My father escaped on foot to the Republican zone and joined the militiamen defending the mountain pass. Over the next months he was promoted through the ranks to serve briefly as Chief of Staff for General Lister, who commanded the best-trained Republican army. What happened to us and to Amparo lay buried under the changes of cultures, languages and families that followed.

A few weeks before Franco's victory in April 1939, my sister Andrea and I arrived in New York with our father. Andrea had just turned three; I was four-and-a-half. Papá, penniless, placed us with an American war correspondent's family, Jay Allen, who he had met in Spain. He departed at once for Mexico City to try to find a job and a home within the growing colony of Spanish exiles there. With the fall of the Spanish Republic, his passport was invalidated and he applied for Mexican citizenship. Because we were not Mexican residents, he could not include us on his application. As of that moment, we became children without a country, technically illegal aliens in the United States.

Meanwhile, Mildred Kenyon, a volunteer with Spanish Refugee Aid, searched for someone who would take us for a longer period, preferably someone with a house in the country where the fresh air and tranquility would help us regain our health. She appealed to her friend Julia Davis, a woman who craved children without being able to bear them. Julia first agreed to take us for six weeks. The months became years, until it was tacitly understood she would bring us up as her own children.

Julia Davis, blue-eyed and slim with graying blonde hair, was thirty-nine years old at the time. Ever since her college days, she had devoted herself to writing. She gathered Nordic tales into a children's book, and followed it with a novel for young adults on the Lewis and Clark expedition entitled *No Other White Men*. In the 1930s, she worked as a journalist for the Associated Press in New York, and for the Children's Aid Society. Unable to place two of her older "cases," she adopted the children herself. Her novel, *The Sun Climbs Slow*, chronicled our informal adoption into her family. In it she presented a fictional version of Amparo's fate: a Spanish mother dies shielding her little boy from an exploding bomb. It was a gentle way, and the only way my father would permit, of telling us we would never see Amparo again.

Julia gave us all the love she would have given children of her own. By the time our father visited one year later, we could no longer understand Spanish.

"You have stolen my children," he said to her sorrowfully when she drove him from the airport to her home in rural Westchester County.

"*Je suis perdue*," Julia replied in French, their only common tongue, and proceeded to lose her way on a road she had traveled for years.

We remained with her even after Papá returned to the United States and married a woman named Florence Hall. They lived in New York for a few years, then settled in Albuquerque where he taught Spanish literature at the university for fifteen years. Occasionally we spent Easter vacations together, but our relationship remained distant.

What had happened to Amparo? All that remained of her was a full-face passport photo of a Spanish woman on the first page of our childhood album. It was a woman we did not recognize. She stared out at us with a sober expression, her brown, curly hair trimmed to her earlobes. I possessed only one other piece of evidence. As a teenager I found a yellowed, typewritten scrap of a press dispatch in Spanish in the box that contained our father's letters. It mentioned the death of Ramón J. Sender's wife and quoted her last letter

> For myself, I do not care because I die for you. But the children. What will become of the children? In haste,
>
>                 – Amparo

The summer I was fourteen the note disappeared. My father was visiting at the time, and my sister thought he destroyed it. However, I remember carrying the fragment in my wallet as a boy, fondling it occasionally, sensing it contained a clue to the mystery of my mother's disappearance. Unfamiliar with Spanish at the time, I was unable to fathom it. Already fragile and torn, it may have finally decayed into shreds or I might have replaced it only to have Papá dispose of it.

As I grew older, I developed a curious obsession: whenever I visited a library, I invariably searched for one name: Amparo Barayón. I found a few references to "the wife of Ramón J. Sender" listed among examples of the ferocity of the fascist beast, but that was all. Constancia de la Mora referred to her in her book *In Place of Splendor*, a passionate account of a mother caught up in the Spanish people's struggle to save their Republic. It was one of the few books written by a woman about that era. According to someone who knew her, the author never forgave my father for abandoning us.

Despite my father's disapproval, I resolved to confront my only relative in North America, the one sister of my father who had emigrated to Mexico City. As small children, my sister and I had lived with her briefly in Barcelona. She showed me a photo of Amparo holding me as a newborn. My mother was dressed in a kimono with an orchid appliquéd to the shoulder. Here at last was the woman I remembered. The long slope of the cheek, the tenderness of her expression – in three-quarter profile she looked totally different from the person in the passport snapshot. The photograph became for me the first tangible evidence that Amparo had ever existed. I was almost forty years old.

My desire for her continued to grow. But to rediscover Amparo, I would have to battle my father's refusal to discuss her. On several occasions he specifically warned me not to write anything about her. I had no choice but to go back to the libraries.

At the University of California, I searched through yellowed newspapers whose pages crumbled under my fingertips. The Spanish headlines named battles whose outcomes had been decided long ago. The photographs showed crowds with their fists raised, their exuberant faces reflecting the optimism of the summer of 1936 when it seemed that the fascist generals would not conquer the nation. I raised my own fist, clenching the tendons tightly. A thrill went down my arm and my chest expanded. My body remembered that gesture! What word did I want to shout?

Perhaps I would find Amparo's face among the marchers carrying banners and chanting victory slogans. Somewhere a newspaper must have mentioned her. I fought the urge to search earlier issues and limited myself to late 1936 and 1937. Her name would not appear in the headlines but on some inside page. I was looking for some confirmation that Amparo ever lived. Even in the midst of Civil War Spain, her story could not have gone unnoticed.

Other images evoked a wordless emotion. On a poster, a muscular, bare-chested reaper bent over a sheaf of grain, blood pouring from a bullet wound in his thigh. In front of him, a grim, shirtless militiaman raised his shotgun to his cheek, ready to fire in defense of his brother. "COMRADES! WORK AND FIGHT FOR THE REVOLUTION!" the message read. I knew I had seen it before as a two-year-old walking through the rubble of a Barcelona street. I threw my fist in the air and whispered, "*Canalla!*" That was the word I wanted, the Spanish equivalent of "scum." I was addressing the Italian and German crews of the bombers that saturated Barcelona with death in March, 1938, eighteen raids in three-and-a-half days. According to my father, we were there. Thirteen hundred dead and at least two thousand wounded.

Another photo portrayed an empty-faced mother seated with her unsmiling children in a Madrid subway during an air raid. She might have been Amparo. In yet another photo, a line of women stood waiting for their milk ration. Their eyes stared into the sky to scan the insignia of the approaching planes, frowning against the light in an all-too-familiar grimace. Ours? Theirs? Thirty seconds later the street might disappear in an appalling thunderclap that would shear bones from their sockets and bury them under tons of debris. "Cousin Mary," "Aunt Pilar," "little Teresa"... each mutilated corpse threw a family into mourning.

After an unsuccessful search in Berkeley, I visited the Hoover Institute of War, Revolution and Peace at Stanford University, a good source of Spanish Civil War documents. In the basement archives, the librarian steered me to the collected papers of a certain Joaquín Maurín. His name seemed familiar. I opened a file box and understood why. It contained a foot-high stack of correspondence between him and my father spanning more than fifteen years.

Joaquín Maurín, founder of POUM, *Partido Obrero de Unificación Marxista*, the Trotskyite party in Barcelona, was taken prisoner early in the war by the fascists. Presumed dead by the Madrid press, a brigade was named after him. When he was found alive in a fascist prison, his wife worked ceaselessly to free him until at last he was released in a prisoner exchange. They settled in New York where he started a literary agency and invited my father to submit articles for the Latin American press. His first letters were stiff and formal, as were Papá's replies. After they met, a warmth developed that blossomed into a close friendship. On one page he wrote:

> "I have met your children and am enchanted! Andrea is
> a charming lass, sparkling with grace and intelligence.
> And Ramón Jr. is a boy who speaks English but over-
> flows with Spanishness in every direction."

Why don't I remember this extraordinary man? I have a vague recollection of "somebody Spanish" visiting us at Julia's. Perhaps my lack of interest concealed the depths of my pain.

In his letters, Papá occasionally mentioned me whenever I managed to elicit parental pride, such as when some music of mine was performed. Another letter told why he resigned himself to our remaining in Julia Davis's care, although the most important reason was "too romantic to tell." A long document locked in a Wall Street safe deposit box supposedly explained everything:

> "In it I also tell why the Russophiles – by Moscow's
> order – proposed to terminate certain people, among
> them myself. The others they killed after the War. So far
> they have not dared to try anything with me but it could be
> that they will try something. If something does happen to
> me, I don't want my children to suffer a new shock after
> having known so many in the Civil War... I will never

forgive the Communists who have deprived me of one of the most legitimate satisfactions of life: to live with my children... Obviously the children know nothing of this. The document must be withdrawn and published on the day anything happens to me. However I believe the Communists have renounced their original intentions and now follow what they call 'civil death,' that is to say, a systematic persecution by slander, etc."

If only he had told us his reasons for not living with us! Or sat down one day and gently described our mother's life and ultimate sacrifice. The truth of Amparo's disappearance, no matter how horrifying, would have allowed the natural mourning process to heal us. All we needed was some acknowledgment, some proof of her existence. But he saw us as living reminders of his greatest failure, his inability to protect his wife and children. He never understood our need to know the reality behind the evasions and lies.

Gradually I built a bibliography for my story. There was my father's book *Counterattack in Spain* which described his life during the last six months of 1936. Surprisingly, he did not mention Amparo's fate until, at the translator's urging, he included a few brief paragraphs on the final pages. According to what he once said, the heroine of his untranslated novel *The Five Books of Ariadne* was modeled after my mother. I began laboriously translating segments of Ariadne's life story. How much was truth, how much fiction? Over the telephone, my sister mentioned a woman character in another novel, *Seven Red Sundays*, supposedly based on Amparo. Also she gave me an address for Amparo's niece Magdalena in Málaga, someone she had met during her own brief return to Spain a few years earlier. This was the first time I had tried to contact someone there myself.

How strange my letters must have seemed. The family only remembered a screaming, distraught two-year-old whose terror reflected their own. Yet if I could reach back through time and tell that child the true story of what happened, perhaps the cloud that obscured my memory of Amparo would dissipate. And perhaps the perpetual winter that existed between my father and me would thaw before death froze our estrangement permanently. I had to try, in spite of his insistence that I leave Amparo's story alone. After all, my affliction was also his.

In the final pages of *Counterattack in Spain* he writes: "I will silence, extinguish, the voices that rise clamorously and imperatively in my heart." Yet the very next sentence states: "I have always written with an indefinite need to reveal myself completely and impartially to the world and not to conceal myself." But were not Andrea and I part of the world? Was it a Spanish trait not to show emotion before your children?

A year before my father's death, I brought my fiancée Judy to San Diego for Christmas Eve dinner so that she could meet him and Florence. Since their divorce a dozen years earlier, they had evolved a unique routine: Papá lived as he pleased in his own apartment, while Florence hovered anxiously from her flat four blocks away, where he came for his meals. That evening, talk at the table had focused on the New York publishing scene.

"It's being ruined by the Jews!" he rumbled. "The last Jewish author of any consequence was King David of the Psalms."

I begged to differ, feeling that at the very least the remark showed no respect for Judy's Jewish background.

"Come on, Papá!" I coaxed. "I can think of at least a dozen Jewish authors worth a mention."

But the old man was in no mood to be contradicted. He stomped away from the meal and fired his parting salvo from the front door.

"Now I know, Ramón, that you have not yet grown up!"

When we returned home, I wrote him a conciliatory note saying that life was too short for misunderstandings. But his final remark, measuring my maturity by my disagreement with his prejudices, remained in my thoughts. The reality of the situation was just the opposite: in order to "grow up," I would have to confront his refusal to give me information about Amparo.

I returned to the Hoover Library with renewed determination. On its shelves I found some of Franco's historians' texts. They gave their version of what they labeled "The Crusade." One book detailed hundreds of atrocities complete with photos of corpses in every conceivable state of dismemberment and decomposition. It was a hard book to look at. In America we are so protected from death that its emptiness confronts us like some alien creature. In Franco's death book, the faces reflected surprise, horror, ravished suffering, even an ethereal ecstasy as if in the last throes the pain had been transmuted into something indescribably blissful. But the dead children were the worst, open-mouthed with white tags around their necks.

I waited impatiently for my cousin Magdalena's answer, but nothing arrived. I decided to try telephoning. Why hadn't I ever called Spain before? During the Franco years I had become habituated to believing it was out of bounds. I listened with deep emotion to the operators speaking in Spanish. When was the last time I had heard Spanish women talk? There was so much drama in their inflections, so much humor as well. Amparo had worked for the telephone company. Perhaps her voice was like theirs, throaty and expressive. At last Spanish Information replied there was nothing. Either Magdalena's number was unlisted or she did not have a phone.

Meanwhile I pleaded with my father for material relating to Amparo. In response, I received a copy of Magdalena's first letter to him. But the letter did not come from him, but from Florence, who guarded his privacy as zealously as she could:

July 5, 1945

Dear Tío Ramón:

Only a few minutes ago I turned on the radio (Voice of America)... and you were speaking on the subject of American independence – such a blessed people! You have spoken the truth to the entire world – this tremendous truth of ours – which so many search for in vain. Many years ago I read an announcement of your death in the papers and my mother and I wept without ever having known you. But during a journey to Madrid in the winter of 1944, a countryman of yours gave me the stupendous news that you were living in Mexico City. I've searched for information about your whereabouts ever since. Finally today we learned unexpectedly that you are in New York.

You cannot imagine the joy and emotions we experienced... What worries us most of all is the fate of Monchín (little Ramón) and Andreita. Mamá often thinks about them and cries. It would bring us incredible joy to know that they are well. I was eleven years old when <u>that</u> happened. I remember Monchín was terrorized by the bombers, and cried in the hallway of the house at the slightest noise. My mother took him to a children's specialist. Both my parents suffered much at not being able to shelter them in our home.

I lament that I cannot give you the reasons for this at this time. I will never forget the last time I saw Amparo. She was happy and talked about taking me to Madrid with her. She always was my favorite aunt and she loved me a great deal. When I showed her some things I had written, she said to me: "In a few days we'll go to Madrid. You'll come with me, and your uncle will teach you how to become a good journalist, you'll see!" I remember everything she said so clearly. Since then, I have written more serious things, which are at the point of costing me dearly. We have here the letters Amparo wrote. They are to me the best pages anyone has ever written. You cannot imagine how anxious we are to hear from you! Mamá doubts that you will reply. She says that it's possible you believe we are of the same sort as that man Sevilla.

I have so many things to tell you! Since I was eleven when my eyes were opened so brutally I have done nothing but hate. For my family and for me especially your respect means a great deal. I spoke several times with the woman who took Monchín to San Juan de Luz, trying to find out something, but... she knows nothing and remembers nothing. Do not delay in answering, please, and give me news of the children. Is it possible they are in Barcelona as Mrs. Maximina supposes? If so, give me their address and I will immediately go to see them. We have to do what is possible to give back the greater part of what they lost. He who committed the frightful deed has died. Wretchedly. Receive the love and the sincere admiration of all the family, especially from your niece.

Magdalena

The letter gave me more information than I might have hoped. What did "the same sort as that man Sevilla" mean? Who was "Mrs. Maximina?" The woman who took me to San Juan de Luz? And who "died wretchedly" for what frightful deed? Had my father received copies of Amparo's letters from Magdalena? There was some sort of cover-up going on. He might have been exiled from Spain for thirty-five years, but I had been exiled for a lifetime from even a single remembrance of my own mother!

A few weeks passed, my father still unwilling to communicate further. It was November 18, 1981: the forty-fifth anniversary of a date carved on the ornate family mausoleum in Zamora. In San Francisco where I lived, the sky sparkled a crystalline blue after the rainstorms of the weekend. This should be a day of darkness, I thought, of counting up blood debts still unpaid. I decided to try to find Magdalena again, this time by telephoning Zamora Information at two in the morning Pacific Standard Time.

Her letter had mentioned three brothers and sisters plus an oblique reference to an Antonio, so I asked the Zamora operator for Antonio Maes Barayón. Names repeat from generation to generation in Spain, so the odds were in my favor. She gave me a number! I dialed but the lines were busy. When I got through an hour later, the person who answered was the wife of Ignacio Maes Barayón, one of Magdalena's brothers. I identified myself to this friendly voice and asked for Magdalena's married name and phone number. She gave me both and inquired after my father. I replied that he was well. Family stuff. How I hungered for these simple conversations that spoke the language of the blood!

Magdalena was out when I called, but a maid told me she would return from her shop at lunchtime. She had a shop! It was now four a.m.. on my clock; one in the afternoon there. Maybe this was why Spain existed only in my dreams, because they were awake while I slept. When I phoned at six, Magdalena answered. At last I was speaking to my mother's niece! My poor grasp of Spanish did not allow me to express my feelings fully.

"I spent a week with your father in Madrid and told him everything," she said. "I gave him letters, documents and photos."

"Papá cannot talk about these things," I explained. "Do you have copies? Did you receive my letters?"

Magdalena's voice was not too friendly. "He does not want anyone writing about Amparo," she warned me. "But I'll send you everything I have."

Compared to Ignacio's wife, Magdalena definitely was cool. Had Papá warned her not to answer me? If there existed a Freedom of Information Act for families, I would have invoked it. In my fantasies I subpoenaed them both and cross-examined them under oath.

Curiously, in my father's novel, *The Five Books of Ariadne*, Ariadne (Amparo) and Javier (Ramón) testify before a surrealistic tribunal. There he lists some possibilities of what could have happened to her:

*The first possibility*
Ariadne (Amparo), wife of Javier (Ramón), surrendered herself to the rebels.

*The second possibility*
One evening there came the horrible Herculana, and Quiñones, nick-named "Lizard." The house was full of papers that implicated her and they arrested her.

*The third possibility*
I, Javier, was guilty, through a type of deferred good faith, for having left those documents in reach of the authorities.

*The fourth possibility*
She was also guilty, because she did not follow my instructions.

*The last possibility*
Ariadne, in spite of everything, lives on, disgraced and amorous, in the style of her ancestors, but always young like the day we separated in Pinarel.

My search for Amparo continued. I drafted a fictional version of Amparo's story as best I could from what few sources I had available – mostly my father's novels and my imagination – and sent it to him with a carefully constructed letter of explanation. I hoped it would provoke a sympathetic response. Instead, my stepmother Florence replied, scolding me for disobeying his admonitions and disturbing him. A few days later, I received a letter from Magdalena. She would not help me. She said my father had everything – names, dates, documents, photos, but he absolutely did not want anyone to use them. She continued: "A short while after the dictator died, an important editor of this country gave me a blank check to write the story of your mother. I told him there wasn't enough money in the world to pay for a sad story of the accursed war about someone of my blood. I feel for you, but search in another place."

Nothing was left but to telephone the old man – the confrontation I had been avoiding ever since I began the book. I was positive Magdalena's refusal was all his doing.

"Magdalena will tell you nothing because there is nothing!" he shouted. "All you want to do is make money out of your mother's bones!"

I drew a deep breath. "If the book makes any money, I'll donate it to the Spanish Refugee Aid, if that makes you feel better."

"Then you want attention! You are screaming for fame!"

I changed the subject to my upcoming marriage to Judy. I invited him to attend and, mentioned that Julia was planning to be there.

"Bah, you are crrrazy!" he growled. "Julia has no respect for you. She will never come."

"She says that she is," I replied, stupefied by his response.

His laughter rasped in my ear, edged with hysteria. "I tell you she will not! You are stupid, an imbecile! The truth is that she hates you!"

This had gone too far! What was he trying to do? "Why do you insult me like this?" I asked.

"Because I am your father!" he screamed.

"Well, then, I'll insult you because I am your son."

He hung up on me. Unbelievable! There was our relationship encapsulated in one phone call. Shaking with suppressed fury, I put down the receiver, my fingertips icy. Such a classic Oedipal struggle! I wrote three drafts of a letter to him until I had vented enough anger to strike a conciliatory tone. He was obviously sick, I decided. I should not hold him responsible for his incredible behavior. Then I wrote to the editor of the Madrid newspaper, *El País,* requesting information from anyone who knew my mother.

"It makes my heart ache to fight with you," I wrote him in that final letter. "Why must we be enemies? Why must we repeat the fate of so many other generations?"

But he never answered, and that phone call must forever remain our last conversation together.

*Florence and Ramón J. Sender, approximately 1978.*

*Sister Benedicta at Ramón and Judith's wedding, 1982.*

## Chapter 2
## Loss and Reunion

My sister Andrea, now "Sister Benedicta" in an Episcopal order of nuns, and I arrived together at our stepmother Florence's home near Balboa Park. The phone was ringing nonstop. Spain's greatest novelist in exile had died, and the Spanish press wanted all the details. Florence, a diminutive, white-haired lady nursing a broken foot, was desolated. Her utter dedication to the man of her dreams had continued in spite of their divorce. To his credit, he had nursed her through several illnesses although he never ceased treating her as a second-class citizen ("Woman! You have just lost a perfect opportunity to keep quiet!"). In his later years, a brief gleam of affection occasionally softened his fierce mockery of her. Also, Florence learned to stand up for herself against the patriarchal tempests.

After supper, we drove to Papá's modern two-bedroom apartment accompanied by Juan, the friend who had found him. It was just the same as always, except for the small bloodstain beside the bed where Papá's heart attack had dropped him. Juan explained how, after the coroner's visit, he phoned the funeral society that Papá had joined, and they whisked him away.

I glanced at Benedicta. Framed by the black veil and white habit of her order, her elongated Spanish features, dark eyes, strong chin and sensitive mouth, expressed the same strange satisfaction I was feeling. A year and a half apart in ages, our lives remained inextricably intertwined in spite of the different directions we had taken. At last we had access to our father's life without his overwhelming presence. That may seem an unusual sentiment under the circumstances, but he had kept us at such a distance, both from himself and from our Spanish family. Now he was dead, the barriers were gone.

I did not appreciate how many Spanish relatives we had until I opened his address book. Among the names I found our half-brother Emmanuel, whose mother Elizabeth had been our first stepmother in France. Emmanuel at last! Papá did not even admit to his existence until Benedicta wrote a story in which my name was "Manuel" and Julia's was "Elizabeth."

"When Julia read it, she asked me what I remembered," Benedicta said. "That made me smell a rat, and I worked out of her the truth about Elizabeth and Emmanuel as she understood it.  Also, I used to dream there were three of us children.  I had been born one of twins, but the other twin was lost in the war.  When I found out about Emmanuel, I stopped having this dream."  She leafed through a stack of papers on the coffee table.  "Did I ever tell you that I had a compulsion at boarding school to tell what little I knew of the Spain story to anyone who would listen?  I would search the dormitories for someone who hadn't heard it or, barring that, who might be willing to hear it again.  The compulsion stopped after I learned about Emmanuel.  I think I must have been searching for someone who could fill in the missing part."

Through the years, we repeatedly had asked Papá without success for Emmanuel's address.  At last here it was, and in Queens, New York!  Five minutes later I was talking to him.  He spoke English well, but with a French accent.  Of course he would fly out for the memorial service.

The downstairs doorbell rang.  Margareta, my father's Colombian woman friend and Florence's nemesis, demanded to see us.  She had already made a considerable pest of herself by insisting the funeral society release Papá's body to her for shipment back to Spain – against his express wishes.  She must have imagined herself first in the procession of mourners at a state funeral in Madrid.  Benedicta would not allow her upstairs, so I went down to the lobby.

Another of Papá's loves, a Central American woman poet I had met years earlier, accompanied Margareta.  One of his letters to Maurín in the Hoover Library archives described her:

> "My friend is (keep my secret) my lover, my chauffeur, my landlady, my colleague (she writes also and not badly), my housekeeper, and also an enchantress and beautiful (a blonde) and fifteen years younger than I.  Not too much, right?  To write the enclosed article I had to lock myself in my room (she doesn't leave me in peace for one minute and comes to the door protesting, saying that I'm a thorny type and uncivil) And it's not more than ten in the morning after having passed, according to my calculations, fifty hours together!  You say that this is delicious?  No.  It's a sort of chaos with both excellent and exasperating aspects.  But that's the way life is!"

I numbered it among my favorite library discoveries because I never had seen this aspect of Papá – flushed with romantic ardor.

Margareta was totally out of control, insulting Florence and claiming to be Papá's only true love. Tearfully she begged for a final viewing of his body. I explained it was impossible. Then she asked me for some of his ashes after the cremation. She had a verbal will on tape, photos of Amparo, paintings, manuscripts. This did not surprise me because Florence and others had described her tendency to trek home from her weekends with him loaded with whatever she could carry. But a verbal will had no legal significance.

Because I hoped to convince her to inventory her memorabilia – and turn over Amparo's photos – I tried to be diplomatic. The conversation continued so long that Benedicta sent the building manager down to make sure Margareta had not added me to her Ramón J. Sender collection. There had to be some way to pry the photos loose. I would have to visit Margareta and her husband, an extraordinarily understanding and generous man.

Upstairs, I discovered to my relief that Benedicta had opted to sleep in Papá's bed and left me the guest bedroom, which he had used as a painting studio. I gave a final lingering glance at the littered desk, the half-corrected proofs on the typing table, the walls covered with his paintings and collages (photos of Brooke Shields figuring strongly in the latter). A copy of Picasso's portrait of Sender as a youth hung over the sofa. When Picasso did not leave him the original in his will, Papá had reproduced it in oils and, with complete aplomb, signed the famous signature in the corner. On the kitchen table I found my last letter to him, as if he had kept it nearby to reread. My throat ached at this proof of his desire not to forget my offer of a lasting peace – or at least a truce – between us. Well, he had gone to find his lasting peace elsewhere. I could only be grateful I had sent these placating words and not my previous angry drafts.

A few hundred pages of manuscript lay scattered about, the left-hand desk drawer stuffed with forty or so book contracts. Didn't he have a literary agent or a business advisor? On an old tax form I found the name of an accountant and phoned. Yes, Mr. Sender had walked in off the street one day six years earlier. Yes, he had seen Mr. Sender just a few days ago. Papá had said, "I'm through with this business of writing books! Now I'm going to have a good time!" He must have felt his life work was finished.

Page proofs of a manuscript titled *Toque de Queda* lay on his typing table, a collection of brief aphorisms. The Spanish dictionary offered "bugle call for curfew" as a translation, a word which in turn derives from the French for "cover the fire." He wasn't ready for "taps," but I think his literary output had reached a final cadence. After all, he had returned in triumph to Spain and been awarded its top literary prizes. Eighty of his books were in print, and only the Nobel Prize had eluded him. The year he was nominated, he kept insisting he didn't care one way or the other about it. But I knew he was deeply disappointed when another Spaniard was chosen.

Throughout my childhood, he contributed only about a thousand dollars to my expenses and not more than six months of his time. Therefore it came as a complete shock to find bank books crammed with deposits in his desk drawer. The total was more than adequate to support one person off the investment income. The thought of an unexpected windfall was not unattractive. For one thing, it would make my trip to Spain a great deal easier. The irony was that, if a will did show up, I knew I would be disinherited. Benedicta also felt the same way. She was certain Papá would not have wanted her religious order to benefit from his death.

I mentioned to Benedicta my plans to visit Spain and research Amparo's story in depth. Also I told her of Magdalena's refusal to help. "She said she told you everything during your visit."

She shook her head. "My Spanish was not up to understanding much. I was only there a few days and emotionally the trip was very arduous. I came back very frustrated, with only the sketchiest of details." Her eyebrows puckered. "I didn't send you the notes I took? No? I will when I return."

We visited the mortuary the following day. Both of us wanted to see our father one last time. We could not let him disappear anonymously into the unknown like Amparo. There was Papá, lying on a gurney, a sheet covering him up to the Van Dyke beard on his jutting chin. We gave a sigh of relief, having braced ourselves for something grotesque. He looked like a medieval crusader home from the wars, his bushy eyebrows curving into space over the granite profile. At last we could have time with him without the distraction of his gaze.

A first cousin arrived from Barcelona that evening, a tall, bearded man just my age. I was delighted to meet a male blood relative, and we talked until two in the morning. He worked as a journalist for a daily newspaper and was married to an Englishwoman with whom he had two daughters.

In the hopes of shaking loose Margareta's grip on Amparo's letters, I set up an appointment with her in Ensenada and drove down. What could I trade her for Amparo's things?  I decided to bring a spoonful of fireplace ashes to masquerade as part of Papá's cremains.  When I arrived, she took me to her study.

"Do you have the ashes?" she asked.

I handed over the bribe, thinking how amused Papá would have been by this macabre chicanery.  She blinked back her tears and, with great moans of bereavement, tucked the box into her bosom.

"These ashes are our secret," I cautioned her.

"Yes, of course," she replied.  "My lips are sealed."

"Now my mother's photos and letters," I said.

"Oh, I'm sorry!  I have been so sick with the flu.  They are not here!"

She promised to mail them to me.  In spite of later phone calls and letters, she never sent them.

"I have a tape I want to play just for you," she whispered.  "I think you should hear it."

She turned on the cassette player, and Papá's voice boomed out through the room.  He had had a few drinks and was singing Spanish songs in a dulcet baritone.  The story he told was the most bizarre he ever concocted.  In it he claimed that Amparo and he had broken up early in their relationship and she had returned to Zamora for an abortion.  That raised my suspicions.  For Amparo with her Catholic convictions to have made such a decision was unimaginable.  Besides, her home town of less than twenty thousand people would have been the last place to go for such an illegal operation.  My father went on to say that she then had an affair, became pregnant again and came back to Madrid.  There she threw herself on his mercy, and he magnanimously took her back, promising to accept the child as his own.  That was me.

When the lurid tale ended, she paused for my reaction.  "Look, Margareta, as far as I'm concerned, I wouldn't mind if he wasn't my father because he was a miserable failure at it."  I shrugged.  "But every time I look in the mirror, I see a Sender."

When I returned to the apartment, the real ashes had arrived during my absence in a cardboard box labeled "Cremains – Ramón J. Sender."  I hefted it – about five pounds.

Benedicta had washed the bloodstain out of the carpet and carefully saved the droplets in a bottle.  "Take this little bit of him back to Spain with you," she suggested.

I promised her I would.

Friday night our half-brother Emmanuel arrived. He resembled Papá more than I, the same bullet-shaped head and tendency to baldness. I resembled my paternal grandfather whom my father hated so much that he left home at fourteen. Such a pity Papá had to die to bring about this reunion. Poor man, how many of life's fulfillments he denied himself.

I made sure to get Emmanuel's mother's address because I wanted to visit her in France. After all, she had been our surrogate mother for a year or more. Only circumstances had prevented us from growing up with her. He described his childhood: Papá's abandonment of them had been total. They had survived the siege of Barcelona and barely avoided the French internment camps where so many Spaniards died.

Later he was shunted from boarding schools to relatives and back. Although Papá always had insisted he never had married Elizabeth, Emmanuel explained they were wed in a civil ceremony. Papá always had disparaged Elizabeth, saying he returned home from a trip to find her mistreating us. That same day he had taken us away and never saw her again. I was eager to hear Elizabeth's version and find out what memories, if any, her face would evoke.

Eight days after Papá's death, we boarded a motorized sloop to scatter his ashes in the Pacific Ocean. A TV crew affiliated with Madrid television accompanied us. Benedicta handed the box to Florence who wanted to be the one to empty it over the side. Florence's broken foot made it difficult for her to turn around so, in actuality, it was I who upended the silvered cardboard container. As the sea wind spattered salt spray in my face, the last traces of my father drifted away. But I had miscalculated the pitch of the boat and a handful of bone fragments landed on deck. When I scooped them overboard, I palmed four or five. These I would carry to Spain with me, to Amparo. The bottle of Papá's blood Benedicta washed out of the carpet I would place somewhere appropriate in Aragón, his birthplace.

The death of a parent, no matter how troubled the relationship, is an ax-blow to the tap root of one's being. Can the old man really be gone? I kept asking myself. It would take me time to accept the reality of his having traveled beyond all possibility of a reconciliation. Most of all, I would miss those mornings when I glanced up from my typewriter to think how, at that very moment, just a day's drive south, he sat in his pajamas punching the keys of his battered Smith-Corona. It had been a distant comradeship at best, but better than nothing, this sharing of the same vocation beside the same ocean.

My obsession with Amparo's story intensified, underscored by the many responses I received to my printed letter in Madrid's *El País*. Also I received the notes my sister had written during her trip to Spain. They offered surprising revelations about Amparo's death as well as new mysteries. She had learned that when the Civil War began in July, 1936, our parents were spending the summer with us at a rustic chalet on the outskirts of San Rafael, a mountain resort north of Madrid. I was twenty-one months old, Andrea eight months.

Papá, so the story went, had gone to Madrid on some errand. While he was there, the battle lines closed and Amparo could not reach him, nor he her. Confused, she returned to Zamora, her family home. En route she tried to phone Papá, but was arrested as a spy and detained a week. During the separation, I became inconsolably upset. Amparo was released, only to be arrested again a few weeks later in Zamora. Andrea remained with her in prison. When it became known that Amparo was going to be killed, relatives tried hard to prevent it, but the danger to them was great.

Amparo had been shot on October 11th, 1936, by a certain Segundo Viloria. Amparo's two brothers had been shot some weeks earlier and their bodies were never recovered. Six years later, seventeen-year-old Magdalena disinterred our mother's body from her unmarked grave in spite of people who threatened her and called her "a Red." She had placed Amparo in the family mausoleum, but her name was not inscribed on the stone until after Franco's death in 1975 because it was not safe.

The notes also revealed my sister's tears and torment. I understood why she had never sent them to me earlier. Rather than answering my questions, they only increased my need to learn the whole story. But now, at least, I knew the name of my mother's killer.

*THAT slays not nor is slain.*
*Greater than great, smaller than small,*
*In the heart of all creatures THAT resides,*
*seen only by one who is free from desire*
*and from grief.*

*Katha Upanishad*

*The author and his half-brother Emmanuel*

## Chapter 3
## Return to Spain

On the trip to Spain, I realized how the film of my life was running in reverse, peeling the layers: Paris, from where we departed for America in 1939, Calais where my sister had almost died of pneumonia in a refugee children's camp during the winter of 1938. And then Biarritz where the Red Cross reunited us with our father in late 1937 and where I now crossed the frontier to stand once more upon Spanish soil.

Finally we arrived to Madrid, my birthplace. At last I understood why it had taken me so long to come back. My father's vow not to return during Franco's reign and his warnings about my safety were partial reasons, but the most important reason of all was that, throughout my life, "Spain" had named the wound in my psyche.

In Madrid, an elfin grandmother opened the door of my cousin Ana María's apartment. She was my Aunt Conchita, my father's older sister, eighty-five years old and still going strong. Her deep-set eyes sparkled from under a prominent brow, her blunt nose an exact copy of my father's. What incredible luck! Of all the Sender relatives, she had known Amparo best.

"I'm living here now with Ana María," Conchita explained. "The doctor has given me a new asthma medicine, which keeps me well." She gave me a loving smile. "Ohhh, Monchín! It's been so long!" Her gnarled hand grasped mine, that same hand that held me as a baby.

Her voice seemed so familiar! I had no trouble understanding her dramatic inflections and emotional turns of phrase.

"I haven't seen you in so many years! Yet, without seeing you, I have seen you grow up." She leaned against me, stroking my thigh. "I always asked myself –" She closed her eyes and her voice softened. "'How are they at this moment?' Also, I knew your American foster mother, Julia. I met her and her husband here in Madrid before the War."

"No, it couldn't have been Julia," I replied. "She has never been to Spain."

"Yes, yes, Julia Davis." Conchita insisted. "They knew your father here. They lived in Conn-ect-ee-coot." She pronounced the word in a marvelous Castilian.

"But they can't be the same people you met here!"

"I knew her." Conchita did not give up her opinions easily. "But –"

"Grandma," her granddaughter interjected from across the room. "Ramón says that the woman you met here was not the one who took care of them." (She used the verb *amparo*, meaning 'to protect or to shelter.')

Conchita snorted. "Well, perhaps since I had met this other couple already, your father thought, 'Because Conchita knows these people, I'll give her this version.'"

Obviously she was aware of my father's tendency to bend the truth for his purposes. I waited until Conchita and I were alone in the room. "Now tell me about the beginning of the War," I coaxed. I had already learned that in Spain 'the War' always referred to the Civil War.

She settled herself more comfortably on the sofa. "Well, for some years we rented a villa in the summer colony of San Rafael – even before your parents met." She glanced at me. "Do you know it? No? It's northwest of Madrid in the Guadarrama Mountains, situated on both sides of La Coruña highway that runs all the way to Galicia. The air is fresh there and the velvet green forests climb up to the sky. We always rented the same chalet, Villa Frutos, the last one on the road toward Avila. Behind it, the valley descends through meadows to the river. The ravines are full of blackberries and tangles of ivy and creepers. But in 1936, Emi, my husband, had suffered stomach problems all winter and was on a special diet. We decided to stay in Madrid that summer and not go to San Rafael. Our children had gone to the Pyrenees with their grandfather to get out of the heat. Meanwhile, your father Pepe, that was his family nickname, rented Villa Frutos in Emi's name to retain his anonymity. He left with Amparo and you children as well as the servant girls.

"A few days later, Emi said, 'We're going to San Rafael.' I said, 'Don't tell me stupidities.'

"'I've just been posted to San Rafael for twenty-five days,' he said. He worked for the telegraph company. 'We have a travel allowance to pay for a hotel. Won't Pepe and Amparo be surprised!' So off we went, four days before the Civil War started."

She snapped open her fan and wafted air in my direction. Its wing-like movements punctuated all our conversations. "The Hotel Golf, where we took a room, was face-to-face with the telephone office. It was there we heard the news that rightists in Madrid had murdered a popular lieutenant of the assault guards. This force was created by the Republic to function as trustworthy city police, as opposed to the civil guard who were of doubtful loyalty. The lieutenant's friends avenged him by shooting the Monarchist leader Calvo Sotelo. These events immediately were followed on July 18th by military uprisings in Morocco and many cities.

"That day we came to the chalet for lunch with your parents. When we arrived, Amparo was seated in the shade of the chestnut tree in the front yard with Andrea asleep beside her in a wicker basket covered with cheesecloth. During the meal, we listened to the radio. The Burgos station was in the hands of the rebels and reported that General Mola had sent troops into the streets of Pamplona. Other generals had taken Valladolid, Zaragoza, Cadiz, and Cordoba.

"'General Franco has declared the constitution worthless,' the announcer said. 'The army can no longer stand idly by and is rising to bring justice, equality and peace to all Spaniards.'

"Meanwhile, Madrid radio insisted that no one on the mainland had taken part in 'the absurd plot.' But Pepe insisted the situation was very grave and the rebellion widespread.

"'The press called for the demobilization of the army a week ago, but the ministers just whine for law and order,' he grumbled. 'Now the workers are screaming for arms, but the government is afraid to distribute them!'

"'Will we be safe here?' Amparo asked.

"You see, San Rafael was a rightist enclave," Conchita explained. "That morning two cars were parked in front of the President of the Council's villa with six police in each, all armed with machine guns. Unpleasant types. And if a general mobilization began, Pepe would have to fight. The Alto de León pass between us and Madrid had to be defended.

"'Amparo, you remain here with Conchita,' he told her. 'Emi has no political reputation and will not be in danger. If things get worse, take the children to your family in Zamora. From there it's only a half-hour to Portugal where you can find passage to France.'"

Conchita frowned. "All through that night we lived beside the radio!

"A rightist general captured Seville and Franco flew to Morocco to assume command of the troops. Sunday at dawn, two announcements

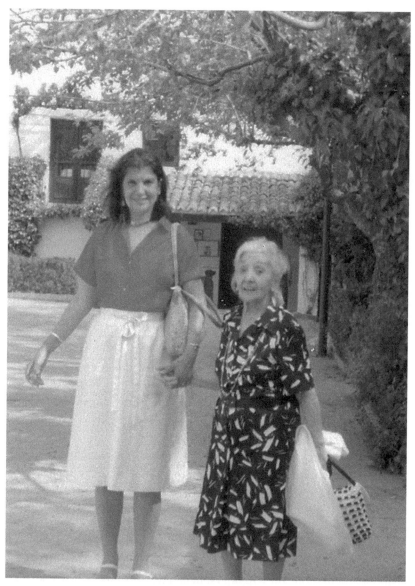

*Judy and Tía Conchita*

prompted Pepe to act – the requisition of all private cars by the workers, which meant a general mobilization, and the arming of all the Popular Front organizations. He left to phone Segovia and place himself under orders of the provincial government. When he returned, he reported Segovia in the hands of the fascists and a confused atmosphere in San Rafael. The civil guards had disappeared from their barracks and armed workers were patrolling the streets.

"Franco himself broadcast a speech from Spanish Morocco: 'I hereby proclaim that the army must respond to the wishes of the majority.'

"He went on to declare martial law. Obviously it meant civil war. All that night and Monday the 20th, we remained in suspense. The fighting in Madrid favored the workers and the rebel general Goded's surrender speech in Barcelona raised their enthusiasm to a peak. Then at five that evening in the hotel we heard a commotion. We were taking a siesta, and Emi left the room to investigate.

"'What's going on?' he asked a bellhop.

"'Civil guards are standing with fixed bayonets in front of the telephone office! You cannot go outside. Everyone's in the foyer with the doors locked!'

"He had not finished speaking when – rat-tat-tat-tat-tat! – machine-gun fire erupted. Everyone was terrified! A half-hour later, the hotel manager went out on the street. Several telephone employees who had tried to escape lay dead on the sidewalk and others were dead inside the building. Someone said, 'They cut all the phone lines and didn't leave one person alive!'

Conchita's eyes darkened. "Ah, what horrors! What were they trying to do? The telegraph office was only some one hundred meters further and Emi was scheduled for duty the following morning!

"'You're not going,' I said.

"'I have to,' he said. 'After all, I'm commissioned to this service. Those of us in charge have to be there in case something happens.'

"'Why are you going to search for a bullet?' I asked.

"We were arguing like this when your father appeared in his pajamas and slippers. 'I've come to tell you to leave everything in the hotel and come to our house,' he said. 'They won't shoot at us there because it's an isolated place. Here you're in the center of town!'

"Emi replied, 'I can't, because the moment we're in a declared war, I'm under military orders. I have to stay here.'

"'Not me!' I said. And I went with Pepe."

My father gave an eyewitness report of this incident in his book *Counterattack in Spain*. A truck of civil guards, rural police hostile to the workers and leftists, had returned to San Rafael. When they were hailed by a squad of militiamen, they opened fire. Everyone took cover except one youth who stood in front of the truck, hands on his hips.

"What you have done is a cowardly crime!" he shouted.

The officer in the truck leaped to the pavement and shouted hysterical orders. "He's their leader! Cover the crowd! Leave him to me!"

But no one was in sight. They had disappeared into nearby houses. Pistol in the youth's back, the officer forced him into the entrance of the telephone exchange and fired two shots into him. The civil guards entered the building shooting, collected their families from the barracks and drove off towards Segovia again.

"*Dios mío*, when Pepe told us this, we were terrified!" Conchita told me. What were we to do? I was convinced I would never see Emi again!"

Early the following day, Victor Rivera arrived with his wife and their two little girls Maruchi and Pepi. As Director-General of Mountains, a post equivalent to being the head of the U.S. Forest Service, he had the forestry residence at his disposal, a short distance from the center of town.

Although Amparo had just met them that year, the Riveras were old friends of Papá, Conchita and Emi. They had come by way of the river behind the town, Victor in an old jacket, his wife in a cook's apron.

"Ten forestry guards surrounded our house armed to the teeth!" Victor told them. "I dared to ask the sergeant who had given the order. 'Sir, the military governor of Segovia,' he said. I decided we shouldn't stay longer because the second order would be to shoot us. So we left casually with our two servant women, and tried to get into the hotel. The manager refused us rooms but agreed to put up the servants. We continued here by way of the river. Pepe, we should get out. A bus load of armed fascist youth have arrived from Valladolid. They'll stir up trouble."

Rivera and my father began to plan to leave San Rafael because both were known government sympathizers. But the road over the Sierras was unsafe. There were armed men everywhere.

"Santiago will get us out of here," Papá said.

Santiago was a retired shepherd who knew the mountains well. When he wasn't working for the family, he ran errands for the sanitarium down the road. But who would go there to find him?

"Look, I'll do it," Conchita said. "I'll take those milk crocks, wear a servant's apron and walk over. If anyone asks, I'll say, 'My master has children and I always come to buy milk at the sanitarium early in the morning.' If I have a dumb expression, they'll let me pass!"

The sanitarium had one hundred beds for children. A dairy on the premises provided milk for them and the surplus was sold. Before anyone could argue, Conchita left. She stayed off the road as much as possible and had no trouble. The lack of traffic seemed ominous and oppressive. It was a stifling day, which promised a thunderstorm. At the sanitarium, they told her that Santiago had gone to El Espinar with a truck but would return soon. She waited until he arrived.

"Santiago, you have to take my brother and another man across the mountain any way you can," she said.

"Nothing doing!" he said. "Terrible things are happening! They'll shoot at us! I'm not going up there. Every time I do I get in trouble!"

But Conchita finally changed Santiago's mind.

"All right, I'll do what you say," he said. "Tell them to wear casual clothes and carry a newspaper or a sack. They should look as if they are out for a stroll to collect pine cones. I'll wait for them by the forest behind the meadow."

She returned to the chalet and reported to the men before joining Amparo and the children in the backyard. Pepi, the Riveras' youngest daughter, was a blonde butterball who liked to mother me and Andreina. Amparo was distraught over the situation. She wanted to accompany Papá, but the children never could have walked over the mountain.

That evening the Riveras' servants, Celes the cook and Adelina the nursemaid, arrived with alarming news.

"The fascist militia are searching for *Señor* Rivera everywhere!" they said. "Also they want *Señor* Sender, but they think he's the secretary of some ministry or other."

Papá laughed, flattered to be given such a dignified post. Celes and Adelina insisted on staying because of the unsettled situation in town.

Everyone ate supper beside the blaring radio.

What happened that night in Villa Frutos can be surmised from my father's novel, *The Five Books of Ariadne*. Here Ariadne speaks for

Amparo, Javier for my father. The autobiographical parallels, Conchita assured me, were unmistakable.

"That night Javier (Ramón) and I stayed awake. I asked him if he loved me. He looked at me out of the corners of his eyes and smiled without replying, as if to say, 'To a silly question, an intelligent silence.' All the same, he knew I enjoyed his silences. I adored him. He was everything that I wasn't... I don't know how to explain it, because the best things of love never have had nor will have any explanation...

"I began to cry without knowing why – sometimes love over-sensitizes me. Javier looked at me smiling.

"'How can you laugh watching me cry?' I asked him.

"'Your weeping only means that you have touched the pinnacle of joy,' he replied.

"'Where have you learned so much, Professor?' I teased.

"Javier removed a paper from a notebook, and read to me a sonnet that he said was by Aldana (famous for his love poems, and nicknamed 'El Divino' by Cervantes) in the times of King Carlos V (sixteenth century):

"'What is the reason, Ariadne, that here
clasped in the maelstrom of love,
tongues, arms and feet entwined,
a vine laced amongst the jasmine
whose vital breath we sip together,
that now and then we are forced
to cry and gasp through kiss-surfeited lips?

"'My love, my lovely Ariadne, inside
our joined souls, you call our bodies to unite
again within this furnace.

"'Yet as water in a sponge cannot pass
from soul to the sweet center,
the mortal shell decries its miserly luck.'

"'It surprised me to discover that what had happened to me also happened to women in the time of Carlos V... I thanked him, because he had changed the name of the beloved from Phyllis to Ariadne...

"Well, I'm going," he said at last."

Conchita remembered how the household awakened before dawn. The radio reported that rebel soldiers had fired machine guns into strolling crowds in Salamanca. Assault guards had captured the socialist leaders of Valladolid. Huelva and Granada were taken, but Madrid remained free – and Barcelona, that citadel of radicalism, as well.

Pepe and the Riveras were drinking hot coffee in the kitchen when Amparo joined them with Andreina in her arms. Pepe zipped up his leather jacket and kissed Andreina's plump cheek. As a going-away memento, Amparo gave him a small photo of herself with an inscription on the back.

"Amparo, be cautious," he warned. "You must burn anything with my name on it, including my manuscripts."

"But some are your only copies!" she protested.

"Nothing must show I was living here with you." He kissed her on the cheek. "Now I must go. Walk with me to the edge of the woods."

"I'm going with Victor," his wife announced. "His health is poor and I don't want to be separated. Conchita, will you be responsible for the girls and servants?"

"Don't worry," Conchita assured her. "I will treat them the same as my niece and nephew."

"Put on your heaviest shoes," Papá told Victor's wife. "And don't carry anything." He held up his binoculars. "This is all I'm taking." He repeated his warning to Conchita. "Burn anything that might define the household as leftist – books, papers. There's a good chance the place will be searched. Above all, do nothing to draw suspicion on yourselves."

In *The Five Books of Ariadne*, Ariadne tells what happened next:

> "We left... Javier asked me to accompany him not only to give the innocent impression of a married couple but also because he had something to tell me. Something important. What? I didn't know. The truth is that he didn't tell me...
>
> "I had one of those moments of inhibition from which I sometimes suffer. I was waiting for him to cross over the silence to me. We walked without speaking. We approached the woods. Near us there was a tree struck by lightning...
>
> "'I'm going on my way without kissing you because I don't wish to call attention to us,' he said. 'I know your kiss is worth some risk, but I don't want that risk to be yours.

It may seem no one is around, but a man with binoculars could be watching us from somewhere nearby.'

"He entered the woods slowly. All at once I lost sight of him. He left at the exact instant he should have left. An hour earlier it would have been difficult and two hours later impossible... I could not remember his saying goodbye, either in the house or outside... I went on thinking that we had separated only for a few days, nothing more... The rent had been paid until September. That thought, so ridiculous under the circumstances, somehow comforted me."

Amparo met the Rivieras at the gate. Victor carried a camera, and was chatting in a low voice to give the impression that they were an unimportant summering couple. A half hour later, the women heard the distant buzz of engines. A convoy of trucks carrying artillery approached along with the troops of the rebel colonel Serrador. Two thousand infantry headed south,

*Judith and the Riveras next to the side gate of Villa Frutos.*

*The meadow across the highway from Villa Frutos where
Ramón Senior and Amparo said goodbye for the last time.*

*The forest near San Rafael.*

## Chapter 4
## A Provincial Childhood

"The most loyal and noble city of Zamora," the fifteenth century king Enrique IV dubbed in perpetuity the fortified town on the banks of the Duero River. The rocky escarpments inhabited since ancient times. Its castles protected the roads from Portugal to the west and Galicia to the north. The city banner was decorated with eight red streamers for the eight battles won against the Romans. From the repeated conquests by and defeats of the Moors evolved the popular saying, "Zamora is not won in an hour." Ferdinand the Great added an emerald ribbon in recognition of the city's help in the final battle that united Spain. Although the twelfth century cathedral was capped by an unusual Serbio-Byzantine dome of feathery overlapping stones, the town did not attract many tourists except for Holy Week when over forty different religious groups marched in procession. Foreigners usually preferred the elegant architecture of the medieval university town Salamanca to the south.

In *The Five Books of Ariadne,* Ariadne tells how she grew up in the shadow of the cathedral. In Amparo's case, it was actually the Church of San Juan on the Plaza Major, a half-block away from her family's Café Iberia. The shadow widened in the morning and then diminished little by little all day long. When the town hall clock struck the hours, the children marked the edges of the shadow on the paving stones with a nail. That way, when the clock was broken, they could calculate the time from their sun dial.

Ariadne's memories of those years were luminous, days full of light and magical nights. Their house had an attic, which the children transformed in their games into a castle or a pirate's ship.

Amparo's father Antonio married twice. His first wife bore three children: Saturnino, Casimira and Magdalena. When she died, Antonio married Amparo's mother, a young woman from the local village of Perdigon who was serving as a maid in the household. She gave birth to Nati who suffered from nervous problems, Amparo, Antonio and Eugenia. This second wife died in childbirth when Amparo was seven.

Among the many children, Amparo's older sister Casimira would play a prominent role in determining her fate. Casimira was the scholar of the family. She had studied in France for some years before returning and marrying a man named Miguel Sevilla. He was an ecclesiastical tailor and a leader of the conservative Carlist *requetés*, the paramilitary groups named after a reactionary nineteenth century pretender to the throne. His name would recur frequently in explanations of my mother's death. Indeed, my father in his novel, *The Affable Hangman*, chose the name 'Sevilla' for a criminal condemned to die by the garrote. There he described the man's final agony in gruesome detail, extracting the vengeance otherwise denied him.

Amparo kept fond memories of her childhood in Zamora. In his fiction, my father recounted Ariadne's earliest recollection – the smell of tobacco on her father's left hand.

> "Everyone treated me as if I were a perfect being, my parents, the household, my neighbors. However I was a little animal, greedy and full of desires, always sniffing the air for colors and superficial pleasures. I owned a piece of white silk over which I would pass my hand and put it to my lips and cheeks... I didn't have the slightest idea of men. I thought of them as a large and hairy hand that smelled in a rare manner and one day would entrap and overtake me and carry me to another house and give me money. After this, I would get fat and give birth to a baby boy, but of this last item it was better not to speak...
>
> "I remember other strange things of that time. When I came in dirty from playing in the street, my aunt would say, 'These people are not from your sphere, child.' I began to believe I lived inside a crystal ball tinted the lightest blue. Outside it the wolves howled, the adults cried, and the guards hung the thieves... I became accustomed to the idea that I was pretty. I remember that, when alone, I thought: 'Well, everyone wants to kiss me, but what's in it for me?'
>
> "My father had his office on a central street. Why do you go to the office so much?' I asked him.
>
> "'To earn money, child, to buy you clothes and toys,' our cook replied.
>
> "After that, whenever I went to his office and saw some bills or coins on the table – change from something he had sent out to buy – I thought, 'This is all he earned

so far today, but later there will be more.' There was something about the earning of money that seemed miraculous and incomprehensible, but which related to the smell of his hand. If I saw no money on the table, I became sad and thought, 'Poor Papá!'

"On election days, I heard people speak about whether they had voted. The expression 'vote' sounded like 'bote' to me, and to us children this word meant a ball game. We would throw a ball into the sky and measure how high it bounced.

'My ball bounced higher than yours,' we would say, and try to prove it.

"There were no classes on election days because the schools were used as polling places.

"'Today the school is full of 'boting'' people,' I said to my father. I imagined the adults throwing balls and jumping about like cats and billy goats. 'What for?'

"'Well, daughter, to elect deputies,' he replied. 'This is a democracy.'

"For many years, democracy meant to me a group of men leaping together like young bulls. No one ever cared to explain these errors to me... But my most persistent memory is of my first communion. I kneeled in my beautiful dress, and from the instant I took the wafer on my tongue, I believed myself semi-divine. Yet suddenly I had to urinate. To be lifted up bodily to God and have to go to the bathroom was a horrible thought..."

In 1912, Amparo's father opened the Café Iberia and moved the family from a house on the square to the apartment above the cafe. As a nonbelligerent nation during World War I, Spain grew prosperous selling food and clothing to both sides. Improved communications brought new ideas that echoed through Zamora's wine shops and cobblestoned alleys. Communism, anarchism and socialism were debated fiercely in the Barayón cafe. For Amparo as a child, it was an important political awakening.

Feliza, a tiny woman who was Amparo's best childhood friend, lived in an apartment full of antique furnishings including a three-story doll house taller than she, with a clock on its cupola.

"Amparo and I were intimate friends because I lived in Number 1 and she in Number 3," she chirped in a voice that mingled with the canary in the other room. "Her father would place a few café tables on the street near his parrot, who insulted anyone who walked by his perch. My father and I would sit there to drink coffee. Amparo would join us because she was a great chatterer. We were very animated and laughed like rattlebrains at anything anyone said to us. All the Barayóns were great *cafeteros* and Amparo was no exception. She loved to talk. I began to stay with her and we became great, great friends. We used to go riding at my family's ranch, Amparo on a horse and me on a burro, just like Don Quixote and Sancho Panza."

One Friday during Lent, rabbit was served for lunch at the Barayóns. Magdalena, Amparo's older half-sister, stared at it and said, "*Andaaa!* What can we do? We can't eat meat!"

"Look, we can't waste it!" Amparo stood up and raised her hand in a blessing. "I now baptize you 'fish!'"

Amparo attended a one-room school for girls run by three single sisters across the back alley from the café. In a class photo, she stands in the back row, full lips visible above the fan she is holding, dark eyes dramatic and mischievous. She must have been eleven or twelve years old. How could this lovable child later be betrayed by those who had smiled at her girlish pranks?

In *The Five Books of Ariadne* I glimpsed more details:

"I had a tutor, María Jesús. She was only three years older than I, and although she was my teacher, in a certain sense I educated her. I had ideas, good or bad. She, no. She only knew what she had learned in books and could not think for herself. Never had I seen anyone as provocative as that woman, but at times the large size of her bosoms made me squirm.

"My father (as a widower) courted her. The day she told me about my father's feelings for her, I felt in her voice something new and suspicious. She talked with great seriousness and without ridiculing my father's pretensions. There was in her remarks a cynical reserve I did not like.

"'Marry whomever you like, but don't play at being an odalisque,' I told her.

"María Jesús was similar to me and my friends in that she loved people with a complete unawareness of sex.

Between parentheses, I have always believed that this sexless love, in which one sees the beloved in a cloud, in a flower or feels his absence as that of God himself, is the unique dignity human love contains. The rest is just localized desires, like hunger and thirst.

"I observed that my father's advances scared María Jesús. Along with her, I felt a mixture of gratitude, repugnance and curiosity. I watched her and thought, 'She has too much bosom, and because of this, she is poised to place herself in those male hands that smell of tobacco, that want to devour and possess her completely.'

"She noticed that her reaction to my father was not what I had expected... One day she said, 'You want me to ridicule your father's advances, but I can't. Just look at what he wrote me yesterday.'

"In the note he told her he was in love with her and could not imagine being old and renouncing life. For him, life was María Jesús. He also said he would only act the part of man and wife with her for one or two years before dying. My father's capacity for love seemed to be the same as in his youth, but naturally to indulge in excesses at his age would have been extremely dangerous. He told her it didn't matter to him if he died after the honeymoon. Furthermore he added slyly that what little money he had would be hers on the day of his death.

"María Jesús looked very serious and repeated, 'How can I make fun of a man like this?'

"To call my father 'a man' made me uncomfortable. It sounded a little indecent...

"We children classified women in several ways. There were odalisques, houris and other Moslem types. Once my friend Carmen asked what an odalisque was.

"'It's obvious,' I replied. 'It's a depilated, undulating, perfumed woman who calls her fiancé "my promised one" and refers to getting married as "changing one's condition." When the fiancé is presented to her family, he has "formalized relations" and calls marriage "that sweet yoke" and pregnancy "an interesting state."'"

"I would not have dared to say 'pregnancy' in the full light, but the room was dark. The boys held their solemn assemblies apart from us girls, and hid some of their slang expressions out of respect. Nevertheless one or two filtered through. We knew that a girl who watched and protected her virginity, but was passed compliantly hand-to-hand to successive boyfriends, was called a 'virgin-harlot.'"

In 1917, when a national strike was savagely repressed, the local Communist Party gained many new members. The following year, the famous influenza epidemic killed many, including Amparo's father. She imagined that, as an orphan, she would go to live with the nuns.

The idea evoked in her a bittersweet emotion, but she remained in the family apartment under the care of her half-sister Magdalena. Amparo's half-brother Saturnino took over the operation of the family café and the ice factory several blocks away.

The younger children sang a ditty about Magdalena:

"Magdalena is very ugly and has a terrible voice.
She doesn't know how to cook, and has an atrocious temper."

Amparo herself had a temper. According to her sister, Eugenia, she could be treacherous. "She would take a glass and say that if we children continued fighting she'd break it. She would throw it. We all laughed so much!"

When she was twelve, Amparo began to study piano, first with her half-sister Casimira, and then with a Señora Muñoz. After taking communion at eight o'clock Mass, she would eat breakfast and then practice until lunchtime. In the early afternoon she came downstairs to wait on customers. Often she was asked to play piano in the café. Later she returned to the apartment to practice again. People would come out on their balconies to listen.

She liked to work in the café and talk to people because something amusing was always happening. The men who gambled at roulette and baccarat in a side room hired her as their lookout. Many pesetas changed hands while Amparo kept an eye peeled for the police. If they arrived, she gave the signal and the men escaped through the alley. When fights occurred, Amparo separated the combatants.

*The Five Books of Ariadne* depicts this period:

"At thirteen, I saw and heard people talking about me in roundabout ways. Well, I did not believe there was anything in life that was ugly or should be prohibited. Our bodies functioned like perfect machines and our souls as well. When I loved someone, it was certain he or she would not lose a moment to love me back. Colors were for my eyes, the breezes to cool my temples. Always I hoped for something, but I did not know what. True, in the street I saw ugly men and women – much too ugly! But I believed they would be able to overcome their ugliness some day. The King and the Pope were to blame for ugly people and social injustices, and I supposed that by devotion and difficult heroic acts – the sort one reads in children's stories– something would be done to cure them."

Ariadne tells of an old curate in the neighborhood who had an absolute horror of flies. So much so that he never opened his garret window except at night.

"The older boys used to go out and trap flies by the hundreds in a sack, using a few pieces of licorice as bait. After dark, they would sneak up under the old man's window where he was hunched over his prayer-book beside the lamp. They opened the sack and the light attracted the flies. Up they rose like smoke right into his room, while he called upon Mary and the Saints."

The lack of a mother during her teens allowed Amparo more freedom than was usual in those times, and she developed into a very independent teenager. The café provided her with a stage, an opportunity to mix with the townspeople who obviously loved her. It served as a meeting place for liberals whose opinions of a modern woman's role helped shape this unusual adolescent's view of what her life should be. The magnetic poles of her existence were San Juan, a mere hundred yards away, and Café Iberia. Within these environs, she grew into a flamboyant young adult, but she drank a lot of coffee, and her liveliness contained a nervous edge. Her fingers sometimes trembled.

Her best friend, Feliza, remembered the musical-literary parties they held as teenagers. "We all smoked, something extremely rare in Zamora. We were too shy to buy the cigarettes ourselves but asked a boyfriend, or else Amparo sent a waiter.

"Absolutely shameless! Amparo would play piano, someone would recite verses, another would read an essay. If someone had written something, they would read it. Another would sing. This way we passed our time together. "There was also a popular tango she sang – 'Smoking, I wait for the man I love...'" She began to sing:

"Smoking I wait for the man I love
Behind the panes of the bright windows
And meanwhile I smoke
So that I don't fret my life away."

"Her eyes were a little sad. They always showed her moods, but she could laugh too.

"In the early 1920s she used to write articles and drama reviews for '*El Mercantíl*' and '*El Heraldo De Zamora*.' She signed them 'Miguelina Ascona,' because her full name was Amparo Barayón Miguel Ascona. She was very considerate. Poor people would come asking for *la señorita niña* to beg for alms. She would always give them something."

In 1923, a cultural club modeled on Madrid's Ateneo began to meet at the Café Iberia. Amparo was among its founding members.

"She had a good friend, a Professor Bientobas at the University of Salamanca. He wasn't a boyfriend, but would come to chat with her because she was a tremendous conversationalist. She loved to talk about everything – literature, music." Feliza smiled wistfully. "*Ai,* those marvelous long summer afternoons with picnics on the knoll!"

Feliza stressed an important point: "I also want to say that Amparo was Catholic from top to bottom! From daily Mass to daily communion, Amparo was the parish priest's right hand. We children sang 'The Flowers of May,' a devotion to the Virgin during the whole month with many canticles about the flowers. Amparo played the harmonium and conducted us. The last day of the Novena of Flowers, we came down from the choir loft to the sacristy and were given little cakes. She taught catechism and prepared children for first communion. In those days, catechism teachers were greatly respected. When the children saw her in the street, they ran up and kissed her. She gave them caramels and little religious cards that she signed at the bottom: 'Live for your friend, Amparito Barayón.'"

Of the many songs the children sang, one included the following verse and refrain:

"A thousand beautiful cherubs form your canopy.
 I want to be with them.
 Virgin, take me with you to heaven.
 My longing will be crowned!  How happy I shall be!
 Take our hearts, Pure Virgin.
 Do not abandon us,  Ever, ever, ever."

Her first serious romance occurred when she was twenty-three, the same year she went to Madrid for the first time and passed her piano examinations with honors.  His name was Aguirre, a sergeant in the army from Salamanca.  He wrote articles for the newspapers, and she liked him because of this.  They went to morning Mass together often, and then in the evening to say the rosary, which was unusual because normally only women attended the rosary.  It was the act of a man very much in love.  Then one day a young lady from Salamanca appeared, obviously his hometown sweetheart.  Through a go-between she asked to speak to Amparo.

"The girl arrived at our house with a neighbor," Amparo's younger sister Eugenia reported.  "We decided to put on a show for her.  I dressed up as a maid to open the door, but I had to hide because the neighbor knew me.  I was going to bring a tray with her visiting card.  So the daughter of the cook – Andrés the waiter's sister – opened the door and interviewed her.  She brought her into the salon where Amparo was playing the piano to make a good impression.  They began to talk and the girl claimed Aguirre was returning to her."

"'I don't want him to spend time with you, because I love him with all my soul,' she told Amparo.  'Tell him you don't want him.'

"'If it's only because you love him and there isn't anything more serious between you – well, then, I love him too!' Amparo replied.

"They said goodbye.  When Aguirre called on Amparo later, he slunk into the room, very ashamed that this young woman had visited her.  Amparo told him that as far as she was concerned, he was free to choose between them.  So he continued seeing her, but she no longer trusted him.  He hadn't told her the truth.  Also, the other woman stayed on in Zamora until he finished his military service – he had only a little time left.  But he kept going to daily Mass and the rosary with Amparo, while the other saw him at the barracks.  This other woman had some sort of hold on him because she had met his family.

"Amparo tried to remain detached.  When he completed his tour of duty, he returned to Salamanca.

*The Barayón family, Amparo standing far right.*

*In her twenties, Amparo accompanies a young violinist.*

*The Barayón Café Iberia.*

*Amparo Barayón, with her niece, Mercedes, and two neighborhood friends.*

A newspaper reporter was a friend of Amparo's, and she paid him to go to Salamanca and check on Aguirre. She wanted to know where he went and with whom. He returned to Zamora and said Aguirre was spending time with the other woman. They were together morning and evening, but at the same time he was writing Amparo every day, and she was answering him. So Amparo returned all his letters to him with a note telling him to go with God and asked him to mail her letters back. He returned her letters and photos with a reply: 'To the woman whom I loved, these photos that I liked so much. Vanity of vanities!'"

After the relationship with Aguirre ended, Amparo took a civil service placement exam in Salamanca. But the job was given to a widow with two children, a native of the city. Amparo was ambitious, however, and preferred teaching piano and catechism to housework, sewing or cooking. Next she took the telephone exam in Zamora in which she placed first. So she began to work long hours for the phone company, but continued behind the café's register for a few hours each day.

Her job required her to visit people in their homes and convince them to install a telephone. The idea of a woman working in sales was something unusual for provincial Zamora, and shocking to the older set. But by then she had cut her hair and was wearing cloche hats, Zamora's first flapper.

She must have demonstrated considerable talent at her work, because she was soon offered a transfer to Madrid. For Amparo, it was a dream come true, a way to escape the confines of her isolated birthplace.

"I saw Amparo only once, when I was seventeen and my father died," Eugenia's husband, a retired civil guard, reported. "She was friendly with my father. All the civil guards of Zamora went to drink coffee at the Café Iberia.

"Amparo held conversations with all the clients. When she heard my father had died, she came to the barracks to offer her condolences, and this was the only time I saw her. When I began a relationship with your aunt, Amparo had already gone to Madrid. She must have left for Madrid in 1930."

So at twenty-six, she took the train to the capital, leaving behind a scandalized family. A single woman striking out on her own in the big city? Shocking! Of course Casimira had traveled to France to attend the university, but she returned home to marry within the Church. Now she shared the view of the other female relatives who were convinced that Amparo was traveling to her ruination, if not damnation as well. Six years later, Casimira would see her prophesy of doom fulfilled.

## Chapter 5
## A Life In Madrid, 1930-1934

In January 1930, the dictator Primo de Rivera had resigned and gone into exile. He had been vilified by everyone including the military and the press, and especially by the students whom he himself had hated the most. Some years earlier he had jailed my father. A rebellion had broken out at the artillery academy in Segovia. Although journalists had been prohibited to enter the city, Papá decided to sneak in. He dressed in the smock and visored cap of a sidewalk photographer and took a camera on a tripod. In that disguise, he had no trouble entering the city. Once inside, friends told him everything about the artillerymen's revolt. His published articles alerted the government, and someone identified him as Sender. They wanted him, dead or alive. When they found him, they locked him up in Modelo Prison. But the public outcry was so loud they had to release him after three months.

When Amparo arrived in Madrid, she found the streets buzzing with talk about how Spain was on the eve of the millennium. The socialist leader Besteiro's manifesto calling for the reestablishment of the Republic had been distributed clandestinely, and the Socialists were the best organized party in the nation. How exciting to be living in this marvelous city with its broad avenues, to be a part of this epoch-making time! She rebelled in her newfound emancipation from Zamora's provincialism, especially from Saturnino who overplayed his role as head of the household.

During the next months she would cast off the bourgeois restraints of her upbringing and become a freethinker. Away from the scrutiny of her family, she was free to embrace a feminist perspective, even to live openly with a man and to bear his child out of wedlock. She expressed her new ideas in frank letters to her family in Zamora, no doubt smiling to imagine the shocked reactions of her half sisters. Yet in six years she would have to return to these people among whom were those who now thought of her as a renegade revolutionary and no better than a whore. And not only return, but depend on them to rescue her from death.

In a photo dating from that year and obviously taken to send to her relatives, Amparo wears a cloche hat of contrasting colors with stylish flaps loose about her ears. She looks like a Spanish Amelia Earhart with a sculpted mouth and dimpled upper lip. Her large eyes stare out in a beguiling manner.

*Amparo Barayón, the year she moved to Madrid.*

What an adventure her life became! Every weekday morning she walked from a nearby pension to her new job in Madrid's first skyscraper *La Telefónica* on the Gran Vía. Its Art Deco elegance underscored her own entrance into the modern world. Whenever she passed through its monolithic lobby and swept her gaze upwards to the artwork on its vaulted ceilings, she must have exulted anew in her escape from her backwater beginnings.

By some miracle *La Telefónica* would survive the siege of Madrid. The fascist artillery used it as a bull's-eye, and it became famous for the number of direct hits it withstood. Arturo Barea in *The Forging of A Rebel* told what it was like to work and sleep while waiting for the shell that would do more than shatter the walls, more than kill the friend on the floor above.

In the evenings, Amparo strolled through the narrow streets off the Gran Vía searching for an available apartment. The neighborhood consisted mostly of older buildings with small bars and shops on their lower floors. One day she spotted a 'For Rent' sign on an ornate redbrick structure just two blocks behind her workplace. Zigzag arabesques and scrollwork decorated the walls and windows. Both the open balconies and the shuttered Moorish *miradors* were adorned with curlicued ironwork. Number 17 Calle del Barco – "Street of the Boat" – a charming name!

When she rang the *portera's* bell, a fragile young woman with a limp answered. "May I see the apartment?" she asked. "Of course! But it's very small." The woman's name was María Cortes. She would become Amparo's good friend.

Amparo fell in love with the tiny two-room flat under the eaves. She immediately hurried over to the owner's address and signed a lease.

María Cortes remembered Amparo well. "She was the best of women. She had such deep feelings, especially for poor people. I had a very delicate back – they had operated on me when I was very little – and would go upstairs to sunbathe on the roof because heat relieved the discomfort. The moment Amparo heard my footsteps, she would accompany me. We shared an enormous mutual liking for one another. She was very Catholic, and often we went to Mass together."

In her spare hours, Amparo treated herself to the movies on the Gran Vía as well as concerts and readings at the Ateneo. There she made friends with many musicians and artists. One night she heard the young novelist Ramón J. Sender reading parts of his just-published novel *Imán*, but she was too shy to push forward and make his acquaintance.

*Amparo's attic apartment
Number 17. Calle del Barco
(Now Number 21.)*

*María Cortes, Amparo's good friend,
her niece, Araceli (my nursemaid's Aisia's daughter).*

Amparo also attended the literary gatherings at the cafés, including the group surrounding Valle-Inclán, the legendary Galician novelist. She happened to be there when he praised Ramón J. Sender's *Imán* as the best novel of the new epoch. Papá, seated in back, complained modestly how, after signing the book contract, he had tried to withdraw the novel because he was dissatisfied with it. He even had returned the advance, but the publisher stuck to his legal rights and printed the book.

They spoke that night for the first time. He remembered her face from the Ateneo and later, when she stood up to leave, offered to accompany her. They walked up San Jerónimo towards the Puerta del Sol. Papá spoke about Valle-Inclán, a writer whose simple, modest nature he admired enormously.

Over coffee at a café, he told her how as a fourteen-year-old he had been suspended from school in Zaragoza and began to live away from the family. He worked in a number of pharmacies, continuing his studies, until at the age of eighteen he traveled to Madrid to escape his father. At the university he enrolled as a law student. When the famous flu epidemic closed the campus, he spent his days in the Ateneo's library reading down one shelf and the next, sleeping on a bench in the *Retiro* park and washing in the fountain called '*La Joya.*'

To pay for his meals, he wrote articles under a pseudonym. Also, he involved himself in the student protests, and was arrested when the police found him nailing up anti-monarchist posters in the park. His father saved him from jail by claiming him as a minor and bringing him back to Huesca. The old man had just assumed the management of a small rural newspaper, "*La Tierra.*" Papá took over as the unofficial editor. When he turned twenty-one, he resumed classes at the University of Madrid. One year later he was drafted into the army. He served in the grossly mismanaged Moroccan campaign, and was discharged a second lieutenant. Out of these experiences, he wrote *Imán* while working as a journalist for "*El Sol,*" the republican daily. Once the novel was published and his reputation established, he earned his living writing on his own. His articles and essays voiced the ideologies of the Spanish anarchists: the workers and peasants only had to free themselves from the Church and the ruling class for their innate idealism to blossom into a classless society of love and comradeship.

My aunt Conchita's daughter, Ana María, described a prank my father played during her childhood: "Once he came to our house when

I was on a walk. When we returned, we found he had taken all my dolls and arranged them everywhere with such charm that they seemed alive! One was peeking through the curtains, others looking out the doors. Some were climbing the heating pipes, another hiding below the wardrobe! It frightened me because it seemed as if my dolls only waited until I was gone to come alive! I said, 'Mamá, why are all my dolls waiting for me?'"

Conchita took up the story. "Oh, if you only knew what my brother was like in those days! Look, I'm going to tell you an episode that occurred some years before he met Amparo. My husband Emi and I had to break off Pepe's engagement to Mercedinas, whose father was Commander-in-Chief of all the Spanish cavalry and an old friend of our father, Don José. He lived in a palace in the Tetuan sector of Madrid and it had enormous gardens. Ah, this is a story! I was angry with Pepe a long time.

"Mercedinas was a great friend of Pepe's sister, Maruja. I treated her like a little sister, but then Pepe started courting her. One day I said to him, 'Listen, don't play around with Mercedinas, eh? She's like one of the family.'

"'No, she's like a sister to me,' he replied. He was already twenty-five or six years old, and the girl eighteen.

Conchita changed voices with her characters. Pepe she portrayed self-important and wide-eyed.

"I said, 'Good! But hold back a bit,' because I had heard the girl was infatuated with him. One day I said to her, 'Listen, Mercedinas, what's going on with Pepe?' Conchita projected Mercedinas in a petulant whisper. "'Look, I want to tell you – I want to say – Pepe and I are engaged. We're going to get married!'

"I thought, 'how is this girl, with her father the Commander-in-Chief of the cavalry, going to marry Pepe? Pepe won't marry in a church! Would to God that he would!' I would have liked that marriage because the girl was like a part of our family, incredibly beautiful, with four or five years of education at Sacre Coeur and a great deal of money. But he kept saying to me, 'Don't worry yourself, woman! I know what I'm doing.'

"'But the girl doesn't,' I told him. 'She's infatuated with you' "So he didn't change his behavior." Conchita picked up her fan. "Then one fine day Maruja said to me, rolling her eyes, 'Do you know that Pepe and Mercedinas are engaged, although they say they aren't?'

"I replied, 'I'm horrified! There's going to be a big quarrel between the families and it will be all his fault!' "And Maruja, who was as big an idiot as Mercedinas, said, 'No, because if Mercedinas' family wants, they'll get married in the Church.'

Conchita sat bolt upright. "'Can you see your brother dressed ceremonially, with a veiled bride at St. Joseph's and all the generals of Madrid seated in the pews? Don't be stupid!'

"A few days passed and then Mercedinas said to me, 'Conchita, you shouldn't call this stupid without knowing anything about it.'

"'*Andaaa!*'" Conchita tootled the incredulous expletive on two posthorn pitches. "'Look, Mercedinas, watch what you are doing. Pepe is my brother and has many good qualities, but I can't see you married to him.'

"'Yes, oh yes I will! And you know how Pepe says he won't go to Mass? Well, he says he'll give me whatever I want, so he'll go to Mass for me! So there!'

"'But he won't go to Mass! The day you marry, he'll stay home!'

"'Off with you!' she yelled. 'It's our business what we do!' Conchita's fan increased in velocity. "Well, some days passed. We were busy planning for summer vacation. Maruja from one side and Mercedinas from the other still insisted Pepe would marry her. When we returned on the first of September, Pepe came to my house and said, 'Listen, Conchita, I must ask you and Emi a favor. You must ask for the hand of Mercedinas.'

"I was astonished! 'We have to ask for her hand and not Papá?'

"He avoided my eyes and stuttered excuses. 'Papá would have to come all the way from Zaragoza, and it's a long trip, and Papá's getting old, Papá – '

"I said, 'No, Papá travels! He always comes here on business. He's an intimate friend of the girl's grandfather. He would do it with pleasure!'

"'No, no, no, I don't want to bother Papá, no, no,' Pepe replied. 'If you two do it, that's adequate.'

"Later, my husband Emi laughed when he heard about it. 'It's like a Hollywood movie!'

"'You might see it like that,' I said. 'But I'm disgusted!'"

She slapped her thigh. "Well, we did it! The father gave Mercedinas a banquet in the garden on her saint's day, with everything beautifully arranged. Pepe had seated me with her and we had brought her a nice present. So we asked for her hand, and then I said to the father, 'Don Bonifacio, excuse us for having to leave early, but my boy has very bad tonsillitis.'

"He called his official car with his chauffeur. Pepe said, 'I'll go with you too.' He turned to Mercedinas. 'Look, I'll come back around eight and we'll go to the movies.'

The car had barely left the palace when Pepe said, 'But I can't marry this girl! I like her very much but I can't!'

"'Wicked!' I yelled. 'You made us ask for her hand! How could you do this to us? Now I understand why you didn't want Papá to come. We can get through this, but if Don José had come he would have killed you! Alive or dead, you would have married Mercedinas!"

My father once told a story about how he spent his evenings at this time among the striking workers, exchanging shots with the police. He was also taking Mercedinas to the movies in the afternoons, Mercedinas would send a note via an intermediary to ask what movie they were attending. Then the police were alerted not to arrest them because it would have caused a scandal for the family.

When he first met Amparo, my father was romantically involved with the daughter of the editor of "*El Sol.*" Amparo had heard tales of his predilection for affairs, but the anarchist ideal of Free Love also influenced her own awakening awareness. In October 1930, he began publishing a column in the CNT (*Confederación Nacional de Trabajo*) union's daily "*Solidarid Obrera,*" aligning himself with the unionists and mocking the Socialists who wished to govern without dissolving the monarchy. A planned rebellion fizzled that December, and the two officers shot, Galan and Hernandez, became working-class heroes. Student demonstrations erupted at the university. Then the April elections swept everyone away in rejoicing. The Second Republic was proclaimed, the royal family went into exile, and the citizenry danced in the streets for days. Not a policeman was to be seen, and yet not a single untoward incident occurred. Everyone wore red scarves and Phrygian caps. They carried flags, posters, even tree branches, and sang "The Marseillaise."

But the euphoria soon passed. Some monarchists met in the central area and played "The Royal March" on a phonograph. This infuriated the Sunday crowds who burned some cars. They marched to the offices of the monarchist newspaper, *ABC*, and set the building aflame. Martial law was proclaimed and the first innocent days of 'the new dawn' were over.

In July 1931, the telephone workers struck. The women were tired of low wages and poor treatment at the hands of the multinational monopoly. The government called out the civil guard and there were some shootings. The telephone workers felt betrayed because the Socialist leaders, who had promised their support, panicked. There was bad blood between the Socialist UGT *(Unión General de Trabajadores)*, which more or less controlled Madrid, and the telephone workers who belonged to the CNT. The UGT provided scabs and in their newspaper "*El Socialista*" attacked the CNT as anarchist provocateurs.

Amparo wrote a childhood friend at this time that she felt very persecuted. Living as she did just a few blocks from La Telefónica, she must have encountered many violent incidents on her street. During the early days of the strike, Pepe spotted her at the CNT offices where she had volunteered as a typist. He invited her to a meal and asked how she was supporting herself during the strike.

"I am teaching piano students at home," she said, not wanting him to know she was in financial straits.

"Why not take a job typing for me?" he asked. "I need a secretary. If I had known what a good typist you were, I would have asked you before."

"Secretary" was often a jokester's euphemism for something else, so she refused. "To help you with your manuscripts is one thing," she said. "But I'm determined to stay with the phone company."

They began to meet at an outdoor café in the Plaza Santa Barbara, just across the street from the Pensión Bilbaina where Pepe lived. Amparo would bring freshly typed chapters of *Orden Publico*, his new book, and pick up his rough drafts. His radical friends frequently joined them, and many intense political discussions took place. Pepe was heavily involved in the clandestine activities of the CNT, which he felt were responding to the will of the people. His job was to relay coded phone instructions to other cities.

Although Amparo never was a political activist, the events of the strike swept her up and she tried to enter the men's conversations. Often she left these meetings irritated by their condescending comments.

Not until two co-workers were wounded by Assault Guards did she become so enraged that she volunteered at union headquarters for a dangerous task. They needed someone to place a bomb on the floor that held the telephone switching equipment. She was given a small package and instructions.

*La Telefonica, Madrid's first skyscraper,*
*which survived many direct hits during the Civil War.*

That evening at the appointed hour, she joined the crowd of protesters at La Telefónica, wearing her blue cloak to conceal what she carried. A scuffle was started at the front entrance to divert the guards. When events were at their most chaotic, she slipped in the side door. She avoided the elevators and ran upstairs. Once she had concealed the package, she returned.

The crowd cried, 'Scab, scab!' when she appeared, also a part of the plan.

Her heart beating wildly, she ran in the direction of the Plaza Santa Barbara café where she found Pepe and a few others.

"Well, you are a bundle of nerves this evening," Pepe said.

Just then a distant explosion was heard and she jumped. "I did it!" she cried. "I placed the bomb!"

My father wrote about the incident in his novel *Seven Red Sundays*. His acquaintance, whom he called 'Graco,' looked at Amparo in astonishment.

"You?" he asked.

"Who else?" she said proudly. "Certainly me. Thousands of lines must be out of action."

Graco made a big fuss over her, kissing her hand and asking her how long she had been a member of the strike organization. "Three months," Amparo replied, getting up and arranging her cloak.

"Where are you going now?" Pepe asked.

"Home to my tiny apartment," she said. "I must get some sleep because tomorrow I rise early to confess and go to Mass."

"To confess?" The men's mouths gaped in astonishment.

"Yes, about the bomb. But I won't tell the priest when or where it was. If he absolves me, well and good. If not, all the worse for him. My conscience is clear."

Pepe burst out laughing, but Graco was enraged. However, they did not taunt Amparo as a petite bourgeoise anymore. The bomb did considerable damage but no one was hurt, and Pepe and Amparo's relationship continued upon the firm base of their collaboration.

"I treated Amparo like a sister from the first time we met," Conchita declared. "Pepe was sick in bed with a flu at the Pensión Bilbaina and I went to visit him. Amparo arrived to deliver a typed manuscript, and he introduced her to me as his secretary. Some time later, Emi and I went to the movies on the Gran Vía, to the Galería. And I said, 'Well, look who bought good seats!' They had those white armchairs in the mezzanine at the time. And Emi said, 'It's Pepe with someone! Where'd you meet her, Pepe?'

"'She's my secretary,' Pepe said and frowned at us. 'I don't remember where I met her.'

"'You're acting just like an American,' Emi said. 'Obviously this is the "secretary" you've been searching for.'

"And Pepe said, 'No I haven't been looking especially. This just happened. She's been working at the telephone company.'

"'I'm going to give classes in piano until the strike's settled,' Amparo said. 'Ramón asked me to be his secretary and I said, "Oh, no!"'

Conchita smoothed her dress. "When Emi and I were ready to leave after the movie, we went back to them, and I said, 'Let's go for coffee.' They didn't even know we were there until Pepe looked up and said, 'No-no-no! We're staying until everyone leaves!'

"We were still standing at the curb when they left hand-in-hand. A street urchin looked up from his shoeshine kit and said, 'Hey, just look at those two lovebirds!' She captured a boy's teasing tone. 'I think there's going to be a wedding!'

"'No-no-no!' they said.

"Later my husband said, 'This time he'll marry, for sure! Even before we get to know her, because she's extremely beautiful and tall.'"

Conchita's fan started up again. "So that was the winter of 1931. If my brother had said they must go to Hell, Amparo would have gone with him. That's the way she was. That summer in San Rafael, Emi and I met a pretty woman, one of those delicate Andalusian types from Murcia, brunette and well brought up. Friends thought of introducing her to Pepe but I said, 'No, no, Pepe already has a love, this secretary of his, and this time he'll marry!' She smiled at the memory. "And by the winter of '32, although they would not admit it, they were engaged."

A sonnet my father wrote in later years described Amparo as he remembered her from this time. Although she is not mentioned by name, the context makes the subject of the poem obvious:

> Instead of the truth came you,
> my bride of strikes and unions,
> all aflutter with your enthusiasms
> and a red star on each shoe.
> You saw me in your competition
> her promiscuity and my innate qualities

doubting between Yahweh and Beelzebub,
you came to give me your contradictions.
I knew no more of the world, beloved,
bristling with spines like a ripe cactus,
than what you told me in your ecstasy.
Yet in that hypocrisy of your silence
I behold myself as on the premature
anniversary of my death you saw me.

The telephone strike failed, and Amparo was out of a job. She wrote letters to several ministries asking for employment, and searched for more piano students.

In September, Pepe left for Paris and Berlin to attend writers' congresses and meet with foreign publishers. He returned pessimistic about conditions in Europe, especially Germany where the depression was playing into the hands of the Nazis. In Spain, many violent incidents occurred between the Civil Guards and the peasants whose situation was desperate. But the general feeling was that the wrongs of centuries could not be corrected overnight. Amparo, meanwhile, concentrated on her music. That winter she played some recitals with her violinist friend, Antonio Arias, and practiced for a concert of Spanish composers.

In January 1933, just after Hitler was elected chancellor in Germany, the Casas Viejas massacre occurred in which assault guards brutally murdered a peasant family. My father immediately left to cover the incident and was the first journalist to arrive. His eyewitness reports, gathered at considerable personal risk, were published in "*La Libertad.*" The government tried to suppress them and put out an order for his arrest. One day Amparo heard a knock on her door.

"Quick, hide me somewhere!" Pepe said, breathless from running. "The police are after me! Azaña is outraged by what I've written. They spotted me outside my *pensión!*"

The police came to the concierge, María Cortes, and asked her, "Do you know a certain Ramón J. Sender?"

"Well, no," she replied. "I can tell you nothing. The name doesn't ring a bell."

After they left, she ran upstairs and said, "*Señorita* Amparo, listen, Don Ramón shouldn't show his face! Don't let him go outside because the police are looking for him."

*Plaza Santa Barbara, with Papá's pensión along the right side.*

*Tía Conchita Sender.*

He stayed with Amparo several days until things calmed down, and during this time, their relationship became intimate. Azaña later admitted that Sender's reports contributed considerably to the defeat of his government.

When parliament decided to investigate the Casas Viejas affair, the police search ended and he was free to roam the city again. But by then he was more or less living with Amparo. Together they attended the May Day celebrations. Not a single car moved in the city, not even a trolley.

María Cortes, the concierge, reported: "One day, in the middle of Mass, Amparo turned to me and said, 'I have to go, María.' And she left. When I returned to the house, I asked, 'Why did you leave, Señorita Amparo?'

"She said, 'Look, I couldn't stay. I believe in God, but since Ramón has been with me, I am totally devoted to him. If I cannot visit the house of God with devotion, I prefer not to go.'

"From then on, Amparo never returned to church. At the beginning, she didn't want me to know she was living with your father. But I said, 'Look, Señorita Amparo, these conventions are silly. Your fiancé can stay here.' So that's the way it was."

Late in May, my father left on a five-month journey to Russia as a guest of the *Unión Internacional de Escritores.* He returned generally sympathetic with the Soviet cause, although his published views avoided a blind acceptance of Marxist-Stalinist ideologies. He praised the egalitarianism he observed, and was especially impressed by a message the writers' organization received asking for help shoveling snow in the streets. He felt it necessary to justify his intellectual career to the workers: "I write books and articles because I don't know how to mix concrete, tan leather or conduct a tram..." Although other visiting Spaniards criticized the lack of civil liberties, my father accepted the explanation that it expressed the spontaneous self-discipline of the masses. For the next three years he would align himself increasingly with the Communists until his final disillusionment during the Spanish Civil War.

In *Seven Red Sundays,* one of the main characters, Samar, writes a love letter to his woman friend, Amparo, an expression of love which my father could well have sent my mother at this time.

> Dearest, forgive me:
> Until now, seven o'clock, I couldn't write you. I'm not going to write much, but you know I love you, little darling, desperately. I am hungry for your arms and your lips. I would like to give you a life filled with

light and peace. But I don't believe it can be... I want
for you all the peace and quietness that shines in my soul
when I lose myself in our love. But how can I give you
the peace and quietness that are so far away from me?...
I have known life in its most secret corners, in sweetness
and in bitterness. I believed my soul held all the secrets,
knew everything, had reached everything... Suddenly, I
came to know you... I was drunk every day with the light
in my own heart... I found in the depths of your gentle
eyes the secret of the universe, immense and everlasting,
and my heart quickened in beats of joy... You and me,
darling! You and me! Others don't exist.

In the general election in Spain that November, the Right gained
more seats than the squabbling Socialists. Street fights occurred
between militant student groups. Many people remained unem-
ployed. But these alarming events swirled harmlessly around Papá
and Amparo, snug in their love nest. They tended to stay home in
spite of friends' complaints about their "overextended honeymoon"
and their "annoyingly bourgeois" attitudes. But the criticisms
bounced off them harmlessly.

"The natural egoism of lovers is threatening to others, because they
see the materialism of their own lives condemned," Papá commented.

María Cortes: "Your parents stayed until she became pregnant with
you. One day she said, 'María, we're going to move to Monteleón
Street. We've found an apartment there because this one is so small.'"

My father told Conchita he was leaving his *pensión* and moving to
an apartment.

"You're taking an apartment by yourself? *Huyyy!*" She shook her
head in dismay. "What dirty sheets and socks you'll have! Who will
buy you a necktie when yours falls away in tatters?"

"No!" he replied with a laugh. "I won't be by myself."

"So then, with whom?"

"You're a witch, you're supposed to know everything! I won't tell
you with whom."

"All right, it's Amparo," Conchita said.

"So it doesn't matter if I bring her over to visit?"

"Of course it doesn't matter, neither to Emi or me. She's a young
woman who's acting stupidly because she loves you very much. And

we'll come to your house also and toast your health! For me, it's as if you are married! Right now! If you tell me later that it was just a passing affair, I won't listen! I won't tolerate it. Don't come by in a couple of months whining, 'Oh look, I don't like her! Now I'm with another.'"

These were the so-called "Black Years," the right-wing radicals in power cynically undoing the few reforms of Azaña's cabinet and selling government favors to their cronies. Spain was overwhelmed with literature on Russia. My father produced two books from his summer journey, *Madrid-Moscú, Narraciones de Viaje* and *Carta de Moscú Sobre el Amor.* In the latter he attacked the repressive sexual mores of the Catholic Church as the cause of alienation and superstition. The erotic symbolism of religion was utilized by old maids and failed lovers for their own titillation. In contrast, he exalted Soviet sex as free from mysticism, 'open' marriage as the means to achieving true tranquility and fidelity in the home. Where sexual liberty was absolute, there existed much less libertinism than within the religiously repressive systems.

Amparo labored long hours at the typewriter that winter. As a result my father published a total of five books in 1934, mostly derived from his articles. By the time the manuscripts went to the printer, she knew she was pregnant. Conchita was carrying her third child and they spent much time together.

Papá placed his most radical articles in *La Lucha,* the daily, which for a year, replaced the banned *Solidaridad Obrera.* It promoted the concept of a single front to unite all leftist parties against the counter-revolution and was frequently confiscated by the police. On several occasions he had to go into hiding after an issue hit the stands.

There was constant turmoil in the streets. That spring, the Rightist leader Robles held a Nazi-style rally at the Escorial, and Madrid's workers expected a Mussolini-like march on the capital, but bad weather kept the crowd below the predicted number.

In retrospect, those early years were to seem idyllic because that October, three events electrified Spain: a general strike, the government of Catalonia's proclamation of an autonomous state and, most serious of all, an armed rebellion by the miners in Asturias.

*A photo of Amparo, dated June 21, 1939, and inscribed "to my goddaughter with love, Amparito." She was twenty-five years old. Courtesy of Antonio Arias.*

Chapter 6
Red October to July 1936

In response to the miners' revolt, the government brought in the Foreign Legion and Moorish mercenaries under the command of General Franco. Press censorship kept the people from learning the more gruesome details immediately, but rumors of the Moors' cruelty and the sexual tortures used by the civil guard horrified everyone. By the end of the month, thirty thousand leftists comprised of Republicans and Socialists were in prison. Most of their leaders were either dead, in jail or in hiding.

My father journeyed north to cover the Foreign Legion's recapture of Oviedo at a cost of three thousand dead, seven thousand wounded. He was outraged by the atrocities perpetrated by the Moors against women and children. When he returned home, Madrid was still under martial law. Three days earlier, Amparo had gone into labor. She left a note at the apartment and went to the clinic. There the nuns seemed more preoccupied with the dreaded revolution than with her labor pains. She gave birth to a son at two in the morning to the accompaniment of machine-gun fire in the street

Two days later, Papá arrived at her bedside. He had walked to the clinic with his hands raised above his head to prove to the patrols he was unarmed. He stared in amazement at the scrawny little bundle in her arms. My head was misshaped from the passage through the birth canal, my skin purple and eyelids swollen.

"He's very intelligent," he muttered, trying to hide his growing panic. "It can be seen in the shape of his head."

Amparo laughed at his expression. "He is just fine, *querido*, although a little underweight. And his head will not remain pointed for long."

According to Conchita, Papá was an exaggerated father, worrying about the slightest thing. My birth created a new problem for my parents because family pressure on them to get married increased, especially from my grandfather Don José. Papá and his father, both strong personalities, had a terrible relationship. As the eldest son, Papá had borne the brunt of Don José's temper throughout his childhood, and his ongoing defiance remained a source of much family friction. Yet ultimately Amparo would be the one to pay with her life for their flouting of traditional values.

Conchita: "What your parents did not want, either of them – this, well, really it doesn't matter but – " She drew a big breath. "They

*General Strike, Madrid, October 1934*

*Amparo with newborn Ramón, October 29, 1934*

didn't want to get married! I remember once saying to your father, 'Look, when one has to go somewhere, Pepe, it's better to take the highway and not strike out cross-country. Why make your children's lives more difficult? You two have the right to live however you want, and to me it's the same, but the children!' But they always said to me, 'We're happy the way we are!'"

She remembered Papá bringing Amparo home from the clinic. It was a brilliant autumn day. After the antiseptic smells of the clinic, Amparo inhaled the fall fragrances with delight. There had been a lull in the street fighting. Crowds strolled along the boulevards in the warm sunshine, as if both violent death and laughter were natural ingredients in the life of a Spaniard. They turned up Calle del Divino Pastor, a street of little shops that connected with theirs. Papá held me with a new father's awkwardness. A pock-faced junkman, remarkable for the long wisps of hair extending from his ears, lifted his cap from beside his cart.

"Welcome home, *señora*," he said. And to Papá he said, 'You are Sender, right? You write for "*La Lucha*" these days." On the steps of their apartment house, children were playing with spent bullet casings they had collected in the street. They clustered around us saying what people always say. "What's his name? What's his name?"

Amparo smiled. "Ramón, of course, like his father. Little Monchín."

"Monchín, Monchín!" they cried.

Conchita visited one day to find Amparo changing me. Obviously I had not emptied my bladder because I let go a fountain across her dress. Amparo was embarrassed, but Conchita was used to it from her own babies. She kept staring at me because I was a perfect miniature Don José – just like my grandfather.

"Please, don't mention the resemblance to Ramón," Amparo begged. "It will cause trouble."

That winter, all of Spain remained polarized, but the Left did not interpret the outcome of the Red October events as a failure. At least it had proved the working class would not tolerate the establishment of a fascist state. However, it had been a defeat for the socialist cause, and the trial of the imprisoned leaders continued throughout that winter.

For Amparo and Papá, these disturbances were peripheral. He stayed home to write his new novel *Mr. Witt among the Rebels*, a fictionalized description of the First Republic's struggles in 1873 to resolve issues similar to those in the 1930s. When I was restless, Amparo lulled me with Chopin waltzes on the piano. She overlaid the harmonies with all her heart's fulfillment, coaxing a beautiful tone from her old upright.

Papá questioned everyone about childcare. "What's that?" he asked. "Why are you doing that? Tell me everything about babies."

He and Amparo bothered their pediatrician so much that when they phoned him he would say, 'What, more nonsense? What's the matter this time?'

In the spring, they took happy rambles with me in a borrowed perambulator. At the zoo, Papá introduced me to the elephants and hippopotamuses for the first time, holding me up to blink over the railing. I did not seem impressed.

"To him everything is extraordinary," Papá explained. "He sees no difference between God and the camel."

Marcelle, my French aunt who later would lose her husband, my father's favorite brother Manolo, to the Falangist execution squad, recalled meeting Amparo at this time. "I met her when Manolo and I returned from our honeymoon in February. She was much taller than your father's sisters.

"When she was dressed to go out, she was very attractive. One day I went with friends to meet her at the theater. We were in the balcony and Amparo was seated below. She was wearing a lovely hat – it was the beginning of spring – a circlet of violets. At the intermission, Amparo and her hat came out to join us.

"Amparo had much character and willpower. She certainly wasn't a coquette like the Sender sisters. Not Amparo. She was a little austere, a woman of intellect above all, more intellectual than the sisters of her husband, more reserved. She became perturbed if other women flirted with your father. Amparo did not confide her fears to me, but obviously Pepe enjoyed the company of other women. He was not the sort who should have married, because he preferred the bachelor's life."

What a happy time for Amparo! Papá hardly went out, her baby was healthy and her milk abundant. In her music, she had an avenue of expression, and her typing was an invaluable help to her lover.

But the political crisis continued, although martial law was downgraded to a "state of alarm" renewed from month to month. The rightists took their cues from the European dictatorships and proposed "a national revolution against atheism and the international threat of the Marxists, Masons and Jews." The leftists saw themselves on the road towards a Russian-style purge of the ruling class.

The reactionary government of Lerroux favored the rich and returned the Jesuits' confiscated properties. They appointed General Franco chief of staff and shelved land reform as well as public education projects. When the hot summer days came, Amparo took the train with me, Conchita and her children to Villa Frutos where Papá would join us on the weekend.

Conchita: "How we loved that first breath of the Sierras after the heat of Madrid, the smell of sage from the rocky hillsides. Our stop, San Rafael, was the first on the other side of the peak of Alto de León. Emi and I had rented the downstairs, and Pepe and Amparo the second floor. We had our new baby Riqui, only a few months younger than you."

When my father arrived with some friends, we picnicked in the pines. I was told I met my first cows there, and looked at them with the same expression I had given the zoo animals, as if thinking, "more strange creatures."

"Yes, you are right," Papá said to me. "They are all as strange as you think they are. And just like us, they did not ask to be born." He looked over his shoulder at Amparo. "We are all innocents, here on this planet without reason or motive."

"But do you believe in God?' Amparo asked him.

"Sometimes, but sometimes not. I see God in the nature of men. Sometimes I believe in men and sometimes not." He grinned. "All without reason."

His paradoxes always annoyed Amparo. "Ramón, why don't you answer me seriously?" she complained.

"I'm as serious as possible in the presence of a kissable angel," he replied.

He thought Amparo a marvelous innocent. Yet if he told her, she would lose the very quality he held so precious. At the same time, Amparo felt he didn't respect her ideas enough. After all, she was a serious person with ideas of her own that she enjoyed discussing. She considered his attitude patronizing and often told him so in a flare of temper. He found her incomprehensible and enchanting.

That day, one of the men had a pistol. They took turns shooting at a distant rock. The women found it nerve-wracking, but the children were fascinated. Suddenly smoke began to drift from the nearby bushes. The crackle of twigs brought everyone to their feet.

"Fire!" Ramón yelled.

He grabbed his leather jacket and began beating at the flames. They labored to contain the blaze, but it had been a rainless summer and the brush was like tinder. The best they could do was escape before they were caught by the foresters and accused of arson.

"A bullet must have struck a spark," someone said.

The fire burned out of control for hours in spite of the arrival of the fire department. The men watched the smoke from the chalet with the guilty expression of boys who knew they had done something wrong. Politics had been banned at the dinner table for the duration of vacation, so instead Papá told a silly story of his youth (which I recall his telling me years later).

"Once I borrowed an old nag to ride to the swimming hole," he said. "We used to swim there naked. After a while, getting cold, I decided to ride my somewhat crazy horse a short distance into the sunshine to dry off. Her broad back was a pleasant place to sunbathe. Anyway, I was stretched out, my eyes closed, when she took off down the main road. I barely managed to stay on, and no matter how hard I pulled at the reins, she refused to stop. It was supper time by her reckoning and she had the bit in her teeth. We came into the middle of town at a canter and completely broke up a procession of the Daughters of Mary. They all screamed and beat at me with various objects while the mayor and the bishop talked about the scandals of liberalism."

"No politics!" Amparo warned amidst general laughter.

I participated in the children's games mainly by interfering. When a wrestling match between two boys bowled me into a corner, I wailed piteously.

Papá squatted down and hit his own head against the wall. "Ow!" he cried, making a clownish grimace and rolling his eyes. By the third repetition, my tears stopped. I crawled to the wall and butted it, sitting back and glancing up for approval. Papá grinned. "See, little son, a man laughs at pain," he said. "He must be courageous in this best and worst of all possible worlds." Gradually, I learned I was something different from Amparo. I must find my fulfillment in the world of men, and be strong and independent. 'No' was the first word I said. I was a vigorous crawler and would disappear in an instant into the flower beds to eat dirt by the handful. Luckily the yard was below the level of the high road, and Ana María old enough to bring me back if I wandered. At night, Amparo put me to sleep singing the lullaby for which Papá

had written the words. She used a melody from one of the canticles of
St. John of the Cross:

> "Four little ducks
> Who had a mama
> Played at skip rope
> Near the water
> Little red beaks
> Little white feathers
> They played and played
> Not paying attention to anything."

When Conchita sang it, the melody evoked an image of Amparo in a
blue and white speckled sweater, her sleeves rolled back, bathing me in
a tub on the kitchen floor. I dreamt this as a child and always treasured
it as the one concrete memory I retained of her, her dark hair tied back,
the sunlight sparkling off the water.

"In the second verse, a wolf creeps up on them," Conchita explained.
She leaned back and smoothed out her skirt. "So that was how it was.
The mountains, the forest glades, the profusion of wildlife all fed our
spirits after months of city living. In the mornings, Pepe walked into
the village for the newspapers. Every three or four days he would grow
restless and take the train to Madrid to pick up his mail, phone a few
friends or deliver an article.

"Because of the censorship, he could only write on innocuous
subjects such as foreign writers or the theater. He always returned
with bad news: the re-imposition of martial law in Barcelona or Franco's
staging army maneuvers in Asturias as a warning to the miners. Azaña,
who had barely escaped with his life after the October Revolution,
spent the summer in front of large audiences, calling for the Left to
unite. Largo Caballero inflamed the socialist youth with revolutionary
rhetoric while Prieto, from his exile in Paris, ignored leftist criticism
and worked for unity with the Republicans."

"Just forget the world for a few months, Ramón," Amparo would beg.
"It won't stop spinning."

He would agree. "Even though after a few days I can't bear the sight
of another tree, another vacuous cow, I know I belong out here," he told
her. "At heart I am a *baturro*, a hardheaded Aragonese rustic."

In September we returned to Madrid where an electrical calm
prevailed. The airing of the Straperlo roulette machine bribery

case implicated government officials and precipitated Prime Minister Lerroux's resignation. With the announcement that November of an even more lurid scandal involving Lerroux himself, the reactionary government found itself publicly disgraced and new elections were scheduled for February. The right-wing parties plastered the streets with posters but offered no platform, confident they would restore the power of the army, Church and ruling class. In contrast, a newly formed coalition of the Left named The Popular Front printed a manifesto. It carefully outlined a program including amnesty for the Red October prisoners and the completion of the 1931 reforms. It took its name from the Popular Front campaign against fascism, which the Communist International had approved the previous summer, an ill-fated choice because other nations were to interpret the Popular Front's victory as a Marxist takeover.

Amparo urged Ramón to complete *Mr. Witt among the Rebels* in time to submit it to the National Literature contest. She was always at the typewriter whenever he slept to make fresh copies of his scribbled-over drafts.

One evening Amparo phoned Conchita. "Ramón has bought a revolver from a friend," she said. "He says we must prepare for the worst. I had wanted to tell him I was pregnant again, that we must find a larger place, but how – "

"Amparo, stay calm," Conchita told her. "Are you sure you're pregnant?"

"Yes, I'm already beginning to show," Amparo replied. "I think the baby will come in February."

"Now you must get married," Conchita insisted. "Otherwise you're only thinking of yourselves. Consider the children! Why place daggers under their feet?"

"You behave as if they were yours!"

"Well, it's as if they were mine!" Conchita told her. "I don't want my children entering life on a bad path. No sir!"

Conchita sat upright with a determined expression. "I must have finally convinced them, because one day Pepe said, 'Listen, the Republic has legalized civil ceremonies so we're going to get married at the Escorial and you have to come along.'

One morning that same month, Papá borrowed a car and drove everyone to the Escorial. The wedding was held in a small parish house, a retired judge presiding. Emi and Conchita were the sponsors and two employees of the judge were witnesses. Amparo wore a simple navy blue wool suit and little matching hat, Papá his usual worn gabardine.

Although Amparo notified her family, no one attended. However, shortly afterwards, her younger brother Antonio came to visit. In a family photo, he wears an elegant suit and rimless glasses, giving the impression of an intellectual young scientist. Supposedly he was the only one in her family who could tolerate her way of life.

"My brother Antonio visited and we went out to supper," Amparo told Conchita. She mentioned how happy she was to see him, to have a member of her family near. He was somewhat shy around Pepe, but alone with her, he told her his electrical business was prospering and the family was doing well.

The civil marriage displeased my grandfather Don José enormously. Conchita's sister Asunción reported, "For my father, marriage did not exist outside the Church. 'No, they aren't married!' he insisted, and continued addressing Amparo as 'señorita.' Of course it didn't matter to me. We often said, 'Look, Papá, you may call her want you like, but we're treating them as a married couple.'"

"There are minds in this world that are outside the usual order of things," Conchita said, speaking of my father. "You can't box them in. Never! I remember Pepe coming over to my apartment one morning in despair. Andrea had not yet been born, your mother having a few more months to go.

"'I'm here!' he said.

"'I see you,' I replied. 'Who have you fought with now?'

"And he said with much drama, 'With whom do you think? With Amparo!'

"I said, 'I'm sorry for her. I'll phone her right away to calm her.'

"'No!' he shouted. 'But since I haven't had a meal, I came here to eat.'

"'Don't even dream of it,' I told him.

"And he said, 'Now I see that Amparo is more your sister than my wife!'"

"'Well, just about,' I replied. 'At least we're faithful and remain in agreement. Even if it's against you. Never come to this house without Amparo, either to snack or have a meal. Either the two of you come, or nobody comes.'

"'I'm not eating at home!' he yelled.

"'Eat where you want,' I told him, 'but here... you don't eat.'" She had captured Papá's inflections perfectly, and her replies were cold

Toledo steel. "'I'm phoning Amparo to tell her, "Rest tranquil, let it be, because he certainly won't eat anywhere the way he is, acting so crazy. You feed your little boy and then go take a nap. After a while, Pepe will show up. When he does, you should say to him, 'Don't you understand that you have met the woman whom God made for you?' Because my brother could not understand this. He had a big heart, he was a good man, but – carrammmba! – to live with him – ! I told Amparo this when she was still single. Before she married him I said, 'Amparo, you are putting yourself in a situation that's going to bring you anguish. Think about it.' 'No, no, I've already thought about it,' she said to me. 'I've thought it through.'"

At the beginning of January 1936, my father was informed that his novel *Mr. Witt among the Rebels* had been awarded the National Prize. His picture appeared in all the papers. And on February 3, Papá's birthday, Amparo went into labor. Andrea was born at home four hours later, an easy delivery compared to the many hours it had taken me to arrive.

Two weeks later, the Popular Front won the elections and the celebrations and parades were endless. The prison gates were forced open by cheering crowds and all the prisoners were freed, both political and criminal alike. Many aristocrats fled the country and took exaggerated tales of communist atrocities with them. Elsewhere in Europe, fascism was on the march. Mussolini invaded Abyssinia and Hitler reoccupied the Rhineland.

Andrea's arrival, Conchita told me, caused me some difficulties. Although I was almost weaned, I was in the habit of returning to Amparo's breast now and then. Suddenly my place was usurped by this squalling bundle. Amparo made a special effort to reassure me. Also she found a fifteen-year-old niece of her old concierge, María, to be my nursemaid, a sweet-faced girl named Dionisia. I called her 'Aisia' and then everyone did. She adored my parents.

María: "One day your father came to me and said, 'Amparo is giving birth.' So I went over and there was the midwife and so on. We talked about my cousin Dionisia becoming your nursemaid. I said, 'Ah, what a pity that she's so young! Well, let's see if she can do the job.'

"Amparo said, 'It's not important how old she is. She just has to be nursemaid to Monchín.'

"'Well, if you want her, I'll bring her,' I said. So I brought Dionisia and she started working there.

Conchita: "I remember you walking beside Aisia, moving your elbow back and forth like a piston and shouting, '*Mi mismo*! By myself!'"

Marcelle: "You moved to the top floor of an apartment house on the Avenida Menendez Pelayo facing the lions' house in the Retiro zoo. When your father had worked all night long at the typewriter, your mother went out on the balcony where she kept a low table and typed there so as not to disturb her husband's rest. A very intelligent woman. And when she arose in the morning, she combed her dark hair with a few drops of water and pinned it behind her head with an aquamarine.

"She always helped her husband whom she loved and admired. She understood he was not like other men. He wrote when he felt like it, sometimes all night long. He made his own schedule, and she adjusted to it. Most women would have found him impossible, but she remained very devoted. To live with your father, a woman had to have all the virtues: good in bed, capable of running the household, of editing and typing his books. All these things Amparo did very well. What she lacked was the flirtatiousness that Pepe found attractive. She would not put on airs or primp. But Pepe liked dressy women, and she did not do enough to satisfy him in this regard. Instead, she cultivated an interest in literature to retain an advantage over other women. She lived in the heaven of her husband. And of course, she had two children on her hands. "

The closeness of the animals excited me, the trumpeting of the elephants and the roars of the big cats. I would stand on the balcony to stare at the giraffes swaying like palm trees. And before falling asleep, I made Aisia tell me a story about the three little boats painted on my crib. But certain things frightened me, such as the peacocks' cries, especially on the mornings I wet my bed. '*Me-yoon!*' they screamed. 'Bed-wetter!' And I was afraid of the Civil Guards in their dark capes in the park.

Sometimes Papá entertained dark men with unshaven cheeks. I looked them over carefully, ignoring their attempts to make friends. Then I would frown and give them their hats. Or tugging them to their feet, I pulled them towards the door. It was my way of telling them to leave.

"I played a game with you," Conchita told me. "I would say, 'Bring me a book of Paye's,' – that was your way of saying 'Papá.' You would go to the bookcase, take a book from the lowest shelf and bring it to me. All the books on that shelf were by Pepe, so you always succeeded at your task. But visitors unaware of this marveled at how intelligent you were. Oh!" She laughed and slapped her knee. "I just remembered something! Don José came to meet your sister. He was very proud of his grandchildren, but Pepe was always ill at ease during these visits. He was especially irritated by Don José's insistence that both you children be baptized. Anyway, you must have sensed your father's mood because you decided to bring Grandpa his hat to encourage his departure.

"'No, no, not yet,' Pepe told you.

"You were disappointed and took the hat back to the hall. Suddenly you had to make pee-pee. Perhaps the hat reminded you of your potty, because you peed in Grandpa's hat, an event that made Pepe shout with laughter. You had expressed his feelings towards his father to perfection!

"However Don José managed to convince Amparo to baptize her children. Behind your father's back, they took you both to a local church for the brief ceremony."

The euphoria of the Popular Front victory soon gave way to rumors of a rightist coup. Groups of youths roamed the streets provoking incidents that could be blamed on the Reds. The government seemed incapable of stopping the political assassinations. When the hot summer days began, the adults all expected the worst, but hoped against hope things would remain calm.

In *Counterattack in Spain*, my father recalled the mood of the days just before the Civil War began:

> "At the beginning of July we were all caught up in confusion and anxiety. Like everyone else, I expected the volcano to erupt. Because it seemed that the military had not yet decided (to rebel) and because the state of Madrid was enervating, I, who did not know how to work in such a stifling atmosphere, once again rented the little San Rafael villa that nestled in the Guadarrama mountains. I assumed it would be a nest of vipers politically, so as before, I put the lease in another's name. I gave my address to no one so that letters would not come to me. Now and then, I made the two-hour train ride to Madrid to collect my mail... far from imagining the importance these lovely landscapes were to assume in the Civil War, and how these events were to strike desolation into my heart."

With Amparo's return to San Rafael, she moved one day's journey closer to Zamora and the unimaginable destiny awaiting her there. If only the Civil War had begun two weeks earlier or our vacation plans had been delayed, we would have remained safe in Madrid.

*Ramón Senior in the late 1930s.*

*The mountain village of San Rafael.*

## Chapter 7
## San Rafael and El Espinar

In July 1982, forty-six years after my last journey with Amparo to San Rafael, I returned once again. I had been eagerly anticipating this search for Villa Frutos, the chalet that played such an important role at the beginning of my life and the war. Maruchi Rivera, one of the two daughters of the Director of Mountains whom Amparo took with her to Zamora in 1936, agreed to accompany me and my wife. Her response to my *El País* letter had helped fill in the story of those panic-stricken days.

It was a beautiful day. The Guadarrama foothills resemble the California Sierras with their golden fields and green swatches of forest. To the west I saw the huge cross that marked *El Valle De Los Caidos,* Franco's monument to the Civil War dead and his own final resting place. Thousands of loyalist prisoners had been condemned to years at hard labor carving the gigantic mausoleum out of solid rock. It was not on our itinerary. Franco only became commander in chief because all others who outranked him were killed. The most grotesque demise was General Sanjurjo's whom the Republic had sent into exile in Portugal after an abortive coup attempt. When the uprising began on July 18, a small plane was dispatched by rebellious officers to bring him back. He insisted on packing his dress uniforms and medals in his suitcase. The added weight forced the plane into the trees at the end of the runway and Sanjurjo died in the crash. 'Vanity of vanities,' as Amparo wrote to her sergeant Aguirre.

The landscape coaxed my thoughts back to the present. We were driving along the La Coruña Highway, Spain's major northwest arterial. Papá and Maruchi's parents had crossed this countryside in a sixteen-hour trek, just minutes ahead of the artillery shells and bombs. The smell of sage from the mountain meadows evoked a familiar feeling instead of any visual recognition of the landscape.

Maruchi sang Amparo's lullaby, the same one Conchita had sung, but only the second verse about a mother wolf sneaking up to grab the baby in the bed. The imagery had darkened into a strange presentiment of what would occur. She gave the date of Amparo's death as October 12, the Day of Pilar in Spain, a holiday that celebrated Columbus's discovery of the New World as well as an important feast of the Virgin. I was convinced Amparo died in the pre-dawn hours of the 11th from what

Benedicta had been told. When I looked up the 11th on the Catholic calendar, I found it commemorated the Council of Ephesus' declaration in 431 A.D. that Mary was truly the mother of God.

We crested the mountain. San Rafael lay beneath us, the exact place I had been forty-six Julys earlier. I had written an imagined description of this town, and stared eagerly at this touristy mountain retreat. We parked on the same main street I had walked as a child. At a nearby hotel we inquired about Villa Frutos. The owner could not help us, but pointed to where the old civil guard barracks and telephone exchange had once stood, now a park and a bar respectively. Between them, a street swerved east to the railroad station and Segovia. The main road continued on towards El Espinar and Avila.

The brisk air smelled delicious. Well-to-do *madrileños* thronged the cafés and stores. We walked towards the northern edge of town because Conchita had mentioned that the villa was situated on the outskirts. Maruchi was undergoing a similar flashback experience. She told how once, when she and her sister were walking with me and my father, we saw some bulls that had escaped from their pasture. My father said, 'Don't move and they won't hurt you.'

The sidewalk ended. An old woman in black was walking up an alley with her market basket. She detoured with us to a shop where an older woman with tight, gray curls pointed north with the feather duster in her hand. She remembered a Villa Frutos further on. Clusters of wild poppies and black-eyed susans bordered the blackberry thickets at the roadside. The towers of the sanitarium came into view just as we spotted a derelict house almost hidden behind a magnificent chestnut tree. A plaque on the wrought iron arch over the padlocked front gate contained the faded words 'Villa Frutos.' We were back to where the nightmare had started on July 18, 1936.

I peered through the bars at the chalet. The second-story windows were framed in red brick. A small balcony with French doors was enclosed with the same curlicued iron that made up the fence. Down the lane, we found another gate, half open and overgrown with brambles. I pushed aside the thorns and Queen Anne's lace. The side door was ajar, inviting me inside. The passage led upstairs. The stairway was half-demolished, rusty nails and broken glass underfoot. Testing each step, I climbed the narrow flight, avoiding roof tiles and fallen plaster. The place felt like a collapsed mineshaft, dark and foreboding. In the upper hallway I saw the roof had caved in.

*Judith and the Riveras in front of Villa Frutos – 1983.*

*Ramón Senior with Maruchi,
Pepi Rivera, and unidentified
boy – 1936.*

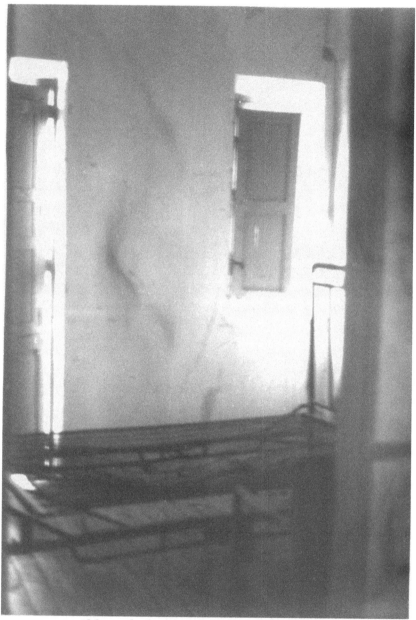

*Master bedroom and frame – Villa Frutos.*

My sense of Amparo's presence increased. She was the last woman to live here. During the War it must have been used only as a barracks. I looked around, half expecting to find familiar odds and ends, pages of my father's manuscripts. In the hallway stood a half-ruined bureau that I thought I recognized. Could the house have remained vacant since the day we left? I started taking photos and drawing floor plans. A back, central room might have been the living room. The master bedroom behind it contained a rusted-out double bed frame – probably the same bed Amparo and my father had slept in for the last time.

One side room was crammed with a jumble of furniture. Could it have been mine? I photographed each area, working my way towards the front. Then I climbed gingerly downstairs and photographed the view from the back door into a garden next to a stone wall. The main kitchen must have been on this floor because it contained a built-in tiled wood stove. Here Amparo had spent her last few days of happiness.

The house had been so overgrown by surrounding trees that it was difficult to take a decent photo of the exterior. Behind it, another gate led to a neighboring house. Below it, the valley unfolded in golds and greens towards the distant mountains. Truly an idyllic spot. I could picture Amparo and Ramón's final walk together to the forest. Across the highway, the meadow rose gradually to the pines. Here, their final parting had taken place.

For me, it seemed a near-miracle to have found the actual site where the tragedy had begun. This whole episode assumed a dreamlike quality, and that night I wrote an article that was published a few weeks later in "*El País*" the Madrid daily:

> A Memory of the Summertimes of Ramón J. Sender
> and his wife Amparo Barayón
> *El País*, Sunday, August 29, 1982.
> During the first years of the 1930s, my father and mother spent the summers in a charming two-story villa in San Rafael. There my parents and friends knew their happiest moments seated under the chestnut tree that hid the garden from the highway. The villa is the last house in the village before the meadows and woods begin.
> We visited the villa almost 46 years to the day when Amparo and Ramón said good-bye forever next to the forest. War suddenly had invaded their paradise. She fled, in twelve anguished

stages, to her martyrdom. He escaped into exile, holding the hands of two motherless children.

Today the house appears as if it has remained empty since that day when terror put to flight all its inhabitants. The garden is overgrown to the point that I had to clear a path through the blackberry thickets to reach the door. Inside the house, the floor was covered with debris.

I cannot describe with what emotions I climbed the ruined staircase, carefully testing each step. What a terrible irony if the roof fell and buried me! Upstairs I entered our apartment. I looked for familiar things in the gloom. In the hallway stood a ruined dresser that I thought I recognized. I remembered the chirps and calls of the swallows in the eaves and the smell of wild sage from the meadows. In the master bedroom stood a rusty double-bed frame, perhaps the same one where Ramón and Amparo slept together.

I dream of the villa renovated with my father's paintings on the walls, with his manuscripts on the desk and his old library on the shelves, which perhaps still exists in some Madrid basement. Perhaps some literary organization in Spain could purchase the property and create in this chalet a small museum commemorating Ramón J. Sender and the woman he loved.

For me, Ramón and Amparo symbolize Spain not only because they are my parents, but also because of their personalities. My mother was profoundly Catholic and, at the same time, independent and liberated, a woman ahead of her time.

### The Ardent Anarchist

Amparo was an ideal mother, famous in Zamora for her open heart for the poor. Papá was, on the other hand, the ardent Aragonese anarchist who scorned ceremony, sentimentality and romanticism from the point of view of a realistic person. But one must recognize some profound paradoxes in my father: music, even the Royal March, could move him to the point of tears. His love for his lost Spain and his lost Amparo scorched his soul. Ramón and Amparo also symbolize their homeland in other ways: Amparo came from upper Castile; Ramón from the Aragonese-Catalán frontier. They met one another in the center of Spain, Madrid. San Rafael was their sylvan summer retreat where they went to forget the thunderclouds gathering over Europe. What an irony that this small village became the front line between the two zones! Some day I hope to return to see the house as Amparo knew it, full of flowers, friends and books. Of course I could help any commemorative effort. I have paintings, my father's typewriter and now, also, Amparo's radio. I think it would be a consolation to offer Ramón J. Sender a little shelter, and revive Amparo in Spain once again.

After my father and the Riveras had escaped, and while the rebel column roared past the chalet, the women quickly gathered Papá's papers and burned them in the stove. Old business cards, envelopes, books, anything that might have given away his political associations. Amparo hesitated over the manuscripts. Wouldn't he be back in a few days? There were some chapters of a new novel and some poems. Did she bury them in the back garden, wrapped in the oilcloth from the kitchen table?

Conchita reported what happened next: "At noon, all the hotels received orders not to serve lunch to the guests because the troops who would be leaving soon for the capital were to be fed first. They put boards across benches with sheets for tablecloths and the soldiers devoured everything. Then the column began to make its way up the mountain. Above them, the defenders had closed the pass and were waiting to ambush them.

"Almost immediately the scattered shots we had heard became a constant rattle. Celes, the Riveras' cook, came running. 'Airplanes!' she shouted. 'Lots of them from over the mountain!'

"The booming sounds, which I had assumed were artillery, now became louder and louder. Bombers! Madrid had sent eighteen planes, all they had, to stop the column. We quickly gathered everyone into a downstairs bedroom. Explosions were coming from the center of the colony."

Conchita slapped her thigh. "*Madre mía*, and Emi in the thick of it! We searched for a way to distract the children and began to sing, but in spite of our songs, the noise of the bombs became louder. They fell on the high road with earsplitting concussions. You, Monchín, screamed and held your head. The planes passed over and then returned to the chatter of machine guns. Bullets whined outside the house and we could hear men screaming.

"'We have to leave!' Amparo shouted over the uproar.

"I certainly agreed. Our conversation was interrupted by the whistle and detonation of a bomb almost outside our gate followed by the crash of breaking glass. Naturally everyone was terrified!" Conchita threw up her hands. "They bombed like they never bombed again! My God! And Emi at the telegraph office! The military armed some townspeople who went around shouting that the village had to be evacuated within twenty-four hours. All civilians had to go to El Espinar – men, women and children.

A short while later Emi arrived looking like a wild man. He had come along the river behind town like the Riveras. "There's a terrible battle going on!" he shouted. "All these generals and captains and colonels are going crazy! They are either dead or out of their minds! Let's get out of here!"

"Those final hours in San Rafael were indescribable! The airplanes massacred the column! Those poor little soldier boys had come in good faith, thinking, 'Let's go to Madrid on a military exercise,' because they hadn't been told the truth. And there arose such screams!

"When we evacuated the chalet, there were forty or so dead in the street. We put the baby in the stroller and piled her clothes on top of it. Amparo carried a blanket and I carried another. We didn't know where we were going to sleep or anything. People were streaming out of town, mostly on foot with just the few belongings they could carry. There was no possibility of finding a ride. So out we went, with you, Monchín, screaming '*No quiero ir, no quiero ir!*' 'I don't want to go!' until Dionisia had to pick you up. Emi carried the radio that Amparo insisted we bring because it was our only contact with Madrid and Pepe. Such a strange-looking group we were, but no stranger than others we encountered."

Bleeding bodies lay along the roadside and screams and shots could be heard on all sides. Truckloads of fascists and soldiers roared past while republican militiamen hidden in the woods sniped at them. The merciless sun added another discomfort to the hysteria and panic. The Rivera girls were old enough to understand what was happening and were appalled by all the dead bodies. They had not taken twenty steps when Amparo remembered something – Andrea's rubber bath. Back she went inside and returned with her face chalk-white.

"Moorish soldiers are in our apartment!" she said.

One of them had put on a sweater of Pepe's over his uniform. Moors in Spain again after so many centuries! Memories of the atrocities they had committed in Asturias had made her hesitate, but he only nodded and smiled at her. She picked up the baby's bath and fled.

"So many people were escaping to El Espinar!" Conchita continued. "Many of them would spend the night on the street. I saw society women from the hotels weeping.

"Finally Emi said, 'We're going to the sanitarium. These children can't walk three kilometers to El Espinar!'

"It was where I had gone to talk with Santiago, and Emi knew many of the doctors. We had hardly gone half the distance when a truckload of loyal militia made a suicidal attack on the rebel infantrymen. We all threw ourselves on the ground until the shooting stopped. A driver was killed and his truck overturned down the embankment. Without the servants, I would have collapsed on the spot, but they were brave souls and kept us moving. As it was, I was trembling with terror by the time we arrived at the large iron double gates. Luckily Emi saw a staff doctor he knew.

"'Let us in, for God's sake!' he pleaded. Behind us, others paused to listen. 'The children can't walk any farther!'

"'Look, Emiliano, the military have taken us over as a hospital,' the doctor said. 'We have strict orders not to let anyone in.' He glanced at the children, then over his shoulder before opening the gate. 'Quick, enter! But you are the very last.' The crowd immediately swept forward but he pushed them away and shut the gate. 'No more room!' he yelled.

"'Let us in, let us in!' they shouted.

"One large man with a child in his arms began screaming, 'For the love of God, open the gate! I am the tenor Fleta with my wife and four children!'

"'Sir, I cannot,' the doctor replied. 'Behind you are a thousand more wanting to enter!' He locked the gates. 'There's nowhere to sleep but the garage,' he said. 'The beds are full with the wounded.' He led us to a low outbuilding that stretched the length of the garden and beckoned us inside. 'Lock the doors,' he told us. 'Unless it is I who knocks, don't open for anyone! I hope to God no one learns you are here!'

"The garage was filthy. We only had the blankets we had brought, nothing else. Celes and the servant girls had some of the children's clothing with them wrapped in newspapers. With the blankets on the floor, we were able to put you children to bed, but that night was like one of those horror movies. You cannot imagine what a nightmare it was! It makes me shrivel inside to think about it! You two little ones went to sleep, thank God, but the Rivera girls couldn't." Conchita's eyes widened. "Next door to this garage, in the same building, they had set up an emergency clinic. We heard some colonel screaming with pain all night long, 'My legs! They've cut off my legs! Give me morphine or else a pistol to end it!' Both of his legs had been blown off in the bombardment. We passed the whole night hearing the screams from the operating tables and the colonel who begged to be killed." She shook her head sadly. "They were not prepared to care for these men – no anesthesia, no surgical saws to amputate limbs. I'm telling you, it was unbelievable!"

At five the next morning, the same doctor came and said he had found us a ride to El Espinar. Amparo asked if there had been any news of Santiago, hoping for word of Pepe. But no one had seen him. We rode in the back of a milk truck to El Espinar, a small town of workers and farmers. In normal times, they served the rich summer crowd at the village. We were let off at the main square that was packed with refugees.

The mayor and all the town officials were lodging people in private homes as well as they could. He assigned us to a magnificent stone house right on the square, the best in town according to Conchita, beautifully furnished with only a few servants occupying it.

"They put us in a Moorish palace!" Conchita declared. "Such elegant furniture and paintings! Also, we needed more of the children's clothes and went back to the mayor. "*Por Díos*, help us go back to the chalet!" we begged him. It seemed safe enough, now that the fighting was concentrated in the mountains.

"He agreed, but said someone must accompany us because San Rafael was full of military vehicles and soldiers. Without them we wouldn't have been allowed into the area. Well, he told us we would have to go after dark. 'Two Falangists will take you in a car,' he said. So we went at eleven at night, and it is something impossible to describe. Amparo stayed with the children. The Riveras' servant Celes, one of the other girls, and I went for the clothes. Celes also wanted to fetch belongings at the Riveras', but the house was in the center of San Rafael.

"I said, 'Look, Celes, do what you want but I'm not in favor of our going. How are we going to get all the way there?'

"'You're right, *señora*," she replied.

"The poor woman wasn't able to get any of the girls' things. However at the chalet it was possible. I always preferred summer homes that were as far outside town as we could find them. We rented that one for six or seven years. But I have never been back. Noooo!" She rolled her eyes. "After that night, I would never put my feet there. I would drop dead on the spot!"

She drew a deep breath. "That night – I can't describe it! Only a marvelous painter could have captured the scene. You don't know what a thunderstorm is like in the sierras. First it gets very hot and then by evening the thunderheads gather. Five minutes after we reached San Rafael, the thunder started and a black cloud partially filled the sky. We had just entered the chalet when we heard the thunderclaps and we said, 'Well, it won't last long. We'll wait. There's only one cloud and it will clear up soon.'

"Then we began to hear all these horses neighing and carrying on. We thought they were cavalry horses, but when we went down to the garden, we saw the most incredible spectacle! I had never seen anything like it in my life! A whole field of horses had broken loose because the fences had been demolished by the bombardments. Look! Over the whole countryside, the road, the horses were going crazy! They were leaping and rearing and carrying on!" Her dark eyes widened. "I'm telling you, it could have been the Apocalypse! Twenty or thirty horses jumping from the fields onto the highway from all sides, neighing and screaming. No one could catch them because they wouldn't respond! They were rearing up like mad creatures with their hooves in the air, insane with terror from so much shooting and so many airplanes dropping bombs!" She flicked open her fan.

"So that was the night of the twenty-third and I said, 'My God, my soul, I will never come back here again!' And I had enjoyed San Rafael a lot because it was so pretty. It wasn't a town – just a colony that depended on El Espinar, but much cleaner and with fewer flies."

Amparo's radio functioned as their major source of news. Madrid reported the workers had overrun the Montana barracks and armed themselves. The hastily formed militia dispersed into the countryside with great enthusiasm, as if going on a holiday. Untrained, they died by the hundreds with incredible bravery as if to prove their loyalty by dying. Although the insurgent generals had captured about one-third of Spain, the four main industrial cities remained under republican control, and Franco's Foreign Legion was stranded in Morocco. The navy's ships were in the hands of loyal sailors who were blockading the Moroccan ports. The Alto de León pass above San Rafael had fallen to the rebels, but fierce fighting continued on the other side of the mountain.

In Madrid, the workers took over the city. They painted their union's initials on the cars they expropriated and drove about in a victory mood. Restaurants and hotels were collectivized, mansions of the wealthy transformed into schools and clinics that distributed birth control information. Pawnbrokers were required to return pawned items to their owners because they were seen as preying on the poorest citizens.

On the twenty-fourth in El Espinar, the women took turns going out to see what food they could find. Whatever was available had to be divided to feed a town that had suddenly quadrupled in size. They would ask for a kilo of bread and be given a half. On the other side of the main plaza from the house was the telegraph office. Emi presented himself there, explaining he had no orders.

"Better stay here than on the street," they told him. "There are armed men everywhere looking for trouble!"

On the twenty-fifth at about one-thirty, Amparo was breastfeeding the baby while the servants prepared the meal. Conchita was seated near her.

"They must have arrived in Madrid by now!" Amparo kept saying with an anxious expression.

"Woman, of course!" Conchita assured her. "Santiago knows the mountain like the palm of his hand. Relax, Amparo. After all, you're nursing the baby. When they get there, they'll send you word."

Emi arrived at noon. "You ought to hear the rumors in town!" he said.

Just as he spoke, machine guns began firing outside, and everyone jumped to their feet. Emi and Conchita tiptoed out on the balcony and saw townspeople with pistols and some civil guards in the plaza. They were firing at the rooftops and others on the rooftops firing into the street.

"Open the windows! Open the windows!" they were shouting. "Stay out of the windows and balconies!" They wanted no opportunities for snipers.

"You can imagine I came inside at once!" Conchita said. "And your mother went to pieces where she sat. 'They're going to kill us!' she began screaming. I took the baby from her breast and said, 'Bring her a glass of water with lemon!' When it was brought I said, 'Look, Amparo, drink this and we'll prepare a bottle for the baby. For God's sake, calm yourself!' Your mother was having an attack of nerves and her milk would become bad. 'If they kill us, it's our hour to die, that's all.' In these matters she was always very fearful.

"We put her to bed and bathed her face with some vinegar. 'We should do this!' Amparo was moaning. 'Do that!' It was a horrifying situation! Such shootings! *Madre mía!* For three or four hours I believed we were in hell! The heat! The people in the streets all huddled together, not knowing where to go! And people shooting at each other! It was Dantesque!"

"There we were, on the second floor of the house. Just then one of the servants came running in shouting '*Señora*! Militiamen are climbing the stairs with bayonets pointed!' I thought we were all going to die! We didn't even have identity papers! So I picked up the baby and I took your hand. These are spontaneous things of the moment when one does not have time to plan.

"'Leave me here with the children!' I ordered. 'They won't harm them. If they kill me, then goodbye, everyone, but it's the best prospect we have.'

"Holding your hand and the baby in my arms, I walked out to the stairs where the uproar was going on. Seven or eight militiamen with bayonets fixed faced me and I thought, 'This is my moment to die!' I was very frightened but not until afterwards because, to tell the truth, I have a certain serenity at times like these.

"'Believe me or not, but I am the sister of the revolutionary writer Ramón J. Sender!' I told them. 'And these are my niece and nephew, his children. We were summering in San Rafael. The others went on ahead and we became separated.'

"'You're telling us stories!' one of them shouted.

"'It's not a story, boys,' I replied calmly, talking serenely but with tears running down my cheeks. 'I beg you for the lives of these two little creatures. Their mother is killing herself with anxiety in the other room because their father is in Madrid. You must believe me. We were put in this house and don't know whose it is! The mayor lodged us here!'

"Go back! Go back!' the one in front yelled. He turned to me. 'Don't worry, you haven't lied!' He waved one arm to the others. 'Back, back! We'll move on!' To me he added, 'Rest assured, *señora*. No one will enter this house.'

"I said, 'If you come in, open a bureau and find guns, you'll kill us! But you can't hold us accountable for what you find, because it isn't our house! We came here grateful for the beds and the roof over our heads, but we don't know what's here! If you find arms, they aren't ours!'

*Sanitorium – 1983.*

*El Espinar Plaza – 1983.*

"'It's nothing, comrade!' he replied. "Don't worry, you're out of danger! I believe what you said, that these children are Sender's. You're really his sister?'

"'Yes, and the mother of these children, my brother's wife, is lying down with a tremendous attack of nerves because she's breastfeeding the baby and doesn't know whether her husband's alive or dead!'

"'Take it easy!' he said. 'I'll put two guards downstairs. No one will molest you further.'

"That moment I felt I had been reborn! This happened around four o'clock. Around seven, the civil guards came back from I don't know where and captured all the militiamen. In that same plaza outside our window, eight hundred militia people – both men and women – were tied up with ropes and machine-gunned – all of them! Because the fascists won that particular battle. At the beginning, many incidents of this sort occurred with the militia. What destroyed them was that they gathered in groups of two hundred or more, armed to the teeth without understanding anything! In San Rafael there was incredible chaos, first one side and then the other gaining the advantage until the fascists killed them all. What these poor militia people did not know was that Segovia, the provincial capital, was already in the hands of the military and well- armed civilians."

The next day, Celes came back early in the morning from searching for milk and bread, whatever food she could find. "*Señora*," she said to Conchita, "We have been saved by a miracle! The owner of this house is the chief fascist of the town!'

"We can't stay here!" Conchita said. "I was able to convince those militiamen to leave, but another time we might not be so lucky!"

When Emi came home she took him aside. "Listen, this house is a powder keg! You stay while I go talk to someone."

She found the mayor and said, "For God's sake put us in another house because this one is too much responsibility. Give us the most modest place you have."

There was an empty summer cottage outside of town on the road to Avila. Conchita accepted it at once. Although the accommodations were minimal, they were lucky to find anything. Everyone moved there that same day except Emi. So he would not have to walk across town four times daily, he found a room across the street from the telegraph office where he could sleep by himself. Conchita went there to cook him his meals on an open grate with sticks of wood.

She chuckled at the memory. "I had never cooked like this! The little old landlady, very agreeable, said to me, 'I'll do it, *señora*, allow me!' But I said, 'No, no, you will teach me.'"

"You see, the El Espinar telegrapher knew that Emi had married Ramón Sender's sister. He said to him, 'The less you come and go, the better. Someone might see you who knows you and do you harm.'

She shook her head with a mournful expression. "Emi was never able to overcome his bitterness. He even expressed it to your father, that just because he was married to me, they would have killed him. He had his own liberal ideas, but politics he never liked. He never belonged to any party. However just because he was married to a Sender, anyone could do him harm. We were put out on the street for twelve years!"

## Chapter 8
## Amparo's Return to Zamora

Conchita leaned back and began fanning herself. "Well, that was the twenty-sixth. Emi and I stayed in El Espinar only two more days because on the twenty-seventh or eighth the order was given that all Communications personnel should present themselves at the military governor's in Segovia within forty-eight hours. This meant Emi had to go, and clearly I wasn't going to abandon my husband!

"Amparo was at the cottage with the children. So I went there – no, I didn't go there – Emi went. He said, 'Look, Amparo, Conchita and I must go to Segovia at once. Take your evening walk with the children and bring everyone to say goodbye.' That's the way it was. Amparo, you Monchín, your nursemaid Aisia, the baby, the two Rivera girls, Celes the Riveras' cook and Adelina their nursemaid – everyone came. They embraced us and I said, 'Amparo, there is no other remedy. You know Pepe is out of danger, because if something had happened, we would have heard. But Emi has to go to his post and I'm his wife! If they kill Emi, they take my life as well! I love him with all my soul.' Together we had eighteen hundred pesetas and we kept one hundred for Emi and one hundred for me. I said, 'Take the rest, Amparo, there's nothing more we can do. Besides, they will have to pay Emi on the first.'

"I explained that we would look for a rented room with kitchen privileges, the most economical we could find. Anything above what we needed to live I would send her with a wagon driver or someone. From Segovia to El Espinar is only ten kilometers.

"'Don't say more to anyone than that your husband is in Madrid,' I warned her. 'None of us have documents, so if they ask for his name, say it's José Garcia, a common name. Like fifty thousand others, you have to stay here while your husband is elsewhere.' The mayor also told her that she could buy bread, milk and meat with vouchers available at the city hall."

Conchita seemed concerned that I understood the details of her break with Amparo. No doubt this event had caused her much anguish over the years. I imagined Amparo's dark eyes staring bleakly from Conchita to Emi. Circumstances dictated they part, but she could not help feeling Emi and Conchita were distancing themselves from her for their own safety.

"'Don't move from here, Amparo!' I warned her. 'At any moment the government troops may break through via Peguerinos and put down the rebellion. Tell them who you are and they'll put you on a truck and – *vamos* – we'll all go! Otherwise stay here in this cottage like all the other women.'

"'That day in the big house on the square!' Amparo moaned. 'If you had not been there, what would I have done?'

"'*Por Díos*, Amparo, stay calm above all else,' I told her. 'Otherwise you can't breast feed the baby. These horrors can't go on forever. Things are so bad they can only improve. But as for us, look how Emi keeps saying, 'No-no-no, we must leave here. They've told me I have twenty-four hours to report or they'll kill me!'"

"I told Amparo, 'El Espinar sends milk to Segovia, and I'll send you notes with the driver. When you find an opportunity, send me a letter.'

"We embraced each other and this was our last farewell. I kissed you all and said to her, 'Don't worry, but be watchful, Amparo!'

"The mayor said, 'We'll send a couple of civil guards with you.'

"'I'd prefer you didn't,' Emi replied. 'The truck's uncovered. If a government airplane comes over – they were always overhead – 'and sees the guards in the truck, they'll shoot at us. Commend us to God's care, but without the civil guards.'

"The mayor saw his point. So we left for Segovia in the late afternoon on another milk truck, ten kilometers of anguish with the Castilian sun beating down on our heads. We arrived around seven, and Emi said to the driver, 'We don't want a hotel or a pension.' Probably we wouldn't have found one anyway because Segovia was crowded with refugees. So I said, 'Look, you drivers know people, and there must be a modest house where you stay that has rooms to rent.'

"And the driver said, 'Right in my house! Because I'm a man of fifty-odd years and a widower. I have two single daughters and the three of us live alone.'

"It was also near the telegraph office. So I said, 'That's it!' We rented it for a hundred pesetas a month. Emi reported to the military government and to the communications sector, which was in a hopeless tangle because telegraph traffic had increased so much.

"The first day he came home from work, he said, 'In the telegraph room there are seven employees and behind us are four fascists armed to the teeth! We have to give them every civilian telegram. They read it, seal it and say, "It stays here forty-eight hours!"'"

"Imagine how many families were trying to get in touch, one in one place and one in the other! The third day we were there, our friend the driver came home and said, '*Señora*, the gentleman at the El Espinar telegraph told me to deliver this to you. Otherwise there would have been a forty-eight hour delay.'" "This man must have been a leftist, although he didn't say so. He treated us very well and his daughters also. In the telegram your mother said, 'We are all leaving for Zamora. I will send you news. Amparo.'

"I began to cry because I thought, 'This creature, how can she go to Zamora?'" She began slapping her thigh rhythmically. "'In Zamora everyone knows she's married to my brother! (slap!)! And Zamora, like all of Castile, was in the hands of the fascists! (slap!) 'Ai, this woman!' The El Espinar telegrapher had sent it on the same paper she had written it. I told Emi when he came home that evening, but I didn't explain how I received it. I said, 'What do you think? I'm horrified! How could she do this?'

"'Amparo won't leave because all the trains are paralyzed,' Emi replied. 'Franco has given the order. No trains depart from Segovia except the one that leaves at midnight.'

"It was a troop train carrying soldiers, but it had one coach for civilians. A person needed a pass to travel on it and it ran only at night, without lights for safety reasons, moving slowly so as not to make much noise.

"All night long!" She threw her arms upwards. "And in the morning, they arrived at Medina del Campo where civilians had to wait all day in a type of barracks!

"The Segovia station was three kilometers from the center of town. 'I'm going,' I said to Emi.

"'But woman, it must be days since they left!' he replied. 'That telegram must have been delayed forty-eight hours or else some sort of espionage is going on, and you'd better not tell me about it.'

"So I said to Emi, 'The driver's daughter told me civilians have to wait for days to leave on this train. The station is crammed with people and it's being bombed daily! There's only one coach available. If Amparo and the children haven't been able to get on − !'

"And Emi said, 'But Conchita, it's been at least two days!'

"'Good, I'm going!' I said.

"'I'm going with you!' Emi replied. 'But if someone sees me, that's the end of my job!'

"Then the daughter said, 'I'll go with the *señora*. I've lived in Segovia all my life. Don't worry, *Señor*. With me everything will go well.'

"So we went together. The place was crammed with civilians and soldiers waiting for that one midnight train. We asked everyone, 'Have you seen a woman with four children, a tiny baby girl, a two-year-old boy, two girls of four and seven (the Rivera girls) as well as some servants?' No one knew anything.

Someone said, 'With luck, they may have left the same day they arrived.' The station was in total confusion with people seated on the floor, but no sign of Amparo. We looked everywhere. The station people said, 'Look, it was night! There were so many people! Between signing safe-conducts and arranging tickets, we don't have time to notice anyone!' So we returned to the house and a few days later they transferred Emi to Burgos. We left Segovia in the same train Amparo had taken but in the opposite direction."

However, Maruchi Rivera remembered that we spent a few days in a recently constructed house in Segovia. It was empty of furniture, and the women collected fruit crates at the market, which they used as tables and chairs. Although it was summer, the nights were cool and it was hard to sleep. Conchita, not knowing where we had taken refuge, had accidentally missed us.

Amparo could not have imagined things worse elsewhere than they were in El Espinar, the constant artillery in the mountains, the random shootings in the streets. Worst of all was the dreaded sound of airplanes overhead and the bombings. The children's terror and Guadarrama's occupation by the rebels on August 1st convinced her to follow her husband's advice: Go to Zamora, the provincial town where life never seemed to change. If she waited much longer, her dwindling cash reserve wouldn't cover the train tickets.

From scattered conversations in the station waiting room, the women learned that German transport planes were ferrying Franco's legionnaires to Seville and Cadiz. Obviously the rebellion was not going to end in a week, perhaps not even in a month.

From Zamora, moreover, it would be easy to cross into Portugal with the help of friends. There she would take a boat and join Ramón's brother Manolo and his wife Marcelle who were vacationing in Biarritz. She looked forward to seeing her family, especially Antonio, her younger brother. It was through him that the radio had come into their lives, even before the telephone. His handmade receiver had connected them to all of Europe. Saturnino finally had allowed him to place one in the café as well in the living room upstairs. When Antonio built a short wave set, he could tune in more distant stations. One day he rushed in excitedly to say he was receiving Russian broadcasts. The whole world seemed to be beaming information towards Zamora.

In Segovia, occasional air raid alerts kept everyone on edge. The railway station was a favorite target for republican aircraft. One day, two bombs dropped on the tracks but did not explode. Armed men patrolled the streets or lounged in groups beside doorways, some in army or Carlist *requeté* (conservative monarchist militia) uniforms, others merely wearing armbands. We ate meals in a nearby café, waiting in line to order what little was available.

"Eat, eat!" my nursemaid Aisia ordered us. She pantomimed devouring a mouthful of food and we copied her with exaggerated gestures.

At last Amparo secured tickets and travel passes. The women packed up their few things, wrapping the radio in newspaper and twine. Evening had fallen by the time we settled ourselves on the train platform for the long wait until midnight. Amparo thought once more of phoning the telegraph office and leaving a message for Conchita but decided it would only increase Emi's anxiety. She talked to Celes of her sympathy for the man. He was living his life braced against the expected blow, the exact attitude that invited someone to strike. Far better to throw out your chest like Ramón and behave fearlessly, Amparo said. Not only did this discourage the cowardly aggressor, but made life worth living. How hard she was trying to cultivate a similar attitude!

Because of us children, we were given seats on the train. It arrived in Medina del Campo at dawn and all civilians en route to other destinations were ordered to remain in a warehouse that had been transformed into a barracks with cots and mattresses.

"But we have to eat something!" Amparo insisted. "Can't we go to the café?"

"No, only to the bathrooms. A man is coming from the station tavern and you can order from him whatever he has. The train won't leave until eleven or twelve tonight."

Faced with a twenty-hour wait, the women made themselves as comfortable as they could, chatting with other travelers. Madrid Radio reported the rebellion had been contained and Amparo's spirits brightened. When the man from the station café came to take food orders, she recognized him as a friend of her half-brother Saturnino.

For days she had been thinking of telephoning Ramón. The early hour was an ideal time because he would be asleep at the apartment in Madrid. Or so she hoped. When the café owner approached them, she introduced herself and asked if she could place a long distance call.

"Of course, *Señorita* Amparo!" He beamed happily because she had remembered him. "It's strictly against orders, but bring the baby as if you need to wash her. Things are so disorganized, how is anyone to know?"

The armed sentry outside the door allowed her to pass with the baby. In the café, she settled herself at the end of the bar with the phone and a cup of strong coffee, Andreina gurgling on her lap.

She dialed the operator. "I wish to call Madrid."

The woman made some comment about 'priorities' but Amparo, from her years with the phone company, was familiar with their procedures and explained it was an emergency. There was a buzz, a loud click and a man's voice came on the line.

"Yes?"

"Ramón? Oh, at last!"

"Who do you want?" The voice was suspicious and unfriendly. Amparo's hopes faded. "I'm calling Ramón Sender in Madrid."

"Why are you calling Madrid?"

"Because I'm trying to deliver a message to my husband, for the love of God!" All the days of agony spilled over in her voice.

"One moment please. Stay where you are." The line went dead. Amparo shrugged. Were the lines tangled? She jiggled the hook. "Operator?"

"One moment please."

A few moments later, an army vehicle pulled up by the door. Two uniformed men approached her.

"*Señora*, you are under arrest," the lieutenant said.

Amparo was terrified. "What have I done?"

"You are suspected of espionage," he said. "We intercepted your call to the other zone."

"But I was just calling my husband! You mean it's not possible to phone Madrid?"

"You were attempting to contact the enemy," he replied. "All such calls are monitored and investigated."

"But – !" Amparo was dumbfounded. "May I at least inform the others traveling with me?"

They accompanied her to the warehouse where she explained to the women what had happened.

"I had no idea I was doing something wrong!" she said to the officer. "How long will I be gone? I am breastfeeding my baby."

He gave an exaggerated shrug. "Bring her, but we must leave at once."

With a despairing look at Celes, Amparo shouldered Andreina and started across the crowded room.

I could read the panic in Amparo's expression and ran after her screaming, "Mamá! Mamáaaaa!"

She bent down to me. "Monchín, it's all right. I have to go away for a little while but I'll come back." She glanced up at Aisia who was hurrying towards us. "You stay here."

I was not convinced. The soldiers frightened me, and I could sense Amparo's distress. "Mamáaa!" I howled, struggling to free myself from Aisia's grip. She had to carry me back kicking and screaming.

Amparo was taken to an army barracks and ushered into the presence of a young colonel lounging behind a desk. He stared at her before beckoning her to a hard-backed chair. The other two men took posts beside the door.

"Name?" he asked.

"Amparo Garcia." She arranged the baby on her lap and glanced at her questioner briefly before swinging her gaze towards the window. "Colonel, I used to work for the phone company. I didn't realize I was doing anything wrong."

"We have to investigate all calls across the lines, *señora*." He picked up a sheet of paper. "You attempted to contact a certain Ramón Sender in Madrid. He glanced up at her. "What is your relationship to him?"

Amparo realized she would have no opportunity to use a false identity. "I am his wife," she admitted. "I was trying to let him know where we were. My children and I were in San Rafael when the trouble began. I'm taking them home to my family in Zamora." She tried to meet his gaze with a frank expression in spite of the terror she felt. "That's all there is to it."

The colonel tapped a pencil on the blotter. When he smiled, one large front tooth gleamed rabbit-like between his lips. "A simple error of judgment, you say, but do you have any proof?" She looked down at Andreina. "What can I offer you? I have four woman and four innocent children in my care." She flung him a haughty look. "For God's sake, *Señor*! If I was a spy, would I travel with eight people? My family in Zamora can vouch for me."

The colonel called his assistant. "Get Zamora on the line, will you?" He turned to me. "Who are your relatives?"

She gave them Saturnino's and Magdalena's names before being led to a bench in the anteroom. The muted voice of the colonel penetrated through the door, and idly she wondered with whom he was talking. When she was ordered back into his presence, he was standing by the window, hands clasped behind him.

"Saturnino Barayón has been detained," he said. "I was unable to contact your other relative."

Amparo was astounded. "Saturnino? But why?"

The colonel shrugged. "We are in a state of war, *señora*." I must keep you here until this matter is cleared up." He crooked a finger at the guard. "Rest assured that you and your child will be fed and properly treated."

Saturnino in jail! Dazed, Amparo allowed herself to be led to a cell in the back of the building. Up until this moment, she had not doubted the wisdom of Ramón's advice that she return home. Could the terror have spread even to Zamora? The jailer, a courteous civilian, brought her a meal. Later in the day, when it became obvious they would detain her through the night, she asked that Monchín and Aisia be brought to visit but was refused.

In the morning, she gave the colonel the phone number of her half-sister Casimira as well as the names of the most influential, conservative people in Zamora she could think of. At midday, she was once more brought before him. He informed her that Miguel Sevilla, Casimira's husband, was willing to take responsibility for her release. She was returned to the station, but tagged as someone to be watched.

Her reappearance was greeted with tears of joy. Celes had taken charge in her absence and bought food until her money ran out.

"We have been living like gypsies!" Aisia said. "And Monchín never once stopped asking for you."

My happiness was boundless. I caught her skirt and held it tight to make sure she would never leave me again. "Mamá, Mamá, stay here!" I repeated over and over.

The train's scheduled night departure from Medina del Campo must have been delayed until just before sunrise. Sections of track had been bombed the previous day and had to be repaired. Although daytime travel was risky, the military situation in the south required that vital equipment and personnel be sent at once. An armored locomotive was backed into position, its boiler protected with hastily welded steel plates. Obviously the commander was gambling that Madrid's impoverished air force could not mount bombing raids two days in a row.

Amparo squeezed up against a window, the baby on her lap. I shared Aisia's seat beside her. The aisle was full, people seated on the floor or on their suitcases, balancing the coach's sway by holding onto armrests or each other. All the women were on the verge of exhaustion. It had been days since they had been able to bathe. Amparo mentioned how there was always a good supply of hot water at the family apartment because of the cafe on the ground floor.

What should have been a two-hour journey took all day because of frequent stops for military reasons and the constant threat of bombing attacks. Finally we crossed the Duero River, and the town of Toro loomed on the cliffs ahead. Amparo stared at it with vague curiosity, remembering childhood outings to the annual wine celebrations. The train hooted twice, running along the river on the final leg of their journey. Two minutes later, the brakes were applied so suddenly that people in the aisle toppled like dominoes. The whistle continued sounding a series of short blasts.

"Out, out!" the conductor shouted. "Air raid! Hide yourselves below the embankment!"

A panic-stricken rush for the exits began. Afraid the children would be trampled, Amparo held back until a whiskery grandfather gestured for her to precede him.

"Women and children first!" he said.

Others took up the phrase. "Women and children!" The jam in the aisle loosened and the car emptied. Pepi began to cry. Maruchi Rivera watched her with the superior air of a six-year-old who had outgrown such childish behavior. Outside, soldiers were helping passengers down the slopes. To the south, the distant hum of approaching airplanes could be heard. Pepi and I began screaming in earnest.

"Quickly!" A fierce-looking officer shouted. "Down the hillside!"

Amparo slid on her haunches, the baby against her chest. Aisia and Celes each held one of Pepi's hands. A large culvert that could hold a dozen people lay under the track bed. "Over here!" A hunch-backed youth gestured at us from inside. He huddled in a ball, hands over his ears with his mouth open to lessen the concussion of the bombs. "Like this!" he shouted.

The sound of the airplanes diminished over the cliffs only to return with the first explosions. They were flying low, parallel to the river. With the whistle of the descending bombs, Amparo clutched both of us, her back towards the culvert opening. An enormous blast knocked us backwards against Celes and the girls. Smoke and dust filled the tunnel, making it impossible to breathe.

Everyone began backing towards the uphill entrance, choking and gasping for air. Another bomb exploded on the cliff above, sending an avalanche of dirt and debris tumbling down. Two women had run out the uphill side and were half buried.

We lay together on the culvert's curved slope. It was easier to breathe within the enclosed space Amparo's encircling arms created. Celes and Adelina were trying to soothe the girls. More bombs were dropping in the distance, but the worst seemed to have passed.

"Don't go out!" the youth warned. "They will come back and gun us down!"

His words went unheeded by several hysterical women who ran downslope towards the river. The officer peered into the culvert. He spotted the two women moaning on the other side and yelled for the medics.

The harder Amparo tried to escape the demon of war, the closer he came. San Rafael had been nothing compared to this! The youth's advice proved correct. The bombers returned to machine-gun the coaches. Bullets sent rows of dirt skyward and tore foliage from the poplars. They pinged and whined from the steel armor of the locomotive and punctured holes in the coach windows.

At last they were gone. Once more death had passed us by. Not so with others, because soldiers were carrying bodies wrapped in blankets. Repairs took several hours before the train, traveling at a crawl, limped the final few miles into Zamora. The rebel commanders had badly miscalculated Madrid's determination to disrupt rail traffic.

We arrived in Zamora in the evening. The most picturesque approach would have been from the south across the ancient Roman bridge with guard towers. Instead we arrived via the northern outskirts where the station was located. Fourteen days after her flight from Villa Frutos – and six years after her departure from Zamora – Amparo had finally come home. Why had she not visited before? She had become such a different person in Madrid, more so after she met Ramón, and she had not wanted to face her relatives' criticisms.

Her youngest brother Antonio was different. As far as he was concerned, she could do no wrong.

Half an hour later, the women pulled up in front of the family café in two taxis. But the doors were shut and there was a 'Closed' notice in one window. At this hour? The café remained open every day of the week!

"What's wrong?" Amparo asked the driver.

He shrugged. "The *dueño* was arrested. He's in jail in Toro."

Of course! Biting her lip in anguish, Amparo peered through the plate glass. Someone was inside and she knocked loudly. Andrés, the teenage son of the cook Señora Gregoria, glanced up from mopping the floor. He came to unlock the door.

"Amparo! What are you doing here?" He glanced behind her at the women unloading the luggage. "Nati and Magdalena are upstairs. You'd better go up. I'll bring everyone inside."

"Where's Antonio?" she asked.

"Both your brothers are in jail," he said. "The café's closed indefinitely."

"Antonio too?" Amparo dug her fingernails into her cheeks, transfixed with horror. "How can it be?"

"Zamora's in the hands of the *Falange*," Andrés whispered, his eyes scanning the street. "Get inside quickly. It's best you're not seen."

White-faced, Amparo explained the situation to Celes and the others. "Wait for me in the café," she said. "I'm going to find out what's going on." She handed the baby to Aisia but I would not leave her side. Rather than risk my yells, she took me with her. I insisted on climbing the stairs by myself.

Amparo's half-sister Magdalena answered the front door. In her mid- forties, she was a dignified woman with a square-cut chin. Amparo treated her more like an aunt. Beside her stood her eleven-year-old daughter Magdalena (nicknamed 'Nena' by the family), Amparo's niece, who exclaimed delightedly when she saw us.

"You should not have come," Magdalena said. "But now you're here, child, come in." She smiled at me. "I thought I would never meet your little ones."

"There are six more of us downstairs," Amparo said. "The train was bombed – we've been through hell." She leaned weakly against the wall. "What about Antonio and Saturnino?" Magdalena's bloodshot eyes testified to her weeping. "They took Saturnino first and Antonio a few days later. It's been a very bad time with many arrests." She turned to her daughter. "Nena, bring the rest of them upstairs."

Amparo described the turmoil of her existence since July 18th. "Finally there was nowhere else to go." Her self-control collapsed and she began to weep helplessly. "It's been too much, first one thing and then the next! Everything's been indescribably horrible!"

Upon seeing her distress I began to whimper and tug at her skirt. "Mamá, Mamá!"

She looked down at me. "The worst has been the effect on the little ones." She bent down and cupped my face in her hands. "It's all right, Moncho," she soothed. "Mamá is tired. Come on, let's take a big bath!"

I sensed her anguish over her brothers and stayed close to her that evening, refusing to go to bed unless she remained beside me. The fearful events of the journey had suffocated my spirit. Also the food in Medina del Campo had upset my stomach. When I fell asleep, Amparo sat by her radio to listen to the local Salamanca station. Little Nena, delighted to see her aunt, leaned against her holding her hand.

The announcer's voice interrupted the music of a zarzuela. " Five shiploads of Foreign Legion troops have arrived from Morocco, and General Franco has flown to Seville to establish his headquarters." There was a burst of martial music. "France has announced a policy of non-intervention and proposes it be adopted by all of Europe."

Amparo switched it off. How could the French socialist premier Blum have betrayed the Republic? It couldn't be true! Otherwise why was she trying to escape to Biarritz? She tried not to think about it. At the dinner table, she found her fingers trembling so much she could hardly get the fork to her mouth. At last she pushed her plate away.

"I can't eat," she said. "I feel caught in a nightmare."

# Chapter 9
## Interviews in Zamora

On my return to Spain, Judith and I repeated Amparo's journey to Zamora from Segovia. "When you go to Zamora, be careful with whom you talk," I had been warned. "There are no middle roads. There are only those who gave the blows and those who received them. Many times those who are guilty will say no, they are not. And if Miguel Sevilla is alive, say to him 'I am the son of Amparo Barayón and I have come to find out how and why she died.'"

The flat landscape gradually changed to foothills. Beyond them, a sloping mesa punctuated the horizon. We clattered on a trestle through the treetops to the north bank of the Duero River. On the cliffs ahead appeared Toro, the town where Amparo's brothers were jailed. Zamora, Amparo's birthplace, lay beyond the violet evening haze. Now, in spite of the warnings I had received, I would find out the truth.

We were met by my first cousin Chori, Magdalena's younger sister, and her husband. Her close-cropped salt-and-pepper hair matched mine, a solidly built woman with a strong chin and deep-set eyes. Her husband was balding, his square face beginning to settle towards his neck. Both seemed more than a little nervous.

Over apertifs at the apartment, Chori brought up her concern that names should not be mentioned in my book. "The guilty ones are dead," she said. "The children should not suffer for their parents."

"Who were they?" I asked. "We heard a certain Viloria – "

"Yes, Viloria was the one who shot Amparo. But Miguel Sevilla, married to my Aunt Casimira, also must bear some responsibility. He could have saved her because he was friendly with the *Falange,* and connected to the Church. Also, Casimira taught French to the sons of the military governor, Hernández Comes."

Sevilla. Magdalena mentioned him in her first letter to my father. "Why didn't he intercede on Amparo's behalf?" I asked.

"He was fearful."

"What happened to him?"

Chori shrugged. "They moved to Seville. The rest of us held them in disgrace."

Would I have preferred him to come to some violent end or to have lived out his years in full knowledge of his guilt? Too late, I had come too late. Whatever dreams of vengeance I might have harbored, of confronting those responsible, I had to forget.

"Viloria died insane in a mental hospital," Chori added. "He was despised by everyone. For so many years we knew nothing about you. Then one night we heard your father on a radio program and he spoke of you and your sister. We were so happy to know you were safe in America! Magdalena wrote to him at once. The second time we wrote was when Magdalena was imprisoned."

"We knew nothing about this!" I exclaimed.

Chori described how Magdalena had been denied entrance to the University of Salamanca in spite of excellent grades because two uncles and an aunt had been shot as communists. Soon afterwards, she was jailed for two years. Her father wrote Papá and told him what had happened. Papá replied saying she should get out of politics because it was a filthy mess. He had seen his political ideals become meaningless. He also said that we children had not been told what had happened to our mother.

Magdalena phoned to say she could not join us. Couldn't we travel to Málaga instead before they left on vacation August 2nd?

"Listen, we never knew you were in jail!" I said. "Chori just told us."

"See what you can do about coming here. I'll call again." Later we took a quick drive past the family café – Café Iberia – now a restaurant, on the edge of the Plaza Mayor six blocks away. I gazed at Amparo's childhood neighborhood, the church of San Juan where she had played the organ. I had imagined all of this. How incredible to be seeing it at last!

Darkness was falling by the time we registered at our hotel. That night I dreamt of a tower full of statues that came alive when I touched them. I was two people in the dream, he who animated the stone effigies and he who discovered them. A blissful mixture of terror and awe awakened me. In the darkness, I reinvoked the feelings by recalling the dream.

The next morning, the family took us on a tour of the city. Another fine day awaited us with rows of clouds similar to yesterday's. We roamed the interior of the cathedral that overlooked the Duero River from the southernmost cliff, late Romanesque with a Byzantine dome of overlapping curved stone shingles. I preferred the sunlit gardens we passed on the way to the cathedral museum.

Later, we walked the parapet for the view south. At the Plaza Mayor we strolled to San Juan's, Amparo's church where she had sung and taught catechism. It was fenced off for repairs, the interior inaccessible. We continued to St. Vincent's Church where Benedicta had been baptized for the second time after Amparo was jailed. The religious ladies in town did not believe her 'communist' mother had seen to it in Madrid.

We drove to the building that used to house the orphanage where my sister and I had stayed. It had been renovated into a state-owned hotel called a *parador*. I walked the polished hallway whose floor-to-ceiling windows surrounded the central courtyard. Nothing looked familiar except the stairs, which for some reason drew my attention. Something about them – walking up? Falling down?

Next morning, we walked with Chori towards the Plaza Mayor for a round of interviews. Near the café, we passed an acacia-like tree in full blossom that gave off a luscious perfume. Its scent and the shrill cries of the darting swallows overhead evoked a memory. As a twenty-two-month-old child, I had smelled this exact same smell.

That day I received one of the best photographs I found of Amparo. She looked about sixteen, her hair in pigtails, her face three-quarter profile over a wide plaid collar. I recognized my sister in her large, deep-set eyes and the length of the face above the slender neck. It was an extraordinary portrait that captured Amparo's artistic sensibility and character.

We also visited the couple who had hired my nursemaid Dionisia after Amparo was jailed. Like everyone we had met, they were extremely hospitable.

The wife described how she had employed Dionisia because she needed a nursemaid for her son. "She stayed almost two years with us and spent most of the time weeping. She would return from a prison visit to Amparo and cry her eyes out. It's not possible for someone to cry more than Dionisia cried for Amparo. I never have seen a better brought up, loving person at seventeen years of age. She read every newspaper and book we had."

She brought out a photo of a moon-faced, attractive girl with a pageboy cut. The little boy on her lap was about the same age I was when I knew her.

Something about her was familiar. "Aisia," I whispered. The name pulled my mouth into a smile. A happy name for a lovable girl.

"This girl was someone very special," the wife repeated. "She was a person – I don't know – of such great kindness. She used to say, 'You're like my parents. Keep me with you.' When we heard later what happened to Amparo, we all suffered because Aisia loved her so much. She sang her praises constantly! We had Amparo's suitcase in our house. It contained photos, clothes, shoes, a large comb. I remember it well because our boy always wanted to open it.

*Dionisia Diaz Cortes, known in the Sender family as 'Aisia,' the young niece of María Cortes. Aisia was hired by Amparo to care for Monchin. Here she is pictured with the little boy she cared for in Zamora after Amparo was jailed.*

*Amparo Barayón, in her teens.*

"Aisia refused, saying, 'This suitcase is sacred to me.' She often rearranged the things inside it. She kept it impeccable. But whenever she did this, she would put her head on the table and weep."

"Then one day some men came asking for her," the husband added. "'We've come to reclaim the children,' they said."

"Dr. Junod of The International Red Cross?" I asked.

"We didn't know," the wife replied. "So I went to the kitchen and told her, 'There are some men here asking for you.' Aisia came out sobbing and they said to her, 'We're here searching for the children.' *Ai Dios*, what a day for the poor girl! She went off with them and came back late crying. She went to bed in tears because they were taking her Monchín and she wasn't able to see him." She leaned towards me. "If one day you meet her, everything I have told you is nothing compared to how she felt. She was crazy about your parents, and even more so about you children."

"How old would she be now?"

"Sixty-two or three."

We must find her when we returned to Madrid. And what happened to Amparo's suitcase? Dr. Junod must have given it to my father.

During two more days of interviews, I began to wonder if my cousin Chori's presence might be inhibiting people from speaking freely about the family's involvement in Amparo's arrest or their later actions. I had told everyone I was writing a book. Could I blame them if they tried to present themselves in a sympathetic manner? But I was committed to this approach. Maybe Magdalena would set things straight. Suddenly I realized how every one of our informants had been a woman. The tragedy of a mother's sacrifice was never forgotten by other mothers. They saw with their hearts the true dimensions of the human drama. Historians, usually male, have chronicled the glorious combats. But it was the anguish of families that enshrined the true saga of humanity.

On Friday I awakened determined to spare the relatives more efforts on our behalf. I could not pressure Chori to do more than she had been doing, but still had discovered nothing tangible about why my mother had been killed. No one wanted to tell Amparo's son the more gruesome aspects of the story. The ten days I had scheduled for Zamora were drawing to a close. Perhaps I should hire someone to continue the search.

That afternoon we broke away from the family and visited the Socialist Party's local headquarters. All indications pointed to a socialist victory in the October national elections, the first time since 1936. Everyone wondered whether the army would attempt a coup. The local deputy to the Cortes welcomed us warmly. He offered us his help and set up an immediate appointment with a *Señora* Chillon.

*Señora* Chillon lived over a clothing store owned by her son Angel, a tall, stoop-shouldered man with El Greco-like features. He took time off from his customers to usher us upstairs. His mother greeted us in a v-neck dark blue dress with white polka dots, her face a foreshortened version of her son's. "My husband Manuel Anton was the first man shot here in Zamora," she said. "He was a well- known socialist."

The lines alongside her mouth were deeply etched by suffering.

Obviously she was devastated by her husband's death. She never would forgive or forget his martyrdom.

Angel returned from the telephone to join us. I photographed mother and son standing beside a bust of the father on the dresser. Then she read a few stanzas from "The Jail Of Zamora," a poem that she wrote in 1936:

> Sad eyes, fastened
> From the doorway on the jailer,
> With what yearning you wait
> To learn if he whom you love still lives!
> You fear the worst.
> Your anguished glance Is fixed on the door,
> Waiting for the notice to be posted
> That you should pick up his clothes.
>
> Yours is the distant stare
> Of someone too fearful to ask
> If he who is detained there
> Needs something you could bring...
>
> His clothes are handed to you
> In silence. The jailer says nothing,
> Not meeting your gaze.
> The signal is infallible.
> The prisoner is no longer alive!
>
> When mothers, daughters, wives
> Receive clothes like this,

They emit such terrible screams!
Why doesn't the earth tremble under them?...

Against your bosom you embrace
Clothes that no longer will cover
That beloved body
Which filled your home with love and hope,

With light and work and bread.
In them his life still resonates
With all its ardor,
Allowing you to feel
His presence next to you...

The intensity of her recitation wove a spell, her words the outcry of a tormented spirit. I was deeply touched because she spoke for those uncounted thousands of Spanish mothers and wives whose suffering had never been told.

Angel listened quietly to her voice. It surprised me he was not more embittered. I could be him, I kept thinking, if Amparo had lived and they had shot my father instead. The doorbell rang and *Señora* Chillon broke off. Angel returned with Dionisio, a man in his seventies, gray hair slicked back above bifocals, his face taut with excitement.

"At last we meet!" he shouted. He walked over to embrace me vigorously and plant kisses on my cheeks. "I was the last to see Amparito alive! I was in jail also, and my job was at the front desk where they checked prisoners in and out. I was there when they brought Amparito downstairs on the way to the cemetery. She said, 'The last moment of my life I dedicate to the memory of my children!' Those were her exact words!"

I made sure I was understanding him correctly. "You heard Amparo say this?"

"She left with those words on her lips!" Dionisio repeated even more emphatically.

I was stunned. Face to face, finally, with the last person to see her alive except for her killers, I had nothing to say. I imagined a frosty October night in Zamora. A squad of uniformed men hurried a lightly clad woman through the prison corridors towards the courtyard where a truck was waiting.

"Amparito was my friend!" Dionisio shouted. "I knew all the girls at the telephone office!" He embraced me again and grabbed my arm. "I was the last one to see her alive! Angel, phone Lolita! You know her number!" He turned to me. "I will take you to meet Lolita and Pepita who worked with her!" He squeezed my elbow. "I remember Amparo coming to my father's fish store! She carried her baby and wore a white dress!" He was a charming fellow, full of goodwill and a desire to help, but overwhelming. "When is the best time?"

"I'll phone you tomorrow," I promised.

In the nearby village of Coreses later that evening, I met a gray-haired workman in a coverall. "Are you Ramón Sender Barayón?" he asked me. "I was talking with friends about your visit, and they said, 'Don't forget to tell Ramón Sender's son that it was he, Hernández Comes, who denounced his mother!' Raimundo Hernández Comes was the military governor responsible for the daily lists of men and women 'released' from prison to the death squads." He leaned back, his eyes half shut. "That's all I have to say."

"At six in the evening they arrived at the jail to select those they were going to shoot," someone added.

The man nodded somberly. "One of Hernández Comes' grandsons once accused his own father. He said, 'How could my grandfather have lived, and you also, with the knowledge that you both have so many deaths on your heads?' The father grabbed a pistol to kill his son, but the cook intervened. 'How can you shoot the boy?' the cook shouted. 'He's only twenty years old!'"

Miguel Sevilla as Judas, Raimundo Hernández Comes as Pontius Pilate and Segundo Viloria as executioner, the cast of Amparo's passion play was now complete. All three were dead.

That same evening I was introduced to a young grade school principal named Fernando Primo. He had been working on a thesis involving some of my father's novels. The longer I talked to him, the more convinced I became that I had found the right person to continue researching Amparo's story after I left.

We made an appointment to meet the following day.

Saturday morning: Walking with Dionisio, once more I passed my favorite tree and inhaled its perfume. A tendril of memory connected me to when I had walked here holding my mother's hand. We turned into the street of the café – *Trascastillas* was its old name, "behind the castle." Now it had been renamed in honor of a local sculptor.

"The only diversion we had when we were young was to take a short walk," Dionisio said. "It was hard for girls to get permission because they led a very cloistered existence, like little nuns. They were not permitted to go out for coffee or take a walk with a man. We lived like primitive anthropoids!" He pointed to an appliance shop. "The telephone office was right there!"

How small Amparo's world was! She lived her early years in almost a one-block area. In the café I explained to the plump patroness that I would like to photograph the work areas and dining room. She agreed, and I began.

Faces turned from the stove to stare in curiosity. In a side room, tablecloths were drying on clotheslines. I caught a glimpse of the back alley whose exit onto the square had served as a shortcut for the Barayón children.

The patroness said something to one of her kitchen staff. He returned holding a heavy china cup inscribed "Café Iberia." She handed it to me, a memento of my visit. I was delighted because I had never owned anything Amparo touched. She might have drunk from this very cup. I imagined a dark- eyed, animated twenty-year-old woman laughing at a table or standing behind the cash register. Or perhaps the muted notes of a Chopin nocturne would be filtering through the ceiling from where she was practicing in her room.

"I met your mother when she was twenty years old," Dionisio told me. "My wife and her sisters went to the same school. They were neighbors."

I had an appointment with my possible researcher Fernando at the Valderey Cafe. Dionisio bade us farewell after setting up a meeting for tomorrow.

Fernando was waiting with his wife and their four-year-old. I discussed a business arrangement: he would continue researching Amparo's life and I would send him a small monthly retainer. I asked him to help us locate several possible informants including my nursemaid Dionisia.

That evening we joined friends for a farewell supper at Señor Pozo's restaurant next door to the old family café. Throughout the meal I kept thinking how, in a paradoxical way, I was the host because we were eating in the very house where Amparo grew up.

After dessert I ordered a round of cognac and made a toast. "It makes me very happy to be here with you," I said. "To share a meal in my family's house." I paused to try to find words in Spanish to express what I was feeling. "I would like to offer a toast to the memory of Amparo. Our being here together is the best tribute we can give her."

Eyes sparkling, they all raised their glasses. What if I had spent my life here with Amparo and her family? Amparo would have been upstairs at this moment reading a story to her grandchildren while I entertained guests from afar. It could so easily have happened.

I said goodnight to the owner, Señor Pozo, and asked if we could return tomorrow morning and photograph the family apartment upstairs. Poor man, he could not refuse.

The next day, Dionisio accompanied us to the apartment of the two Muñoz sisters whose mother had been Amparo's piano teacher. The older one explained how, like Amparo, she graduated from high school and went to work for the telephone company.

"Amparo was one of us," she said. "Our mother loved her very, very much. She didn't want to teach piano to Lola here because she said they would come to blows. So she said, 'Amparo will give classes to Lola.'"

"She gave me classes in solfège," Lola explained in a husky voice.

The older sister told how she studied French with Casimira. "The half-sister who married Miguel Sevilla, *el sastre* – the tailor."

"*El desastre* – the disaster," Judy commented, a good Spanish pun. "He could have saved Ramón's mother."

"Because they were inhuman!" Dionisio added.

"No, no!" the sister insisted. "If they had told us something, my mother and my father would have been the first to have claimed them! No, sir!"

"There were the sisters of his mamá, Magdalena and the others! Did they know?"

"I think the family was very fearful," I said.

She shook her head. "I firmly believe that my mother, knowing her as I do, would have said, 'Amparo's boy will stay with us!' She wouldn't have let a moment pass without bringing you here."

"And the baby girl! The baby girl!" Dionisio said. "She was still being nursed when they took her away and killed her mother!"

The conversation turned to how Amparo was denied absolution after her final confession. Both the sisters didn't believe the story. According to them, there was no way the priest would not have absolved her. He was an intimate friend of their father.

"How ignorant you are!" Dionisio shouted. "Excuse me, but I know how these things were done! I worked in the prison office! I detested that man! He was responsible for many bad things. Because of this, I don't want to discuss him."

I explained how a highly placed cleric begged my sister's forgiveness on behalf of the Church during her visit to Spain because of this priest's actions. "That's right," the older sister replied. "I remember he was disciplined and transferred to a bad position before retiring. He lives in a small village far from here. Paradinas. He's probably almost ninety years old."

Our time was running out. Dionisio walked as far as the Plaza Mayor where he embraced us with great warmth. His eccentricity probably protected him better than a bulletproof vest during the Franco years. When we arrived at Señor Pozo's, he was just returning home with an armful of groceries. His face fell at the sight of us. What traumatic memories did we evoke? I reminded him of my request to photograph the family apartment. It was a very personal demand to make of a Spaniard, but he could only agree.

I took both color and black-and-whites of the interior. The hallway was paved with five-color octagonal tiles that had survived since Amparo's time.

Out the back window I took a shot of the jumbled rooftops. These also had not changed, I thought. Amparo had stared at this same view. All my senses were turned up full because I had spent some weeks here with her. These walls echoed her excited, girlish chatter, and the music of Granados and Albeniz she played on the piano. How many similarities existed between her life and mine! Throughout my teens I practiced piano three or four hours a day, no doubt many of the same pieces.

Which room was hers? I was hesitant to open doors because Señor Pozo seemed so nervous. I satisfied myself with the kitchen, hallway and living room. No doubt he thought I was wondering how he came to inherit the place. I assumed that when the government confiscated everything, they auctioned it off to the highest bidder.

I could elect myself judge and jury. I could play out a Sicilian vendetta fantasy and track down whatever person still survived who had been even distantly implicated in Amparo's murder. What if I demanded an admission of guilt – from whom? A doddering priest whose senility could only awaken my compassion? I had come too late. Amparo's murderers had remained in power for forty-odd years, long enough for the world to have turned its attention to fresher atrocities.

We thanked *Señor* Pozo, and walked down the Calle de la Reina behind the apartment to tour the neighborhood. A block away I photographed the old city wall and the nearby building that once had housed the family ice factory. It too had been auctioned off as "war goods," and now had become a hardware store.

So far, my breakaway from the family had not brought me any closer to the truth. People had talked more freely of Sevilla's role, but that was to be expected. I had collected the names of others who made up the execution squad with Viloria – Sebastián the druggist, Mariscal the postman, but nothing more. What else could I find?

I had to keep reminding myself that no matter what I found or how much I heard, Amparo would remain a shadow. Nothing would bring back her voice, her laughter, her touch or smell.

The following morning we went to the Civil Registry with Angel Chillon to search for Amparo's birth certificate. We were walking an upstairs corridor when a man dressed in a suit approached us. A dignified type in his late sixties, he greeted Angel with a nod and a word.

"That is Hernandez, the son of the military governor Hernández Comes," Angel whispered. "As a young soldier, he delivered to the jail the execution lists signed by his father."

Hernández Comes' son! What a strange feeling, passing him on the way to verify Amparo's birth date! I should have stopped and introduced myself.

What could I have asked him? "Did your father know, when he signed the prison release for my mother, that it meant her death?" "Were you the person who delivered it?" I would be the last person to whom he would speak openly. What must it have been like for those who had to live in such close proximity with the men guilty for their relatives' deaths? A parallel situation in America could be found in the South where black families resided in the same town as the Klansmen who had lynched a father or uncle.

At the Civil Registry we gave the approximate year of Amparo's birth to the clerk. He hauled out one leather-bound register after another, running his finger down the columns. In 1907 her younger brother Antonio's name appeared. At last he found her, born on May 8th, 1904. That meant she was thirty-two when she died and not twenty-nine as I had estimated. I accepted an official copy and we returned to the sidewalk.

"Where is Hernández Comes' son's office?" I asked. He shrugged. "Not far. Just a few blocks."

I decided to pay the man a visit. It was my last opportunity before we left town to confront someone at least indirectly involved with the guilty ones. But I wouldn't tell Angel because he had to live there. We bade goodbye to our friend and five minutes later rang Hernandez's doorbell. A maid ushered us into a well-appointed apartment and a book-lined study. The man behind the desk, white-haired with a clipped mustache, looked every inch the prominent attorney.

"May I be of service?" he inquired.

"I am the son of Amparo Barayón," I explained. "I have been told that you might be able to verify some facts regarding my mother's death."

"Amparo Barayón," he repeated, gazing thoughtfully at the ceiling. "That name is familiar. Was she Casimira's sister?"

"Yes, that's correct."

He nodded with a smile. "I know her name because Casimira was my professor of French. But I did not know Amparo personally."

"She was arrested and shot in 1936," I continued. "One version of the story reports she was detained for insulting your father, the military governor."

He spread his hands and shrugged. "Of this I know nothing. Perhaps it is possible, but so much time has passed."

I tried again. "She was the wife of Ramón J. Sender, the novelist. I am here to find out if this was the reason she was murdered." His open gaze protested his ignorance, yet something did not ring true. I was convinced he knew more, but what could I do?

Would you permit me to take your photograph?" I fully expected him to refuse, but he seemed flattered by my request and agreed. Would he have done so if he had something to hide?

Afterwards, there was nothing left to say. Judy had checked the books on his shelves and found numerous official histories of Franco Spain. This meeting would be the closest I came to confronting anyone even distantly responsible. But as Chori asked me, must the children pay for the sins of their parents? Even if as the military governor's son this man had carried the death lists to the prison, could I accuse him of complicity? Every attempt I had made to pin down concrete facts about Amparo's killers had ended in frustration. Either people did not want to mention names or else the passage of so many years had dimmed their memories.

That afternoon we returned to the Plaza Mayor to talk with Waldo, a poet and flamenco scholar we had met. From an outdoor table I watched the wind rustle the three flags on the city hall, Spain's, the province's and the city's. Zamora, Zamora! As the old saying went, "You don't win Zamora in an hour." Amparo's story also could not be won in an hour, a week – or a year.

The bells rang out a hymn. Everyone was taking their stroll, the street crowded with walkers, young married couples with their children, teenage boys cruising in tightly bunched squads. Waldo came to join us, a gray-bearded man with a kindly face.

"*Hóla, amigo!*" I called.

"In all honesty, I deeply sympathize with you but I cannot help you in your search," he explained with ornate Spanish courtesy. I will try to find you someone who knows more." He raised his voice to override the motor scooter revving beside us. "The story of your mother is one of those incomprehensible things. Your father was connected with the anarcho-syndicalists, but your mother was a religious woman!" He pointed across the square. "She taught catechism in that very church! She came home thinking that because she knew everyone there would be no problems, and instead went to her downfall without knowing why." He shook his forefinger. "Without knowing why because she had not participated, according to what everyone knew, in any political movement. Naturally she had her sympathies for this or that idea, but she was never an activist in any sense of the word."

He sighed and smoothed back his hair. His features were so similar to mine that we could have been related. "You see, we felt great hope when World War II finished. Everyone thought the Allies would open Spain." He leaned forward. "And no one opened anything! They sold us down the river!" He glanced at a squad of young soldiers strolling past. "We called ourselves 'The Accursed Generation' because we were all under lock and key. There were those who were imprisoned, those who were orphans, those who were drafted in the Blue Legion and forced to fight for Hitler on the Russian Front – and us. Imagine!"

Pedestrians swirled about us. If only I could have reached into their minds and filtered out what each one knew about Amparo! All the information I needed was passing before me in the memories of these people.

"Was anything ever published about the killings in Zamora?" I asked.

*Hernández Comes' son.*

Waldo shook his head. "Unfortunately not. An interesting fact is that when this current opening occurred, this liberalization, those of the Right had a terrible fear that we would hit the ball into their court – that we would take vengeance. But the reaction of the Spanish people has been fabulous." He stared at me. "You must hear this, Ramón, because this is the great lesson the Spanish people has to offer you." Waldo was telling me Spain had put away the nightmares of the past. Here there had been no Nuremberg tribunal to judge the guilty and satisfy the victims of this particular holocaust. Of course there still existed those individuals who could not forgive and forget, who played the loops of their personal tragedies over and over. I myself ran the risk of becoming one of these, of endlessly cycling on the theme of Amparo's death.

My father, during one of his return trips said: "I can forgive the fact that my wife was shot, but I cannot forget the deed. Only God can forget such an act; man's nature forces him to remember."

*Hernandez Comes,*
*Military Governor*
*of Zamora – 1936.*

## Chapter 10
## The Betrayal and Arrest of Amparo

I had heard many opinions and theories, but in the end I gathered the following facts:

A few days after Amparo arrived in Zamora, she and the other women were brought in for questioning and then released. However, Amparo had announced her intention of applying for a passport to leave for Portugal. That, plus the fact that she was known to be the wife of Ramón J. Sender, the radical author, resulted in her being placed under a type of house arrest whereby she had to sign in at the police station daily. She remained at the family apartment with the two of us and Nati, her neurasthenic older sister.

Magdalena, her husband and eleven-year-old little Magdalena lived just across the street. Meanwhile, the Rivera girls and servants moved into the small cottage of the waiter, Andrés, and his mother who cooked in the café. Every day more and more people were being arrested. Magdalena was in anguish because her husband expected to be imprisoned. Fascist execution squads were dragging people out of their houses. Mutilated and bullet-riddled bodies were being found along the roadsides and in the river.

Little Magdalena, or 'Nena,' remembered watching the adults burn books and papers in the café one evening. They also burned a statuette of a woman with a Phrygian cap, the symbol of the Republic. Her mother found a list of local Communist Party members hidden in Amparo's piano. Antonio was a communist and in charge of the archives. We children watched our elders in astonishment as they searched frantically for incriminating items.

Two women friends visited Amparo. They found her seated by the radio listening with great excitement to a clandestine broadcast from the other zone. The announcer had reported things were going well for the Republicans and Amparo was euphoric. She was very animated and spoke in a great hurry, a temperamental sort. The war would end in four days, she told them.

When they left, she accompanied them onto the landing and continued talking. Her guests walked downstairs but she shouted after them, still very agitated, "No, no, the uprising will be over almost at once! We are winning!"

"Oh my, Amparo shouldn't be talking like this in public!" the women said to one another. "Because if they hear her – "

The government confiscated the café, the family ice factory and Antonio's electric shop as "war goods." Magdalena was advised to renounce her Barayón inheritance so that her husband would not also be fined.

According to Amparo's younger sister Eugenia, Amparo was arrested on St. Augustine's day, (August 28th), the same day they killed her brother Antonio. "She went to protest what they had done to Antonio. She took the baby with her because she knew they would not harm her with the child in her arms. Then suddenly she understood what they were like in there and left on the run. She understood she had not shown proper respect to the governor and had to escape. On the street she fell. They grabbed her and took her to jail. People later felt the governor had the option of noticing or ignoring her action. If she had left tranquilly – "

But Magdalena told a slightly different version, which was confirmed by Palmira who as a fifteen-year-old shared Amparo's cell: Amparo had asked her brother-in-law Miguel Sevilla to use his influence to help her acquire a passport.

On August 28th he contacted her.

"Amparo, the military governor wants to talk with you about your request," he told her. "But don't take the baby when you go down."

"But I always take her wherever I go," she replied. What a strange thing for him to say!

"There is apt to be a long wait and – well, I just thought I'd mention it," he finished lamely.

His tone of voice convinced her to do just the opposite. With my sister Andrea in her arms, she started down the block in the late afternoon.

"Amparo!" Her half-sister Magdalena hurried up to her. "Oh, Amparo! Antonio has disappeared! They were transferring him along with twenty others to the Fermoselles jail and they never arrived. Someone reported seeing many bodies in the fields outside Toro."

Amparo was dumbfounded. "You mean they just took them and – "

"When they disappear like this, it can only mean one thing." Magdalena moaned, wringing her hands. "Oh God! I've got to talk to Casimira. Maybe Sevilla told her something."

Dazed, Amparo walked the six blocks to the provincial office building, now under the administration of the military. Ushered into Colonel

Hernández Comes' office, she stood with the baby in her arms while he stared at her.

"I spoke with your brother-in-law regarding your application," he said. "Because of the unsettled state of things, we are not issuing passports at present."

"Are you also the one who authorizes the transfer of prisoners?" she asked.

"Yes, but why do you ask?"

"Because my brother Antonio disappeared today while being transferred to Fermoselles."

Hernández Comes spread his hands helplessly. "Ah, these matters are tragic but there is nothing I can do. According to reports I received, all the prisoners involved in the transfer have been found shot."

Antonio murdered? Amparo drew herself up, eyes blazing. "I feel it is my duty, sir, to inform you – " She took a deep breath – "that you are – all of you – vile murderers and scum!" She spat the epithets at him. "I hold you personally responsible for his death!"

Realizing that her fury had bested her, she turned and ran out, slamming the door behind her. She had to get away! Andrea clutched to her chest, she walked quickly back to the apartment. Dionisia had just begun to feed me. Amparo joined us at the kitchen table, breastfeeding Andrea while staring bleakly out the window. Dionisia went downstairs to the café to do the laundry, leaving me dawdling over my bowl of farina. When Andrea fell asleep, Amparo put her down in her bedroom before returning to retake her seat.

In *The Five Books Of Ariadne*, my father wrote of how the sun still shone upon her childhood paradise, but the streets had been invaded by shadows, shapeless forms that she could only see out of the corners of her eyes. As a girl, she would have laughed at these dark ghosts, but now they threatened to engulf her.

After weighing all my informants' versions, I reconstructed the following:

A hammering at the door jolted Amparo upright. "Open up! Open up!" a gruff voice shouted.

Throwing a crocheted dark blue shawl around her shoulders, Amparo undid the latch. A police sergeant forced his way past her followed by three men with rifles. They searched the rooms, staring briefly at Nati semi-comatose in her bed. "*Señorita*, you must come with us," the policeman said. "We have an order for your arrest."

"But my children – "

"Leave them." He seemed nervous. "Come along now."

I clutched her skirt, wailing. She murmured soothing words and tried to lead me into the hall, but I threw myself down, arms thrashing.

Hands grasped her arms and lifted her.

"Monchín!" she screamed.

She was half-carried to the waiting car. Behind her, I was climbing down the stairs backwards, bellowing.

"I can't abandon the children!" she shouted. She leaned out the window. "Dionisia! Magdalena!"

The policeman faced her from the front seat. "*Señorita*, as a suspected Red, you are without any rights whatsoever." He shrugged. "You should have thought of this before having children." He said something in a low voice to the driver, who burst out laughing.

In the laundry room, Aisia heard Amparo's shout and ran outside just in time to see the car turn the corner. My screams echoed from the landing where I had fallen and cut my lip. She picked me up and brought me upstairs.

At the police station, Amparo was placed in a holding cell with a wooden platform for a bed and a slop bucket. The rationale for her arrest was that she was implicated as a relative of Saturnino and Antonio, and that she had a clandestine radio transmitter in her possession.

The following morning, she was brought upstairs and told they were transferring her to the prison a few blocks away. Prison! Her breasts ached with milk for her baby! She gazed wildly about her, searching for a way out. She waited until both policemen were occupied and then flung herself out the door.

"Halt! Halt!" The shouts were followed by gunshots.

She ran towards the apartment. In front of the post office, her toe caught in the cobblestones and she fell. Half-stunned, she lay there, pain searing her forearm and knee.

Footsteps. She was seized by the elbows and dragged to her feet. "Got her!" the policeman yelled. "Don't try that again!"

Later that morning, Dionisia took Andrea to the prison because Amparo was breastfeeding her. A café neighbor in Zamora saw Dionisia return with me from a visit to Amparo, both of us crying.

Amparo's sister, Eugenia, who lived in nearby León, left for Zamora immediately. "When I arrived at the apartment, you were seated under a little table screaming in outrage. Your fits of anger lasted such a long time that my mother took you to a children's specialist and he gave her some medicine for your nerves.

"You had seen many bombardments in the previous weeks. After two or three days, your mother's aged aunt Maximina took you to her farm in the village of Perdigon. Dionisia could not remain responsible for you because she was a minor.

"Maximina was an old woman and half-blind. But she and her husband were childless and delighted to have you. You were sickly – you didn't want to eat, but you ate very well for her. At her house there were chickens and a pig, a garden with a well and fruit trees. You would call for her, 'Tía, Tía!'"

While I stayed with Maximina, Amparo endured the hardships of Zamora's prison. Two women who knew her there – Palmira Sanjuan and Pilar Fidalgo Carasa, lived to tell of her fate. Their accounts were later printed in newspapers and magazines. Together they provide a collective testimony of horror.

Palmira, whose father and brother both were shot in Zamora, later was sentenced to a long prison term for distributing pamphlets condemning Franco. "I met Amparo when I was jailed with my mother," she told me. "She had long dark hair, very thick, which she twisted into braids to keep clean. I was a youngster of fifteen, and Amparo treated me as another daughter. She was very loving to me. I always wanted to hold the baby and feed her, but Amparo wanted to be with her as much as possible. I was only able to hold her when Amparo had something else to do. I was always saying, 'Amparo, Amparito, give me the baby!'

"All I know about Amparo's story is what she told me. She always accused an in-law named Sevilla. 'It's my uncle Miguel Sevilla who is guilty.' These were the exact words that came out of her mouth. Amparo said, 'He told me to go pick up my passport at the Civil Governor's office. And the strangest thing was that he told me not to take the baby along. Why did he not want me to take Andreina?' These were her exact words! She talked with my mother about it.

"Sevilla was friendly with all the killers. He knew who had been condemned to die and when they were going to be shot. Amparo always said, 'Sevilla is the guilty one!' She named him just like that. He knew days ahead that they were going to kill her.

"Amparo did not care for her family because none of them concerned themselves with her situation. They brought her none of the things that families usually supply to their loved ones in jail, no soap, nothing! There was only one person who came to visit her, a young girl who was in service to your family. She brought her sandwiches and was always weeping. She was the only person who cared after Amparo in prison. She also brought her a little soap occasionally.

"Amparo's family did not behave well. Normally, the moment a loved one was arrested, the mothers, the sisters, the children went to the door of the jail to weep, to find out news, to try to see who was inside. They did not visit Amparo. They abandoned her when she needed them, and for this they should feel remorse. But not Amparo's husband. If they had captured Ramón Sender – hah! They would have cut him into tiny pieces! Poor man, he had to escape.

"They killed Amparo because they could not kill him. I'm very sorry I wasn't able to talk with him just to tell him he shouldn't feel guilty. Amparo always said that she loved him very much. There was a lullaby she sang to her baby. 'The words were written by my husband,' she said. 'And I put them to music.'

Palmira described how Teresa the jailer brought coffee around eight. Then the women went to the patio where they sat on the ground. Those who had soap washed their things in a large basin, but soap was as precious as gold. Amparo did not put the baby's things in with the other clothes. Instead she washed them in a small bucket to avoid infections. Bathing facilities were primitive, and some of the older women never bathed. They wanted to hold Andrea but Amparo would not let them. She was very kind, very loving, but said no. But Palmira would sit down and Amparo would put the baby on her lap.

"Don't get up, or you'll fall with the baby!" Amparo would say.

She used these moments to comb her hair and retie her braids. The prison provided combs and powder because of the lice. After the midday meal, they were locked up. Late in the afternoon, they descended to the patio and waited for supper. The men cooked the food over a wood fire in the kitchen. The lentils or other beans were brought in a large kettle and the women lined up for a bowl apiece. After the meal, they returned to the cell and awaited the hour of the "*La Lista Negra*," the Black List that named those condemned to die.

Palmira remembered another mother with a baby in the jail who was named Pilar Fidalgo Carasa, "a lovely woman with blue eyes. They jailed her right after she gave birth and her tiny newborn baby was with her. She was well-known in Zamora because her husband started reclamation proceedings and succeeded in having her moved to the republican zone. Your father could have done the same but he was unprepared. He could have gone to the French embassy and given Amparo's name and perhaps reclaimed her."

During the first period of the war, many persons who found themselves caught 'on the wrong side' of the conflict were switched across the lines via the intervention of the Red Cross or a foreign nation. Prisoner exchanges were also accomplished and, in theory at least, Papá could have applied to have Amparo brought out to France.

Pilar later described conditions in the prison: "On my arrival in prison, I was compelled to climb a narrow, steep staircase to a cell already holding thirty-five other women prisoners. I was left there in a half-fainting condition until, under the pretext of being interrogated, I was obliged to climb up and down this staircase several times a day. Because of my recent confinement and my weak state, this brought on a severe hemorrhage and a descent of my uterus. Also, I contracted a bladder infection that totally prevented me from urinating.

"I had not been allowed to bring any clothing for myself or my child, and since there was neither mattress nor coverlet, I had to sleep on the cement floor – even when winter came, and the climate of Zamora was one of the most rigorous in Spain. I tried to wrap up my child so that she would not suffer too much. The temperature in our cell fell below freezing, and her hands and face turned blue. I had only a piece of blanket that a companion had given me to protect us from the bitter cold. Because I continued hemorrhaging, I constantly begged the warden for help. Finally she brought the prison doctor Pedro Almendral who merely came as a matter of form. Upon seeing my suffering, he commented that 'the best cure for the wife of that scoundrel Almoina is death.' He prescribed nothing – neither for myself or my baby.

"The warden, Teresa Alonso, was nicknamed 'the Hyena' by the prisoners. Her daughter was secretary for the Falangist Party, and because of this, Teresa had been hired as supervisor of the women prisoners. She insisted we address her as 'Doña Teresa' while treating us with brutality and overwhelming us with the grossest offenses. In our presence she insulted our husbands and seized every opportunity to be cruel. Her helper Ludivina was serving a life sentence for infanticide. The prison regime was barbarous. Two days after my arrival, I gave up trying to breastfeed my baby, because all these emotions had dried up my milk. Every afternoon I was given only a little cup of goat's milk and water. The child had to drink it cold, for we were not allowed to make a fire. I was attempting to coax her to drink the evil-smelling liquid from a baby bottle when the Hyena entered the cell.

"'You don't know how to be a mother!' she shouted, and pulled my daughter from my arms.

"She thrust the bottle so violently into the baby's mouth that the baby, unable to breathe, turned blue and began to suffocate. I fainted on the floor. When I came to, I was surrounded by my companions. Meanwhile my baby, freed from the claws of the warden, went into convulsions. Not surprisingly, she later fell ill of dysentery and bronchitis.

"One child died of meningitis in our cell. He cried piercingly and died without any medical attention. The day after, both the mother and grandmother were shot.

"At times we were forty prisoners in a cell built to accommodate two people. There were two benches, each capable of seating three persons, and the floor to sleep on. For our private needs, there were only three chamberpots. They had to be emptied into an old rusty cauldron, which also served for washing our clothes. We were forbidden to have food brought to us from outside, and were given disgusting soup cooked with soda ash that kept us in a constant state of dysentery. We were all in a deplorable state. The air was unbreathable, and the babies choked many nights for lack of oxygen. We were not allowed to go into the yard to dry our washing, so we had to spread it out on the cement floor of the cell. Then we all squeezed ourselves into a corner so as not to walk on it. We tried to soften the heart of the warden and begged to be permitted at least to place the babies' linen in the sun. She replied that we could dry it on our bodies. That is what we had to do, so that the infants should not suffer from wet clothing.

"To be imprisoned, according to the rebels, was to lose all individuality. The most elementary human rights were unknown and people were killed as easily as rabbits – indeed more easily, because to kill a rabbit, a hunting permit was required. But to kill people you only had to go into the street and fire on them as a diversion."

"In other towns it wasn't like in Zamora.," Palmira explained. "The military revolted and that was that. They arrested people certainly. They killed someone here, they beat up someone there. But in Zamora they shot twenty or thirty every night! They should be covered in shame for everything they did.

*Palmira Sanjuan Misis, who as a young girl was imprisoned in the women's cell with her mother and Amparo.*

*Pilar Fidalgo Carasa, whose testimony about Zamora prison conditions was published in 1939.*

"It didn't matter if you were pregnant or not. Engracia del Río was eight months pregnant, a schoolteacher. She came upstairs with two others and they said, 'Go see Don Justo.' Don Justo, the administrative secretary, asked her whose baby she was carrying. 'Mine!' she replied. 'Come on, it's what's-his-name's,' he said. 'I'm not going to say,' she said. A few days later they shot her, in full knowledge of her condition."

Pilar: "The first three women murdered in prison were Engracia del Rio, Carmen N., a beautiful seventeen-year-old with lovely black hair, and María Salgado, a widow and mother of a seven-year-old boy. These last two were led to the cemetery by a band of Falangists who, once there, told them to run. If they succeeded in escaping, their lives would be spared. The two women were shocked but, urged on by the instinct of self-preservation, they ran madly from tomb to tomb, jumping over graves and hiding behind crosses and little chapels. Meanwhile the Falangists, young *señoritos* of good families, pursued and fired at them as though on a hunt. Wounded, bleeding, victims of an incredible madness, the two women fell dead from the bullets of their hunters. The *señoritos* roared with laughter and recounted their exploits at the casino. On the following day, they took communion at their parish church where the priest impatiently waited to congratulate them on the zeal they had shown in defense of 'Holy Religion.'

"Every day a new and frightful trial began at twilight. With growing horror we watched night fall, wishing the sun would never set. At eight or nine o'clock we all began saying goodbye to one another. Some tied up their belongings in what scraps of material they possessed and used them as a pillow. Some already had given away their jewels, earrings, wedding rings, religious medals to their relatives through the bars of the interview cage. One can guess with what emotion these belongings were received, as well as the final messages for those soon to be orphaned. Others who had not been visited turned over their souvenirs of happier days to those among us whom they thought would be the last to be killed.

"Herminia de San Lazaro, a young married woman and great beauty, was held prisoner until the month of October. When they released her, she fell seriously ill, either because the suffering she had endured had weakened her or because of the emotions she had undergone. Then they accused her of having thrown a statue of the Inquisitor Diego de Deza into the river.

"For those who had reestablished once more the Holy Office of the Inquisition, that was a double crime. The clergy and the bigots would not rest until Herminia was dragged from her sick bed and again imprisoned. She entered our cell at dusk and for three hours was prey to intermittent convulsions. That same night they took her to the cemetery and murdered her. She was killed to avenge an offense against a block of stone, the statue of the most infamous among Spain's inquisitors. For a long time thereafter, persons considered to be of the Left were obliged to search in the river for the statue. The searches were in vain, and many of the people drowned.

"For mothers who had a baby with them – and there were many – the first sign that they were to be executed was when their infant was snatched from them. Everyone knew what this meant. A mother whose little one was taken had only a few hours left to live. These were heartrending scenes. For the last time the condemned woman pressed her little one to her bosom and covered her with kisses. It was necessary to wrest the child away by brute force. Then the tears ceased. The woman fell into a state of semi-consciousness, of frightening silence, losing all contact with her surroundings. Many were led to their death in this condition, and it happened almost every night. In frozen stillness we heard the first steps in the corridor, and tried to discover within those treads which of us would be chosen to die that night. Then the door opened. Civil Guards and Falangists appeared. To hear the list better, we held our breath and so that our children would not cry, we gave them the breast.

"They read out the list very slowly – with a tortuous slowness. With the calling of the first name, terror seized us all. Those called gave their bundles to us, and asked us to see their family received it. Those who once more had not been named uttered a sigh of relief at the twenty-four more hours of life assured them, a small concession that seemed such a precious gift. We who had to stay behind, fearing the murderers would prolong their stay amongst us, begged the condemned ones not to delay their dressing. They knew, and we knew, that they were about to be killed. We all were anxious that the scene should end, because when the victims delayed, the executioners hurled the grossest insults and threatened to take us all. Tragically, the unfortunate ones about to die understood this very well and so went quickly, some even without their shoes. However long, however full of change my life will be, neither I nor any of the survivors shall ever forget those moments.

"In the province of Zamora they murdered about six thousand people, six hundred of them women. Bodies appeared on the roads, in the meadows, in the fields, under trees and in the thickets. Some were left as they fell, others disinterred by animals from hastily dug graves. Widows and orphans had to hide their grief for fear of being killed. They begged in secret, because anyone who helped the survivors of a 'Red' exposed himself to being shadowed. Only the Social Assistance organization could officially allay material needs, but only by imposing moral suffering. They obliged the orphans to sing the songs of their fathers' murderers, to wear the uniform of those who executed them, to curse the dead and blaspheme their memories."

## Chapter 11
## Amparo's Death

At the beginning of October, the ground froze and northern Spain's bitter winter set in. As the skies darkened, so did the climate in Zamora's prison. And for Amparo, the worst was about to begin.

Pilar: "One of the most sinister nights I spent in prison was October 9, 1936, when the greatest number of my friends from Benavente were killed. Along with many others whose names escape my memory for the moment, they shot Epifanio Rodríguez Rubio, Felipe Martínez Abad, Ildefonso Lopez, Enrique Villarino Santiago, Francisco Fernández, Luciano García Guerra, Marcelo Carbajo Lora. There was the son of a cobbler named Burgos who was only nineteen years old, Feliz Vara, the painter Ibañez, Alejandrino Perez, Teofilo Infestas and Venancio Alonso. The wife of the last-named, María Garea, was imprisoned with us. The men spent the whole night shut up in the chapel, which also served as a torture chamber for the condemned. From our cell, grouped around the poor wife, we heard their cries and screams. Then they came to take María Garea to accompany her husband. I was present at this scene and shall never forget her charging us with the welfare of her two small boys. But worse was to follow. She was taken to the chapel where, along with the others, she found her husband. We heard them moaning as they embraced for the first time since their imprisonment, and also the last time because the moment of meeting was to be the moment of parting. At dawn their bodies, clasped to each other, were thrown into a common pit.

"It was in the same chapel that all the prisoners heard Mass. Throughout the ceremony, we had to kneel without turning our heads towards the area of the chapel where the men were. During the long sermon, the priest frequently insulted us by calling us 'Red bitches.' Behind us, our jailers kept guard. In this dismal spot, which had been the scene of so many martyrdoms and sufferings, we found small pieces of paper with a few words of goodbye written by feverish and trembling hands, a last vow or a final request. On the floor and against the walls were splashes of blood. Sometimes, although not without incurring great risks, we could gather up these papers and carefully preserve them."

Palmira: "At six at night they took the men out. I don't know how because I never saw the men's part of the prison. They put them in the chapel next to our cell where we could hear them calling, each one saying things about himself so that we would know who he was. One time my mother thought the voice was my brother's and almost fainted because he was shouting, 'Mother!' Every night there were these dramas, with the men calling their final messages to us.

"Later, when the tower clock struck midnight or one o'clock, they came for the women. From the bottom of the spiral staircase they called out the names of the women they wanted. When someone resisted coming down, they went upstairs. Each one went according to her manner, some bravely, others tearfully, others talking of their father and mother, brothers or children. At that moment they spoke of the persons they loved the most in the world. They went downstairs and what happened to them we didn't know. If the killers told others and these others spoke, then we would hear something. But no loved one really knew how the chosen ones died or how they were killed. If you knew, you were an accomplice."

Pilar: "The story of the Flechoso sisters is no less moving. Angelita was fifteen, her sister eighteen. It tore one's heart to see those two young girls, so ignorant of the fate awaiting them. We did not think there would be any executions that day because generally they did not come on Sundays for victims. Also, we wanted to persuade ourselves that no ill would befall the two children. We advised them to rest and make a bed on the floor out of clothes and rags we loaned them. They slept in each other's arms and we watched over their innocent sleep. But towards nine o'clock the executioners came to look for them. Upon hearing her name called, one girl, very gentle in appearance, asked what it meant.

"'Angelita, if you do not feel well, lean on me,' the older one said. "Together they dressed quickly. We were so upset we could hardly say goodbye. We listened to them descend the staircase and then, as they realized what awaited them, we heard their cries. The following day we heard they had been killed together, clinging to one another. A month later, an order came to set them free.

"I also remember some young girls of the Figuero de la Torre family. Serafina and Aurelia, along with their mother María, were still in the women's cell as if they were dangerous criminals when I was released. A brother, seventeen, had been killed but the family did not know about it.

*Pilar Fidalgo Carasa's testimony, published in France in 1939, cover by Picasso.*

"All the members of the Flechas family, both men and women, were killed, a total of seven persons. A son succeeded in escaping, but in his place they killed his eight-months-pregnant fiancée Transito Alonso and her mother, Juana Ramos. In Transito's case, even after she was dead the baby kept moving and they shot through her body many times."

Palmira: "The next day the nuns came to teach us catechism and to love God. 'They killed Transito last night,' they said. 'Shall we say an Our Father for her?' 'Ah, did they?' someone replied with much sarcasm. 'Good, good!' In general I grew to hate nuns.

"Those few months were the worst. They were killing mothers who had small children, even old grandmothers. It was excruciatingly painful emotionally. The fish-sellers, Juana Ramos and Emilia, were both over eighty years old. They were foul-mouthed old ladies and joked about everything, although they knew that in spite of their age they were going to be killed. 'So who are you taking to old Cacabel today?' they would ask the Hyena. But after her daughter Transito was killed, Juana fell silent until the day they called her name. When they took her away she kept crying, 'I have children who love me! Why do you kill me if I have children who love me?'

Pilar: "They did the same with the family Carnero; the mother, two daughters and the fiancé of one were all killed. A tailor named Silva, well- known in Zamora, was shot along with his wife. I could cite many families who were completely annihilated.

Palmira: "Many priests acted very badly. The bishop of Zamora in 1936 was more or less an assassin – I don't remember his name. He must be held responsible because prisoners appealed to him to save their lives. All he would reply was that the Reds had killed more people than the Falangists were killing."

Pilar: "A priest heard the confessions of the condemned and accompanied them to their execution – not as a devout duty but in the spirit of collaboration. Statements were taken from the prisoners and were the occasion of fresh arrests and executions. I recall in this connection that a priest took it upon himself to speak with the prisoners. By his insidious questions this cleric extracted names and facts that he conveyed to the Falangists. He even employed this procedure with those soon to be shot and whose fear and nearness to death inevitably inclined them towards religion. Another priest was the one who said Mass. All his sermons were inflamed harangues against the 'Reds.' He covered the Republicans with insults and said that we were not to be killed because we were robbers but because we were connected with men just as infamous as thieves. His imprecations were terrifying, and the most terrible curses came from his lips during the Offertory. He refused absolution to Amparo because she refused to declare that her husband was scum."

Meanwhile, Conchita and Emi had heard of Amparo's arrest.

Conchita: "A month after Amparo returned to Zamora, we were transferred to Burgos. They put Emi in front of the telegraph key, but there was almost always a guard. He waited until one day at three in the morning when they were less busy than usual and the guard was on a break. Then he wired his Zamora comrade that he wanted confidential news of a relative. It was a dangerous thing to do, because once he gave the man Amparo's name, the man could harm him. He had no way of knowing whether the person at the other end of the wire was a fascist who might turn him in. But he received a friendly answer: 'I'm always at your disposal. You can count on my discretion because I would like to ask about someone in your zone.'

"So Emi said, 'Her name is Amparo Barayón, married to Ramón Sender.'

"And the other man answered, 'She's in jail but there are those who are trying to get her out.' Things remained like this for a long time. Every three or four days Emi asked after her whenever his shift coincided with his friend's at the other end. 'The baby has been taken to her in jail. Little is possible but there are those who have hope.' So that was how Emi learned that Amparo had been arrested, but he didn't tell me until much later when the worst had happened."

Palmira: "Of course everyone hoped to survive, but basically Amparo was fearful. I remember her talking one day with my mother – we were seated on the floor – and she said, 'Yes, they're going to kill me.'

"'Come on, Amparo!' my mother said. 'Don't say that!' "I have always remembered this conversation. She was a strong, intelligent woman, but she knew Ramón was writing in Madrid. She was afraid he would write something against Franco that would destroy her chances. But most of all, she felt her brother-in-law had led her into a trap."

If the military governor Hernández Comes dangled a passport as bait, it was a man named Viloria who killed Amparo for a reason, as we will ultimately learn, worse than any we could have imagined.

Pilar: "Segundo Viloria was a lawyer who represented the Conservative Party in Zamora. Everybody knew him and until then had considered him normal. However, he was responsible for bringing in hundreds of women – it was his specialty. Among these unfortunate women was a certain Eugenia. He had beaten her so violently that when she entered our cell, her body was black and her underwear stuck to her wounds. After he beat her, he raped her, but he didn't stop there. When he was again on duty at the prison (as a member of the Falangist death squad), he once more sought out his victim and repeated his terrible acts. Some weeks passed, and then this monster came again one night to look for her. He led her to the cemetery and there killed her.

Palmira: "Viloria was a beast. He was paid to kill and he killed my father. He was one of a group of men who were paid to murder.[1] They shot without knowing who their victims were. 'Kill this one,' the Falangists would say. They would grab them and shoot twenty, thirty, forty, whomever they wanted. But he was not the one to denounce her. He shot her, but the person responsible for her death was he who denounced her. If there had not been denouncers, there would not have been assassins."

Pilar: "Another case of sadism worth mentioning is that of an assassin named Mariscal. He went freely about Zamora and committed so many terrible crimes that even his accomplices became afraid. Mariscal became one of the worst of the executioners because of the long succession of

---

[1] "The cruelest Falangists in the province used to belong to well-off families from the south of the province. They were young men, new graduates in law or medicine. These organized 'camions de muerte,' trucks of death that traveled through the villages in search of victims denounced by the political bosses from the town. One of the bloodiest trucks was the one that took care of the area of Sanabria political bosses, a notorious truck known throughout the province. One of the leaders of the same, along with Mariscal, was the lawyer Viloria. In the 1936 elections, Viloria was elected for a delegate. He defended the anarchists, but when with the State of War was declared, went to the phalanx, and pretended to make merit with his performance.

"This death truck was composed of thirteen people, eleven men and two women. These two women ended up as prostitutes after the war, one of them the jailer Teresa Alonso, nicknamed 'La Hyena.' Some of the men: Viloria, lawyer; Sergeant Luis Valera Nieves (Sergeant Poison); Mariscal, postal official; Campal, countryman from Corrales; the judge of Madridanos; Piriz, son of a teacher from Arcillos y Rueda, from Zamora capital." – Laura de Dios Vicente: *Control y represión en Zamora (1936-1939). La violencia vengadora ejecutada sobre el terreno* (1936-1939) ... Historia y Comunicación Social Vol. 7 (2002) 47-74 atrocities he perpetrated without regard to age, sex or the condition of the victims. These two murderers, Viloria and Mariscal, would have made an interesting study for psychiatrists."

Eugenia, Amparo's younger sister, hurried to Zamora when she heard of Amparo's arrest.

Eugenia: "When they decided to shoot Amparo, the military governor Hernández Comes told Sevilla to take charge of Andrea. 'I can't take the baby,' Sevilla said. Hernández Comes asked why. 'How could I face my wife with the baby in my arms and tell her that her sister was going to be killed that same night?' So they took Andrea to the orphanage."

Pilar: "Amparo Barayón, wife of the distinguished writer Ramón J. Sender... had with her in the cell her baby daughter Andrea. At six o'clock that evening, Justo, secretary to the administrator of the prison, dragged her child from her arms, saying, among other witticisms, that 'Reds did not have the right to nourish their children.'"

Palmira: "Justo snatched Andreina from her mother in the patio. Amparo tried to stop him but she couldn't. We were eating, and – ... At this moment Amparo understood that she was going to be shot... The thing is that I don't remember much. These were moments of confusion. Moments that – you don't know what's happening – you're not trying to record these events. One doesn't think like this. They happen, and I have been told I have a trauma about this incident. Also, when someone was going to be shot, my mother protected me from the information. What happened was terrible."

Pilar: "Amparo, powerless to defend the baby, struggled and wept, a prey to indescribable madness. Then she wrote a farewell letter to Sender that I kept for a long time, but had to tear into pieces and eat because of the continual searches to which we were subjected. In this letter, she delivered her children to his care and held Miguel Sevilla responsible for her death."

The text of Amparo's note:

> Beloved Ramón: Do not pardon my assassins who have robbed me of Andreina, nor Miguel Sevilla who is guilty for having denounced me. For myself, I do not care because I die for you. But what will become of the children? They are yours now. I love you always, Amparo.

Pilar: "When she finished writing, Amparo fainted. When she recovered, she remained in a state of semi-consciousness, crying for her little girl."

From the article in *INTERVIU* magazine: "Hours before her assassination, Amparo was confessed by a priest... who explicitly refused her absolution, alleging later in public that she had always lived in sin because she had not been married by the Church... In later confessions to the murder, Miguel Sevilla... said that 'Amparo's confession damaged her case very much.' One has to ask whether the secret of confession was so devalued in those days, or whether Sevilla only pretended to know, to excuse himself for not having moved a finger to save his sister-in-law...

"Minutes before midnight in the women's cell, the clattering of *Senora* Teresa's keys was heard. Shortly after the town clock struck twelve... a man's voice shouted the names of three women from the lower level of the staircase: Amparo Barayón, Juliana Luís García and her cousin Antonia Blanes Luís. When one of the women summoned delayed in coming out, the voice shouted: 'Are you coming down or do you want us to come up and get you?'

"The Falangists in charge of the execution put them in a bus. They were not handcuffed. Some minutes after midnight, the bus left on the road to Salamanca en route to the cemetery."

Eugenia: "I believe Amparo left for the cemetery weeping and shouting, 'My children, my children!'"

Zamora, 1982: The time had come to visit the cemetery, the moment of truth on my pilgrimage. I didn't feel ready for it, but it had to be faced. We stopped to buy white gladiolas and red carnations at a flower shop. Earlier that same day, my researcher Fernando had told me that during the first few years after Amparo's death, some unknown person regularly had placed flowers on her grave.

South a few kilometers towards Salamanca, a high wall loomed up on the left. The gate featured a statue of San Atilano, the patron saint of the city. The graveyard contained rows of family tombs arranged between cypress trees. Amparo's final resting place consisted of a flat slab of ornate marble in front of a twelve-foot-high headstone topped by a black cross. Below the cross, a thorn-crowned head of Christ was carved in high relief and below that, the words "Familia Ignacio Maes" – Magdalena's and Chori's grandfather. It was by far the most ostentatious tomb in sight. On the elevated center slab, a plaque read:

Amparo Barayón Miguel 18-11-1936
Q.E.P. ("Rest In Peace")
From Her Husband Ramón J. Sender

According to my sister's notes, the plaque was not added until after Franco's death because it was dangerous to do so. And the date was wrong, some obscure family mix-up at the time. The grave lay in full sun, the light reflected by the white stone blinding. 'She's in there,' I kept thinking. I put the flowers in the receptacle below the agonized Christ. In my pocket I had a small box with the last bits of my father's bone and ash which I wanted to leave with Amparo.

"Oh no, we can't open the tomb!" Chori's husband exclaimed. Chori pointed to a diamond-shaped ventilation hole in the front.

"Would it fit in there?"

I measured the aperture. "Just barely."

She handed me a twig. "Push the box with this and it will fall inside." She explained how the interior consisted of a series of shelves, three on a side, and below them a bone pit, the ossuary. When the shelves were full, the first to have been interred was the first into the ossuary, a simple, practical system.

"So if I push the box far enough, it falls into the ossuary?" I asked.

"That's right."

Either I was going to make a production of this by insisting on an appointment to have the marble slab lifted, Amparo's casket opened and the ashes placed inside, or I was going to behave myself. I attached the box to the twig with the rubber band holding it shut and inserted it into the aperture.

When I withdrew the twig, I heard the echo of its landing far below. It sounded very empty inside. Empty and far away. What should I do now?

How could such a beloved, endearing woman have been shot in the midst of her childhood paradise? Given what she remembered of Zamora, the logic of her decision to return was unassailable. "I'll go home where everybody loves me," she had decided. "Where I'll be safe." To have been betrayed by the relatives to whom she had returned for protection must have been the final disillusionment.

The heat was intense. I had never been so uncomfortable in my life. More than anything, I wanted to claw open the tomb, lift the lid off the casket and take Amparo's poor bones to my breast. I wanted to wrest her out of the clutches of the three entities that had killed her: her family, her church and her town.

"Where was she originally buried?" I gasped. "Where did you find her?"

"They have completely redone the cemetery," the husband said. "It's not possible to see the spot."

I took photos to distract myself. If only I could have come out alone in a cab in the cool of the evening. And then what? I wanted to avoid people hanging around waiting for me to be through with something I hadn't even started. What utter frustration to have come across all these years, these thousands of miles, only to be stopped by a few feet of stone! But I had to understand, at last, that she was beyond my reach. I could never be next to her again. I had to acknowledge that my hunger to touch, to be with her, would never be satisfied.

On another day I returned to the cemetery, determined to spend the afternoon alone with Amparo. Seated beside her, I thought how the priest's refusal to give her final absolution must have brought her to the ultimate horror of her religion, a death without hope of redemption. According to the teachings she had professed throughout her early years, she would burn in hell for eternity.

Silently I offered up a prayer for Amparo. I did not pray to the Catholic Mary, nor to the Mary of the Crusades or the Inquisition, but to the Divine Mother of peace and gentleness who is offended by pomp and ceremony.

Amparo left the church because it became unclean. If somehow she erred in this, I asked pardon for her.

Instead of the sign of the cross, that rack of pain upon which man's nature has been crucified by the priesthoods, I made the sign of the circle, placing Amparo within the shimmering blue sphere of Ariadne's childhood paradise.

Pacing up and down between the tombs, I wondered where Amparo could have drawn her last breath before Viloria pulled the trigger.

"Where did the fascists shoot them?" I asked several people. "Against the far wall," an elderly couple told me. "Beside the tall stone cross beside the entrance," two maintenance men replied.

I closed my eyes and allowed my intuition to lead me to... a spot on a side path that inexplicably attracted me. It might have been here, on a cold October night, that Amparo finally crossed the frontiers of Spain, but not into Portugal or France.

*Family pantheon,
Zamora.*

*'The spot.'*

*Zamora bishop and Military Governor Comes, 1937.*

*The author in front of family pantheon.*

## Chapter 12
## Eugenia's Visit and Uncle Manolo's Execution

Two hours north of Zamora in the cathedral town of Astorga, we met with Amparo's younger sister Eugenia and her husband Delfín, a retired civil guard. They remembered the tragic aftermath and added even worse details.

Eugenia: "When I arrived in Zamora on October tenth, I went first to the café. Casimira phoned me there to invite me to spend the night. I wanted to go to the jail to visit Amparo right away, but Sevilla said, 'Don't go.' He already knew they were going to kill her that night. 'They'll argue with you about a safe conduct pass from the governor. You can't just go at any hour.' And the next morning, he no more than left the house when he came back and told me Amparo had been shot."

Suddenly the room in which we sat listening to these horrors filled with a chorus of rasping shrieks, like fingernails clawing slate. The swallows nesting outside the window were just settling down for the night, but it sounded like some mythical creature beating its wings against the walls. Everyone fell silent, waiting for the avenging angel to pass. It was *lubricán*, the twilight hour when, according to my father, men in Aragón turned into wolves and murdered their loved ones.

I tried to regain my composure by asking the next question on my notepad. "And the date for Antonio's death?"

"We knew nothing!" Eugenia protested. "I was living in León, and my husband had been ordered to his barracks!"

I was surprised by the sudden vociferousness of her response. Obviously she was replying more to some inner voice than to me. Had she also felt that instant of horror?

"In those moments there was nothing we could do!" her husband sputtered. "I was a civil guard and had to be where I was posted. I couldn't even accompany Eugenia on her trip to Zamora. Also, I did not know Amparo, but they judged everyone in the family the same." He was speaking as if I had accused him for not having rushed to Amparo's assistance. "I thought this way: 'I should go beg for my in-laws' lives, but the Falangists will start believing that... and I have two infant children!'" He paused, frowning to himself. "These were moments you cannot understand unless you lived through them. The Civil War was a despicable thing. They took people away for nothing!" His voice subsided into mutters behind the general conversation.

"We have Amparo's radio put away," a cousin told me. "Would you like to see it?" He brought out a large box tied with twine.

I hefted it. Heavy! How had Amparo managed to carry it all the way from San Rafael? I unpacked it and stared at it in awe, a Phillips in a wooden case. The dial had yellowed. The tubes were the size of pint bottles. At last something from her past! Amparo's fingers had touched these knobs, and no doubt mine also. How many long hours had she spent beside it, her head bowed beside the speaker to listen to forbidden broadcasts from Radio Madrid!

"Take it with you," Eugenia offered.

"Perhaps just the case and speaker," I replied. "The radio probably won't run on American current anyway."

On the way to the station for our return to Madrid, Eugenia mentioned another grotesque detail: "Two years after Amparo's death, the news spread that Franco was going to visit Zamora. He wanted to find out who was responsible for all the murders. The Falangists decided to cover their tracks and appear innocent, so they brought in Casimira and Magdalena. They forced them to sign a certificate stating that Amparo had died of pneumonia."

Our train stopped at Medina del Campo, where Amparo was first arrested. Red-bricked Castle de la Mota glowered over the landscape as if daring someone to besiege it. Queen Juana la Loca holed up here after traveling all of Castile with the corpse of her husband King Philip I. When my spirits were low, I could identify with her because I was crisscrossing Spain carrying an unavenged and unshriven mother in my heart. According to the tenets of Amparo's religion, the best she could have hoped for was to enter Purgatory. Or perhaps she remained earthbound because of her concern for her children. My sister once told me how, as a three-year-old, she had awakened at daybreak one morning to see the dark silhouette of a woman pacing the floor at the foot of her bed. She always believed it was Amparo who had visited her.

At my cousin Ana María's, Conchita welcomed us home. "Oh! I have something for you! Here! Here!" She handed me a photo. "It's the only one like it in the whole world." She stared over my shoulder. "She was prettier than that. She had a lovely figure and she was tall."

I was looking at a picture of my father and Amparo. Never before had I seen one of them together. He looked very natty in a full-length double-breasted leather overcoat and gloves, Amparo in a rakish hat and black coat. She was taller than he by perhaps two inches, although she might have been wearing heels. He looked every bit the successful young journalist, while she had a stoop-shouldered, delicate air about her. Incredible how different she seemed in every photo! Perhaps her hair was the reason, because here she was wearing it shorter than elsewhere.

Conchita described how she and Emi had been transferred to Burgos, the capital of the rebel zone, a month or so after Amparo left for Zamora. "All this time I thought my brother Manolo was in France with Marcelle and her family. They were supposed to have gone there in early July on vacation with her parents. Anyway, a delegation arrived from Huesca to Burgos and I was eager for news." She smoothed the wrinkles of her dress. "You have to remember that all communications had been stopped, even telephone conversations and telegrams. So this commercial delegation arrived from Huesca to ask for help because the town was being besieged by republican forces. They knew Emi had been transferred to Burgos and phoned him at work.

"'Well, Emi, we're here for twenty-four hours!' they said. 'Let's meet at one of the Plaza Mayor bars before lunch.' Emi agreed and phoned me to join him. 'Perhaps they'll have news!'

"They were all acquaintances of ours, so I went down around two o'clock. 'Well, Santa María,' I said to one of them. 'Any word about Manolo? He's in France, right?'

"'You don't know about Manolo?' he asked in amazement.

"'What?' I said in growing alarm. 'What has happened?'

"'They shot him in Huesca on the thirteenth of August!'"

She slapped her thigh. "Right there, in the middle of the plaza with all the bars filled, I began to scream! 'Assassins! Scum! You're all a band of scoundrels, from Franco right on down to the bottom!' I had kept quiet for so long, so quiet, making excuses for what was happening.

"The others began pleading with me, 'Conchita, *por Díos*! Conchita!'

"Emi was signaling desperately for a taxi. He found one and put me in it. One of them re-entered the bar and said, 'Look, she suffers from nervous attacks. She can't control what she says – sometimes she even says she's a saint!'

"Emi said, 'They'll never leave Burgos because we're all going to jail!'

"In the taxi, poor Santa María said to Emi, 'If you had warned me I wouldn't have told her!'

"When we got back to the house, I was still acting like a crazy woman. 'We must get away!' I was screaming. 'These people are all assassins! We have to leave this zone! I'll live anywhere else, even in an open field! We're living among killers!' I couldn't stop!" She sighed. "That's how I learned about my brother."

"Poor Emi said to me, 'Don't you realize you're endangering everyone? They can have us all shot!'

"This is why Emi told me only much later in Zaragoza of how he learned of Amparo's death from the telegrapher in Zamora. He said to me, 'How could I have told you about Amparo? If I had told you then...'"

From family members, including Manolo's widow Marcelle, I learned details of Manolo's arrest and murder. On the night the Civil War began, he worked late at his office.

Marcelle phoned a sister-in-law. "Listen, we haven't left on vacation because Manolo has so much work," she said. "Let's come have supper at your house."

When they arrived, everyone talked of going to the movies, because in Huesca they only had movies on Saturday. But that night, Manolo remained glued to the radio in amazement. The announcer was reporting the uprisings in all the cities. Suddenly all over Spain everyone was in the streets with weapons.

"Come to the table!" Marcelle called to him. "We're eating!"

"Let me be," he replied. "Things are very bad."

When the news was over, he asked Marcelle to go directly home with him.

"Aren't we going to the movies?" she asked.

"This isn't a night for the movies or anything else," he replied.

When they left, the town was in an uproar, the workers and the fascists threatening to kill each other, firing shots in the streets. He stayed at home quietly for a few days. Then the police came looking for him. Since they were all friends of his, they encouraged him to escape.

"Manolo, you'd better leave the country. Do you have a passport?"

"If I go, it will look like I'm running away," he replied. "I've done nothing wrong. I don't have to hide myself." He was very noble. "I don't have to escape because no one can harm me. Go ahead and do your duty."

They arrested him and put him in the guardhouse of the jail. There, on the thirteenth of August, without a trial or any formal accusation, he was taken to the cemetery and shot along with three others. The bodies were dumped together in a common grave.

Marcelle: "Manolo's assassins were four men. One was from Canfranc where I lived, where my father was Director of Customs. His family had a bakery and every day he brought our bread. I knew him by sight. But he was a fascist, and they paid him. Don't believe they were volunteers. They were paid killers. He told someone, 'I hunt wild goats in the mountains. I'm a good shot. Assure the lady whom I have seen so often that Manolo did not suffer. I killed him with one bullet.'"

With a tapered index finger she pointed to her head. "It entered here and exited behind. It wasn't necessary to give him the coup de grace. The night they shot him, I was awake. I heard the cars leaving the jail. I thought, 'They are going to kill someone.' They were already killing many people. At three in the morning I heard shots. It's because of this that I still awaken many times at this hour."

We arrived in Huesca on the thirteenth of August, the forty-sixth anniversary of Uncle Manolo's assassination. Our visit coincided with The Feast of San Lorenzo, the town's patron saint, a week-long event that brought thousands of visitors. A hotel room was out of the question, so we had phoned my Aunt Carmen, my father's youngest sister, at her summer place in Jaca. She and her husband would be glad to pick us up at the Huesca bus depot. They drove us to the cemetery through festive crowds of young people wearing the traditional green caps and neckerchiefs of the saint. I wanted to spill the drops of Papá's blood that Benedicta had washed out of his bedroom carpet beside Uncle Manolo. It would be a symbolic reunion with the brother he loved so much.

From *Counterattack in Spain,* I remembered my father's eulogy to a fallen comrade:

> The soldier had fallen forward on his face and in his death agony his fingernails had scraped the loose earth into small mounds. His open eyes stared at the soil of Spain, as if to memorize the precious substance he was dying to protect.
>
> There was a passionate frenzy in his expression as if he was clutching his beloved to him in an outpouring of love.

I thought, 'Our dead are not repugnant to me. Go, comrade, take with you that precious earth that you grasp. It's yours, now and forever. The land is yours by a divine right greater than that of kings, than that of Franco's filthy, vulgar pretenders. All they have done is mortgage your soil to the German and Italian generals. But their own lies will condemn them and the land will be ours. Enriched by our blood, the calcium of our bones, it will nourish another strong generation in whose songs you will live, in whose lives you will be remembered.'

Before our departure for Málaga and Barcelona we paid a final visit to Conchita in Madrid. Standing by the elevator, I took her hand.

"Best of all on this journey has been meeting you," I told her.

"If only you knew how long I waited to see you again! How many times I wondered how you and your sister were. When your father returned to France in 1962, the whole family went to visit him in Pau, and I said to him, 'You must put me in contact with the children.' And he said, 'No! Because I know how you are and you'll tell them the truth of the tragedy of their mother. I don't want them to know! Perhaps when they're old, but I don't want their childhood, their youth, to be embittered.'"

She stared up at me with great tenderness. "You cannot know what a mother you had in Amparo. She did not die just once, but three or four times. She was such a mother! For her, the most horrible was to think of her children uncared for – *desamparados* – abandoned."

*Uncle Manolo Sender.*

*Amparo's radio.*

*Magdalena Maes Barayón, niece of Amparo Barayón - 1983.*

## Chapter 13
## Final Details

As the train pulled into Málaga, my anticipation built. At last I would meet Amparo's niece Magdalena, the person who had kept her memory most alive. Her testimony, delivered with quiet authority, would resolve many of the conflicting details I had heard from others. Would Magdalena meet us? I didn't even know what she looked like.

"*Hola*, Ramón?" A thin woman with her gray hair done up in a topknot approached us. She had a long, intelligent face.

Beside her stood her husband, a bushy-browed, professorial type with a briar pipe in his mouth. He drove us through downtown, pointing out the harbor and lighthouse, the flourishing park across from the two ancient fortresses the Alcazaba and Gibralfaro that had protected the coastline in olden days.

Their apartment, two blocks from the beach, was lined with books. One bookcase contained the most complete collection of my father's I had ever seen.

Over apertifs, Magdalena kept glancing at me with a bow-shaped smile on her lips. I thought of the tensions fostered by my father in our relationship. God only knew what he had told her. In his San Diego apartment I had found her correspondence reporting my requests for information and including photocopies of my letters. Now that he had died, I hoped she would prove as loyal to me.

"Eugenia said Amparo was arrested after insulting the military governor." I told her.

"This much is certain," Magdalena replied. "The police came to the house and arrested her. I know because I went to the apartment every day to see you. One morning when I arrived, the servant girl said, 'No, she isn't here. They took her away.'

"I told my mother. That afternoon they transferred Amparo from the police station to the jail, but when they told her they were taking her to prison, she tried to escape. She was fearful of leaving you and Andreina. When she started to run, she tripped and fell in front of the post office."

Where could she have run? Where in such a small town could she have hidden with two children? Despair had overwhelmed her, and she had responded like a hunted deer.

"Who visited Amparo in jail?" I asked.

"My father, and Aisia many times. My mother, Eugenia and Nati did all they could to help her. You see, Amparo was arrested twice in Zamora," Magdalena continued in her subdued manner. "The first time she told them who she was and that she wanted to go to Portugal. But it wasn't possible – the frontier had been closed – and they let her go because she hadn't committed any offense. The second time, someone in the family denounced her."

"Miguel Sevilla."

"Miguel Sevilla was against everyone," Magdalena admitted. "The family was very divided. Sevilla was not one of us. I believe he was very guilty for Amparo's death. Very guilty. Because he knew all about the killings ahead of time." Her mouth tightened into a thin line. "It's very sad to have to say this to you."

"So Sevilla was the one."

"Something like that," Magdalena replied. "My mother kept saying he would save Amparo, that he would do what was possible. Also, Casimira could have done something. She was the French teacher for Hernández Comes' children. My mother said to her, 'Please, let's go talk with him.' As military governor he was the one who signed the releases for those in prison. He gave people permission to leave and then they would be taken to the cemetery and killed." She gestured helplessly. "But Casimira said no, and explained that the governor had been informed and would not permit anything to happen to Amparo. She wouldn't be released to the death squads. Why was Casimira like this? Because she thought if Amparo was put out of the way, she and Sevilla would get more of the family money." She shook her head sorrowfully. "It's horrible to have to admit that a family member could do such a thing. But I was present in the café the night Miguel Sevilla came in and said, 'Tonight they are killing Amparo.'

Shocked and incredulous, I leaned forward. "He said this to whom?"

"To everyone." She hesitated. "I was overcome with emotion. Casimira and Sevilla came to the café because we were making an inventory. The court had seized everything as war goods. We were holding a family council, and they had an interest in the property, although it was in the names of the uncles. They said to my mother, 'Tonight they are killing Amparo.' And my mother couldn't do anything. It was horrible! Between the two of them, Casmira and Sevilla could have saved her."

Perhaps Sevilla, head of the local *requeté* militia and with close connections to the church, could have interceded for Amparo, something he was unlikely to do after having denounced her. And Casimira, with her easy entrée into the Comes family, might have wielded some influence. But I believe the truth lay closer to what Palmira Sanjuan said: Amparo was given up for lost by her family after her arrest, and the surviving members distanced themselves from her. Magdalena's parents were paralyzed with fear, along with the majority of the citizens of Zamora. Her father expected daily to be arrested himself.

Later I mentioned how I had heard two versions of where I lived while Amparo was in jail: with Amparo's elderly aunt Maximina and in the orphanage.

"Both are true," Magdalena said. "Maximina took you first, and then after Amparo was killed, you were taken to the orphanage at the governor's order. My mother went every day to bring you things and see how you were. The nuns were very kind. Then when Dr. Junod came, the director of the Red Cross's Spanish relief effort, they arranged for an ambulance to take you and Andrea to France.

"When Dr. Junod asked, 'Why was Amparo killed?' they answered him, 'It was a mistake. An error.'"

"She was killed by mistake?" I repeated, stunned.

"An error. We had then a type of open proceedings called 'political responsibilities.' My mother was called to appear, and since this Red Cross man had come to search for you, they called for Amparo also. They cited Amparo as if she was alive! They sent a subpoena as if she wasn't dead and said to my mother, 'Why doesn't this Amparo present herself with you others?'

"'I don't know,' my mother lied. 'They took her from the house one day and we don't know anything else.'

"It was necessary to pretend ignorance because there were those who would have shot my mother also." Magdalena paused. "I remember seeing you and your sister leave together with Dr. Junod, Tía Maximina, Andrea's wet nurse and a Swiss count. Also, Sevilla went with you."

"What? Sevilla?"

"You didn't know that?" Magdalena asked.

What unbelievable gall the man had! To denounce Amparo and then accompany us to the frontier!

"But why?" I exclaimed. "That's the most bizarre thing I have heard!"

"He did it to prove he was kind," Magdalena admitted. She went on to describe how, when Antonio was shot, no one knew where his body was. "My mother went with Casimira in a taxi to visit Saturnino in the Toro jail. When they had gone halfway, they were stopped by a Falangist with a rifle. 'Could you take me with you?' he asked. Clearly they couldn't say no. So he got in. 'I come from burying some pigs that the dogs dug up,' he said." Her face stiffened in anguish. "My mother had to listen with all the pain of knowing they had killed her brother. When they arrived at the jail, the warden said, 'Please, don't enter dressed in black! No! And don't tell Saturnino his brother is dead! Say he's in another jail, because there are Falangists here who will arrest you too.'

"The warden was a good man and took them to his wife who gave them normal clothing to wear. They put them on and went to visit their brother, but there was a Falangist listening to everything that was said. When Saturnino asked 'Where is Antonio?' they had to answer, 'Don't worry, he's all right. He's in the Fermoselles jail.'" Her mouth drooped. "Later they shot Saturnino along with thirty-six others in reprisal for a civil guard's son who was killed at the front – near where you were in San Rafael. When the father heard the news of his son's death, he went to the Toro jail and began saying, 'This one, this one, this one!' without knowing who they were. Thirty-six were shot, among them my uncle and many of my uncle's acquaintances."

The conversation shifted to the priest who denied Amparo absolution.

"He was a young man because now he's over eighty," Magdalena said. "He lives in a residence somewhere. On the day after they killed Amparo, my mother went to find where they had buried her. Since she had already lost both brothers and had not been able to recover their bodies, she was very distressed. She was weeping by the pole where they shot their victims and there to one side was the grave."

"A pole in the cemetery?" I repeated.

"They put a light on top of a tall pole in the middle of the cemetery to shoot by, and there they killed people. They buried Amparo next to the light, which they did many times. There was a mound of earth of the sort they put over one and that's where she was. There was no marker – nothing. My mother ordered that a cross be placed there." Magdalena paused. "My mother was there crying and this same priest came by. 'Are you related to Amparo?' he asked.

"'I am her sister,' she said.

"'I heard her confession,' he said. 'I definitely did not give her absolution.' "This was what that priest said – to my mother! And she asked him why. "'Because she was not married by the Church,' he replied. Her voice trailed off. "It was I who went some years later to recover the body. My paternal grandfather had died. He was in his final illness when the tomb was being built, but he died before it was finished. When they gave us permission to move his body into the tomb, we also asked permission to move Amparo. The same day we disinterred them both. My mother said, 'You dig up Amparo's remains.' I was seventeen years old." She paused, her face suddenly gaunt. "The bad thing was they put quicklime in with her. There was no coffin or anything, just the body and quicklime."

I pondered the image of a seventeen-year-old girl forced to recover the remains of her favorite aunt. She had to brush the dirt off the bones and gather them together, to perform the ritual every part of me yearned to have accomplished. All at considerable danger to herself. Perhaps that was one reason she was jailed five years later.

I mentioned how in Zamora we met the son of the military governor in the Civil Registry and questioned him at his office.

"I knew the elder Hernández," her husband muttered around his pipe. "He was a man inflated by his authority. As military governor he had all the power in the world to stop the killings, but he was a weak man."

"He signed the exit papers that allowed the death squads to take their victims," Magdalena said. "But not the death orders. He authorized their leaving prison, but did not know where they went." She placed her hands in her lap. "I imagine he did know, but he didn't sign for their deaths."

"Those who provoked this catastrophe were very few," her husband added. "Very few from one side and very few from the other."

"The Right did much more than the others," Magdalena said. "The coup attempt on the twenty-third of February – "

"However!" Her husband used the word to slice through her response. "People died on one side and died on the other. But the majority – they were horrified! They had to continue living together. Today, if you were to ask in Zamora who the guilty ones were, there were only six, seven, or nine men. No more!"

"True," Magdalena agreed. "There weren't more. It was just that one half of the city confronted the other half."

"Who were the killers?" I asked.

"The one who shot Amparo was a lawyer," Magdalena replied. "Segundo Viloria. He courted Amparo at one time. He fell in love with her. But Amparo told him, 'No!'"

I gasped in amazement. "What?"

"That's what happened," her husband concurred. "That's history."

What a grotesque twist! Viloria was doing more than following orders. He was avenging himself on the woman who had resisted his advances. Unbelievable!

Magdalena gave a quirky smile. "One day I looked out the window and saw Viloria on the street below, talking with some men – I must have been twelve or thirteen. I took a flowerpot and dropped it – plaff!" Her eyes twinkled with amusement. "The pot missed him, but it was a big one and shattered. He looked up and saw me. My mother said, 'But child, they'll come and kill us all! They know who lives here!'"

Her husband relit his pipe. "I returned to Zamora in 1937 and Viloria was hated throughout the city. He had passed his lawyer's exams, but he did not work. People would not bring him their business – nothing at all. He was totally repudiated and rejected by everyone."

"The other part of the guilt for Amparo's death must be your father's – a disagreeable thing but true," Magdalena said. "He should never have told her to return to Zamora."

I nodded. "I've been told Amparo was afraid he would write something for the Madrid papers that would seal her fate. Did many people know Amparo was the wife of Ramón Sender?"

"Yes, everyone knew. It was a small town and your father was very well known. I read his books when I was young, even before the war. The bookstores carried them."

"If Amparo knew that people in Zamora knew she was Ramón's wife, why did she return?"

"Because she didn't think there would be trouble. Zamora had always been so peaceful."

"When she arrived and found Saturnino and Antonio in jail, why didn't she try to escape?"

"How? There were no possibilities. You needed a safe conduct pass to go anywhere. To go to the university in Salamanca for my exams, I needed a paper like a passport. And that was many years later." She got to her feet. "I have copies for you of the letters Amparo wrote to Aisia." She crossed to the desk and handed me some pages.

The letters at last!  These were the first words of my mother I had
seen since I lost that typewritten copy of her farewell note as a teenager
– and the first time I had ever seen her handwriting.  The first letter was
dated September 9, 1936:

> Dear Aisia,
> I have so many thing to tell you but they are only
> moments of anguish.  I enclose a letter for Ramón's
> grandfather.  Address: José Sender, Huesca.  I don't
> remember the street.  Put on the letter, 'If you can't
> find him, please forward to Joaquín Monrás at the
> wine shop.'  Joaquín is my sister-in-law's husband.
> Regarding the children, I would like you to have every-
> thing you need until you can return them to their father.
> With or without me, don't separate yourself from them.
> At best you all may be able to return before me to Madrid,
> depending on the freedom (to move about).
> Other food – please observe: in the morning some Neave
> cereal, at midday after three-and-a-half hours, one-half
> a broth of vegetables or a bouillon without fat, the other
> milk and for last another portion of Neave.  If he has
> more appetite, milk, but I think this is enough.  To one
> spoonful of Neave add two of sugar.  Don't forget to tell
> Ramón that I love him very much.  Kiss this Monchín
> and don't forget that I love you with all my soul.  Write
> to my brothers...
> Many kisses to all.
> Amparo

The second letter is undated but obviously written later because of
its context:

> Dear Aisia,
> I received your letter for which I thank you with all my
> soul.  I don't think you're telling me the truth because
> you ask for the address of Ramón's father.  The address in
> Huesca I don't remember, as you know, – I have quite a
> bad head.  That of Miss Maruja is in a suburb of Madrid –
> I believe it is Canillejas.  Doubtless they have been at her

mother-in-law's house for a month and there she'll give birth. Moreover, since he is a lieutenant in the artillery, he isn't going to leave her alone in the house. As far as Huesca is concerned, because Don José Sender is a lawyer and well known, it isn't difficult to find him, if he is alive. You know what it must mean to have one son on each side at seventy years of age. Write me often and tell me everything. Baby Andreina yesterday was peevish.

I'm sending you a letter that you must carry in a sealed envelope to Don José Maria Cid who lives next door to the Barayón house.

Kisses to everyone, with my heart for my son Ramón,
Amparo

Amparo's letters were treasures, making her more real to me than even her photographs. Her instructions regarding my diet, written after weeks of nightmarish confinement, displayed her motherly concern for me even more than her messages of love.

In her desperation she had been trying to contact anyone who could help her because she mentioned people to whom Aisia was to forward notes. Why to my Aunt Maruja? Probably to find out where my father was or to let him know what was happening. Why did she ask Aisia to write "my brothers" if one was dead and the other imprisoned? She must have meant her brothers-in-law. Her concern for my grandfather Don José whose sons were fighting on different sides showed her compassion for others in the midst of the hell in which she was trapped.

The writing was hurried, distracted, the words hard to read. The last paragraph of the first letter was finished in pencil, as if her pen went dry. The originals either had been destroyed by my father or, more likely, remained in the hands of his compulsive archivist, Margareta. Why hadn't I received these letters years ago? What a difference it would have made to have read my mother's caring words!

"Do you think my parents had a happy marriage?" I asked Magdalena.

"I doubt if Amparo and Ramon's relationship would have lasted," she replied. "Personally, I don't think they were even married."

What an ironic twist! Did Amparo suffer months of anguish for a husband who would have ultimately abandoned her? As far as their having been married, Conchita's description of the wedding contradicted Magdalena's statement.

"Your father had a woman friend in Madrid during the summer and fall of 1936," she said quietly. "I was with him when he was signing books at the Book Fair in Madrid in 1974. This woman gave him a kiss and said she was his girlfriend during the War. I wasn't able to find out who she was."

So my father had been unfaithful while Amparo was in jail. All those months while Amparo was sleeping on the floor of a crowded cell, he had been leading the life of a carefree bachelor in Madrid. And writing his important from the front, any one of which could have sealed her fate if they had fallen into fascist hands. Even if I acknowledged his need for a sexual outlet as natural, the image left a bitter taste in my mouth.

Later, Magdalena handed me a wrapped parcel that contained a large full-face portrait photo of Amparo in an oval, gilded frame. This was her special present to me and was the best photo of all because it delineated Amparo's features in detail, the indentation between the mouth and nose that I had inherited, the same upper lip and chin. I judged her to be in her mid-twenties. Although her nose was too Roman to type her as a classic beauty, her eyes were large and expressive.

On a visit to friends, I played some Chopin nocturnes on the piano while everyone sat in the patio arbor. I chose them especially for Magdalena because I was sure she had heard Amparo play them. It was my way of telling her that Amparo lived on in her son. I tried to give the phrases the same shading and lilt that I imagined Amparo might have given them.

When the time came, it was hard to say goodbye. Our few days together had put to rest much accumulated misunderstanding. The moment Magdalena and I met, our distrust dissolved because we sought and found in each other aspects of the woman we both loved.

In Barcelona we visited Asunción, the tiniest, brightest (according to all family opinions) and feistiest of my Sender aunts. A red-haired, elegantly coiffed lady, she stood with the same military thrust-back shoulders of Papá and Conchita. From the way she kept throwing emotion-packed glances at me, it seemed my visit was of extreme importance to her.

"I lost everything under Franco," she stated. "They took away my degrees, my right to work. I had to teach in Switzerland because no Spanish college would give me a job. I was in prison for a year and a half. A year and a half! I have nothing from before the War – no photos, no belongings." She stared at me with that peculiar intensity

I had noticed earlier. "Come with me into the other room, Ramón. I have something I must tell you."

She was dead serious. What secret could not be bared before her husband and my wife? Seated in the hallway beside me, she continued.

"Many times I was on the verge of telling this to your father, but I could not bring myself to." She fell silent, frowning. "Now he has died without my having done so, but I want you to know." She drew a deep breath and leaned closer. "I was in jail a year and a half in Zaragoza and San Sebastián. They transferred me to San Sebastián with my son who was just a baby at the time. I entered prison handcuffed to some civil guards." She inhaled deeply and sighed. "I stayed in the San Sebastián jail for eight months, and in these jails you eventually hear everything. If you stay a day or a week, you learn nothing. But when you're in there a long time, you hear all the news. In that jail, there was a Basque woman who had been in prison with your mother. She told me a detail that I have not heard anywhere else. I don't know if it's the truth, but it seems to me that you have the right to know."

She had me hanging on her words in suspense. Come on, out with it! I screamed inwardly. But if anything, the closer she approached her topic, the slower her words.

"She told me that... on your mother... they used..... psychic torture."

"Psychic torture?" I repeated in stupefaction.

"And that she died insane." She pierced me with a glance. "Can you bear to hear this?"

"Huh," I grunted, as if punched in the diaphragm. Her disclosure, horrifying as it was, only verified what I had already sensed. "What do you mean by 'psychic torture?'" I asked.

"Brainwashing," she replied. "And she died insane." She grasped my shoulder. "Your father suffered such guilt, and yet I always felt he had a right to know. But when I arrived at the moment of telling him, I didn't dare. You are younger and stronger..."

"I always believed the worst," I muttered half to myself. "I believed she was raped and tortured physically."

"Physical torture, no."

"But then what?"

"The type the Gestapo used in the concentration camps. They dedicated themselves during Amparo's last days to torturing her psychically, saying things such as that she was jailed because of your father, that he had denounced her, telling her horrors she could not possibly understand until finally she lost her reason." She paused to allow the image of my mother, crazed and out of control, to burn into my mind. "I just couldn't say this to Pepe because he was always so dejected when he spoke of Amparo."

"So psychic torture consisted of – "

"Speaking badly of the family and presenting lies as if they were the truth, just to make one suffer. Telling horrible things, gossip, as if they were poetry."

"According to Pilar's testimony, the woman jailer in Zamora was terrible," I replied. "They called her 'the Hyena' and she always taunted the married women by telling them their husbands were sleeping with other women or by describing the death agonies of those they shot."

Asunción nods. "The same in Zaragoza and San Sebastián. If one was bad, the other was worse. These are things one wants to forget, but they form the course of one's life." She leaned against the wall, her eyes half closed. "They also used psychic torture on me regarding your father. This I could never tell him. They took me into a room and said, 'Your brother is killing, he's raping nuns...' I knew nothing, but I knew what they were insinuating. With me the torture wasn't so deep, so strong. I could deal with it. But with Amparo, because they were thinking of killing her, they forced it more."

According to Asunción, psychic torture consisted of taunting and verbal bullying rather than sleep deprivation, bright lights, solitary confinement or other refinements. Of course the Spanish Inquisition had included all these subtler forms of pressure among their gruesome repertoire, and no doubt the Civil War refined these brutal techniques. The terrible irony in Amparo's case was that, when she was told her husband was sleeping with other women, it was unfortunately true. Pilar had described how the nuns also harangued the women: 'You have sinned against the Holy Spirit, you are damned forever, your soul will be in torment.' Their accusations were designed to wrest a full confession and a change of heart. But the worst suffering for Amparo must have been her deep worry and concern for her children and her husband. To be told he was dead or had abandoned her must have pierced her like a knife.

I could see where after weeks of imprisonment, from within that vacuum of total isolation, the repetition of such brutal remarks could have brought Amparo to the breaking point. She was a woman with a high-strung temperament. I could only hope that when she finally lost control, she had told her torturers exactly what filth they were.

"They also were going to kill me," Asunción admitted. "They pushed me along the corridor with rifles in my back. 'Let's finish her off!' they kept shouting. But they didn't do it because they hadn't been given the order. They were only amusing themselves a little at my expense. You have no idea how terrible it was inside those walls! We would hear screams when the death sentence was read to the prisoners."

"My hope is that Amparo lost consciousness during those last hours," I said. "The body has its own anesthesia." I paused because Asunción's words had brought me to the cutting edge of rage and grief.

When I could speak, I said, "I always have been caught between two impulses – vengeance and forgiveness. In Zamora I felt at times a terrible thirst for revenge, but at the same time, I thought how important it is for Spain to forget what happened and start afresh."

Asunción gave a fierce snort. "Now listen to me! Those rightist beasts are the ones who injure others, while those of the left are always asked to pardon the injuries done to them. The rightists always inflict pain for no good reason and we, who have suffered so much, have to forgive and forget! They, in the meanwhile, without the remotest cause, nothing, pick up their weapons and go out on the sidewalk to shut down democracy!" She sat bolt upright. "And today it's just the same! Right now! On February 23rd, 1981, when the Cortes were invaded, my husband Daniel and I were here in this house and he said, 'Now it begins again,' and in this we were in agreement. Daniel also was condemned to six years." Her lips tightened. "The killings didn't stop when the war ended. Even on September 25th 1975, just before Franco finally died, the government shot five political prisoners!"

*Amparo, approximately twenty-two years old (1926).*
*Folds in the photograph show that it had been rolled up*
*and hidden for many years before being framed.*

*Asunción Sender (Tía Suni), who was imprisoned by Franco, with the author in Barcelona, in front of a sketch of his father.*

Chapter 14
My Father From July 1936 To April 1939

And what about my father? In *Counterattack In Spain*, published in the middle of the Civil War, he described how he and the Riveras crossed the mountain safely on that hot July day when they escaped from San Rafael. In Guadarrama, the Riveras caught a ride to Madrid. Ramón volunteered for the militia and spent the next days with a rifle helping to slow the rebels' advance towards the capital. Then he returned to the offices of "*La Libertad*" and wrote up his experiences. He enrolled in the Fifth Regiment and returned to a Guadarrama half destroyed by enemy artillery. His life fell into a rhythm: time at the front and then Madrid to write articles. After spending one sleepless night at the apartment haunted by memories of Amparo and the children, he took a room in the mansion that had been assigned to the *Cultura Popular* team. Occasionally he traveled with them to battle zones where they distributed pamphlets and periodicals.

In August, his patrol was assigned to an artillery battery at Cabeza Lijar near Peguerinos. Through his binoculars, he could see Villa Frutos in San Rafael below him. He adjusted the focus and caught a hint of movement in the lane. Soldiers. It was impossible that Amparo was still there. She must have taken his advice and returned to the safety of her family in Zamora. A few days after, fascist bombers decimated the battery and they had to move the guns by hand under cover of darkness. Back in Madrid for the funeral of the Peguerinos commanding officer, he met a woman soliciting donations of bed linen for military hospitals. Before the afternoon was over, they had slept together. She or someone like her became his lover over the next months. His patrol elected him captain and they were transferred to the Tagus River lines. There he rose in rank to Major (*Comandante*).

In early October, Franco boasted of taking Madrid by October 12th, but the day came and went without any important victory. The roads to Madrid were choked with refugees. They camped in the subway stations while thousands of men dug trenches on the outskirts. Morale among the troops remained high in spite of rumors that the government was preparing to flee to Valencia.

The Luftwaffe bombers came over daily. They were painted white, the traditional color worn at children's funerals, and seemed to prefer to drop their loads on the narrow streets of the workers' suburbs. Militiamen shouted for everyone to take cover in the nearest cellars. Often that was not protection enough, because frequently a two-hundred-pound bomb smashed through the upper floors before exploding in the basement.

On the morning they bombed La Cuesta de Santo Domingo, thirteen children were among the thirty killed. On a little street close to the Cava Baja, a bomb fell on a line of women waiting to buy milk. Eleven died, one with a baby in her arms. Never before in war had a civilian population been so vulnerable to violent death because never before had airplanes been used for such gruesome purposes. Sometimes the bombs dropped on a 'school group,' the little shelters in gardens, and seventy, eighty – in one instance three hundred and nine children were killed. In this last case, the whole city was thrown into mourning. Why the children? Why tear life away from five and six-year-olds? The only explanation was that Franco and his generals hoped to exploit terror in the same way Hitler and Himmler used it, and they made the same miscalculation. Dying Spanish mothers called out to their sons, "Grow up quickly and learn to shoot a rifle before the Beast devours everything!"

Ramón witnessed scene after scene of desolation. He saw a militiaman weeping over the ruins of his home. The man had returned on a three-day furlough to find his wife, his children and parents all dead. "Those tears will create a barrier against which the fascists will find no successful weapon," Ramón wrote. "They give a strength to the heart and a tone to the muscle that become an insuperable obstacle to the science of the modern army."

At the end of October, Russian tanks, planes and officers arrived in Madrid. In return, the Bank of Spain's gold was sent to Russia under tight security. What other country could the Republic trust with the coin and bullion bars? Valued at 500 million dollars, it acted as collateral for the purchase of arms, oil and other necessities. Stalin threw a banquet to celebrate its arrival at which he said, "The Spaniards will never see their gold again, just as one cannot see one's own ears!"

Ramón's company, transformed into a battalion, received orders to become part of a brigade going to Valdemoros south of Madrid. He had been appointed Chief of Staff under the communist general, Lister, a quarryman who had risen rapidly through the ranks. In spite of Lister's heroism and intelligence, the wheel of fate had handed him a series of defeats. Although Ramón professed great admiration for Lister, he was not altogether happy with his post. They were to attack at dawn, their objective the village of Seseña before moving against Torrejón. In the early morning hours of October 29th (my second birthday), Polikarpov I-15 planes strafed the enemy positions. Fifteen fast and heavily armed Russian T-26 tanks led the infantry.

From the command post, Ramón watched their troops advance under a covering artillery barrage. He hoped this would be the beginning of an offensive that would change the tide of the war. When the sector chief telephoned to report unidentified troops attacking neighboring Torrejón, Ramón's optimism faltered. Enemy bombers added more chaos to the hordes of panic-stricken militia retreating from the front. Gradually he realized that his men had attacked the wrong town and been hit by their own artillery. On the Seseña side, they had been ordered to return and defend Valdemoros from attacking troops. One by one, all their morning hopes crumbled.

Lister was furious. He personally collected the scattered militia and placed them in position. The attack on Seseña, a tactical disaster, was turned into a victory by the Republican press. But the truth was that, three days later, Valdemoros was surrounded by the enemy, and Lister's battalion had to fight their way out with bayonets and grenades.

From this point on, my father's and Lister's versions differ. Lister was outraged. They had lost ten miles. In his book *Nuestra Guerra*, he writes that when the fight at Valdemoros seemed hopeless, Ramón left for Madrid. He goes on to complain of my father's lack of enthusiasm, of humanity, of comradeship, before accusing him of cowardice under fire and desertion from the front.

> Sender, calculating that I would not escape from the circle in which the enemy was enclosing us, retired tranquilly to his house in Madrid and, after a night's rest, presented himself at Fifth Regiment headquarters. There he displayed the commander's insignias, which he said I had given him before dying. (Since I was still very much alive,) he was demoted on the spot, which was the least he merited, and his military career cut short.
> It then appeared that the air of Madrid no longer agreed with him and he took another 'retirement' to Barcelona and, a few weeks after, another to Paris where he 'resisted' for the rest of the war writing his book *Counterattack* where he tells of the Seseña operation and his own personal performance, placing himself in the most advantageous position.

My father did disappear precipitously from combat during early November. The incident at headquarters may have been his desperate attempt to wrest control of the regiment from the communists and Russians who were arriving in ever greater numbers. Lister's accusations of cowardice and desertion were the most powerful insults one Spaniard could level at another. My father never responded.

Among the replies to my original *El País* letter asking for information, I received one from a man who had served under my father in the Shock Battalion, "Commune of Madrid." He wrote he had met Sender on November 7, 1936, at the defense lines at the Manzanares River. This casts doubt on Lister's words that "his military career was cut short."

> Your father arrived at 9 p.m. in his blazing new uniform of Major (*Comandante*), and to his adjutant and political commissar he confessed his belief that Madrid would fall in 48 hours, that there was nothing that could be done about Franco's army. Also he had just received news that his wife and children had been killed by the fascists in the rebel zone. They had cut his wife's hair to the skin, had administered castor oil and shot her as the wife of Sender...
>
> Your father wished to tell you nothing because – and it is sad to have to tell you this – during those moments at the front he acted as a coward; he suffered from a dreadful fear of dying and, overpowered by terror, he disappeared that night and left us without a commanding officer...

Maruchi Rivera pinpointed November 6th or 7th as the day her father told Ramón of Amparo's death. She added that, upon hearing this, he left immediately for France. This might well have been the reason for his disappearance, although it seemed odd that he had not applied for leave in the normal manner. He must have been in a terrible state of nerves even before the news of Amparo's death reached him, what with the Seseña fiasco and his abortive effort to wrest control of the brigade from the Communists. Could I fault him for bizarre behavior at this point?

In one letter to Joaquín Maurín, my father stated that "the Russophiles... now follow... a systematic persecution by slander." I believe the truth lay somewhere between his and Lister's versions. The Communists had been systematically eliminating by whatever methods they could Republican officers who favored competing ideologies. Obviously, when my father made his ill-advised attempt to take over the brigade from Lister, he was demoted and placed with another unit. At the same moment, he heard of Amparo's death and his first priority became to go to France and recover his children. He always claimed his departure at that moment saved his life. By his disappearance, he avoided being found mysteriously shot at the Manzanares River front lines in the days that followed.

Amparo's last message to Ramón via Pilar never reached him in its original form. Pilar guarded it carefully until one morning the women were lined up to be searched. Faced with forfeiting her own life if it was discovered, she went to the bathroom, tore it into shreds and ate it. However my father in an interview once mentioned that he did receive a few lines Amparo had hidden among Andreina's clothes.

In his book, *Counterattack In Spain*, my father describes how he heard that a militiaman (Victor Rivera) had arrived in Madrid and was looking for him. With an inexplicable feeling of foreboding, he kept the appointment. They met at dusk at the top of the Castellana. In the distance, the clamor of machine guns increased and diminished on the freezing gusts of wind.

Victor greeted his friend with a warm embrace. "Ramón, I bring you bad news," he said. "Amparo is dead. We went to Bayonne to reclaim our children through the Red Cross, and contacted your brother's widow Marcelle as you suggested. She referred us to Dr. Marcel Junod of the International Red Cross, and through his good offices we tracked down Maruchi and Pepi in Zamora where Amparo had taken them. He managed to rescue them along with our maid Celes and we returned to Madrid with them only yesterday. They brought the terrible news of Amparo's arrest and death." He put one hand on Ramón's arm. "She died bravely, Ramón, with your name on her lips. She was denounced by her sister Casimira's husband and shot by Segundo Viloria, a member of the Falange execution squad. Andreina was taken to the convent orphanage, and about Monchín, the only news we have is that he is safe. I know how this must pierce your heart. Believe me, it pains me to be the bearer of such news.

"Dr. Junod was unable to retrieve your children with ours because the Zamora authorities require your signed authorization. You will have to go to Bayonne and apply to the Red Cross in person."

Ramón stared across the city to the firefly flicker of the guns. "You have done me a service," he murmured at last. "At least I know the names of whom I must kill."

He walked away with rapid steps, needing time alone to allow the ice in his chest to thaw. Why had Amparo not found safety among her family and friends? The answer condemned him with its obviousness. "I have killed her," he moaned. Grief-stricken, he stumbled bleakly onwards. His first impulse upon hearing the news had been to draw his revolver and shoot himself. No, he would return instead to the front and take as many of the enemy as possible with him into death. Better yet, he would track the killers down one by one.

But his life was no longer his own. Amparo's death compelled him to live for the children's sake. Above and beyond any thought of revenge, he must get Andreina and Monchín to safety. He returned to the dugout that served as his command post beside the Manzanares River and lay down on his cot.

Years later he would confess his turmoil in *The Five Books Of Ariadne*, placing his words in the mouth of Javier:

> "You know, Ariadne, if I express my feelings in words, I violate them. For this reason I rarely spoke to you of love... You used to wonder, 'What does Javier think of me? Does he love me or not?' I had no idea if I did or didn't, nor did I wish to have one, because if I had told you what you meant to me, my definition would have killed those feelings... I didn't want to say if I loved or hated you, nor those other things which at times I was so close to saying and then said nothing...
>
> "What I wanted to say to you was that in a certain way your life made me fearless. Don't be scandalized, my dear. I'm telling you in all seriousness, there was nothing sweeter than your thighs. Your whole body was mine. You were all mine and, in a certain way, you were my creation... But your life was of no importance to me... (I see now) how your death was a distinct possibility, staying on as you did... but your death and your destruction seemed two separate things. I don't know if you can understand this. Perhaps there are things a woman cannot comprehend, things only a man can feel... Your death was not necessarily going to be your annihilation."

He could hear Amparo reply, as she always did, "This is absurd, Ramón!"

The next day, he left for Bayonne to contact Dr. Junod at the International Red Cross. At the Hotel de L'Europe, he met twenty-year-old Elizabeth who would become his second wife. Their friendship blossomed around the radio in the drawing room where Ramón listened to the daily news.

Elizabeth: "I grew up with my uncle's family in Guernica. He was a Basque scholar and served several terms as mayor. When hostilities broke out in our province in the fall of 1936, we sought refuge in France."

Much to her family's disapproval, she fell in love with the radical journalist from Madrid. Ramón himself must have been swept off his feet by the remarkable beauty of this convent-educated young woman. He accompanied her on her way to Mass and back, waiting outside for the services to finish. Also, he must have been motivated by his desperation to find a mother for his children.

Dr. Junod, meanwhile, returned with us from Zamora. He brought me immediately to Bayonne while Andrea remained in San Juan de Luz because of a severe skin rash that had to be treated before she could enter France. My old aunt Maximina met with my father and delivered to him a letter from Amparo which had been found among Andrea's clothes by the nuns in the orphanage.

It was a hurried farewell in which she recommended he marry a friend of hers in Madrid who she felt would care for us as her own.

"Ah, no! She's much too ugly!" he replied, according to Maximina's report to the family in Zamora.

Elizabeth: "You were very traumatized when Dr. Junod brought you to us. Very withdrawn. Your father and I took you almost at once to your Aunt Maruja's in Barcelona. On the flight from Toulouse, you kept saying, 'I want to get off,' much to your father's amusement. He returned immediately to wait for your sister."

Marcelle: "What you, Ramón, liked best was to ride the trams in Bayonne. Your sister came later. The wet nurse who had come with her was not given permission to exit Spain. Because of this, a cousin of mine who had recently had a baby, breastfed her. Also we began bottle-feeding her. Poor little thing, she never cried and was so very small. My father loved children and played a great deal with her. She used to laugh when he caught her by the fingers. He would say, 'How can she know, poor sweetheart, what has happened?'"

Elizabeth: "After your father arrived in Barcelona with Andrea, we were married at the end of December before a member of the Catalán parliament. Our witnesses were your Aunt Maruja and my brother Sabino. My family only agreed to the civil ceremony because there were no priests in Barcelona at the time, and because Ramón promised a church ceremony when we left Spain. We departed immediately with you children for Pau, France, where Ramón rented a furnished apartment on Blackbeard Boulevard. He had signed a contract with an English editor to write the book *The War In Spain* (titled *Counterattack In Spain* in the American edition). He dictated it to me and I took it down in shorthand."

At the beginning of 1937, we moved to a cottage in Louvie-Juzon, a picturesque village close to the frontier of Aragón. My father wrote another book there, probably *A Man's Place.* In November, Elizabeth gave birth to Emmanuel. During that winter my father made two trips to Paris to help with the International Congress of Writers. Also he traveled to the United States in April 1938, on a fundraising tour for the Republic.

Elizabeth: "Andrea was very sweet, very adorable. She was much more trusting than Monchín. Monchín was very different, because he had participated in the drama. In June, Ramón returned from Barcelona and told me the war was lost. He would return to the front 'to strike a last blow,' but we could not go on living together. In the same manner as Amparo, he told me to go to my father's house in Barcelona. I left at the beginning of June 1938, and since that time I lost all trace of him and you children."

"In the same manner as Amparo..." The coincidence was indeed strange. And why did he send Elizabeth and his infant son back to Spain when, in his own words, "the war was lost?"

Papá took Andrea and me to Paris briefly before placing us in "Duremont," a camp in Calais for Spanish refugee children. Andrea almost died of pneumonia that winter. Meanwhile, he struck up a relationship with a Viennese journalist named Anya Herzog, who Elizabeth felt might have been the true reason for his abandonment of her. Now that my memory had been jogged, I recalled an attractive blonde coming with Papá to the camp for visits.

In March of 1939, Papá booked passage on the USS Manhattan and brought us to New York on his diplomatic passport. He left us with Jay Allen and his wife, having met Allen during his stint as correspondent in Spain for "*The Chicago Tribune*." He also left a note that described me as obedient and gentle, if my wishes were respected. If I became obstinate, it was best to leave me alone. "His experiences had given me a timidity that did not represent his real character, yet his sense of beauty, of color, of nature and music, are enormously developed."

Andrea he described as the opposite of me, very sociable and open; but he warned against spoiling her because then she became a tyrant. She should be spoken to gently but with authority. "When you talk to them about me," he finished, "I beg you to tell them that I have gone to Mexico to buy them a little house."

*Ramón, 2-1/2 years old*
*Louvie-Juzon.*

*Tía Maximina's gate in Perdigón where Ramón stayed as a two-year-old.*

*Cottage in Louvie-Juzon, French Pyrenees.*

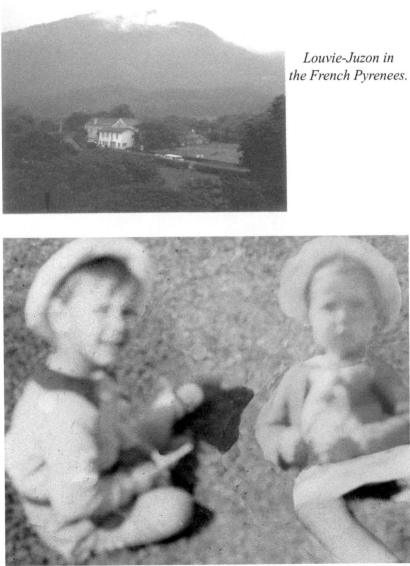

*Louvie-Juzon in the French Pyrenees.*

*Louvie-Juzon 1937.*

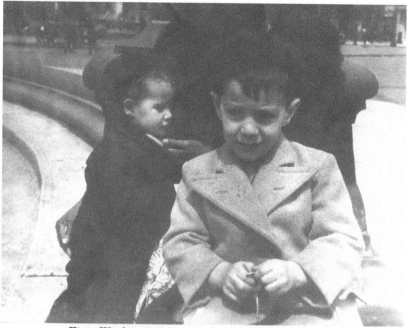

*First Week in USA – Washington Square Park, 1939.*

*Bedford Village – 1940.*

# Epilogue

Upon our return to the States from Spain in August, 1982, Judith and I stopped on the East Coast to visit my American mother Julia in the Berkshires. She and her husband were delighted to see us, tired after a busy summer of grandchildren and putting up vegetables from the garden. At eighty-two and eighty-six years respectively, it was no longer easy to do everything they would like to do.

"I have to remind myself I'm no longer a young girl of seventy," Julia told me with a twinkle in her eye.

She was relieved that my trip to Spain was not as emotionally stressful as my sister's. I explained it had been just the opposite. True, the journey had been painful at times, but in a good way like the excising of a boil. For so many years I had lived not knowing, not experiencing the part of me that had suffered through the death of my mother. Judith's presence and her language skills helped me enormously. Without her, the terrors of the past might have overwhelmed me. Instead, she was always beside me with her love and understanding. In a way the trip was harder for her because she was not experiencing the healing of a wound, but just hearing the grim details over and over.

Also, I returned with a deepened appreciation of Julia's mothering, of everything she gave me. Before we departed for home, I wrote her a note: 'No matter how much I have rediscovered Amparo, I am also your son.'

So much of a child's remembrance depends on continuity, on the adults saying, 'Remember when...' or paging through the family photo album together. On the first page of ours, beneath Amparo's passport portrait, was one of two children in white sunsuits glowering at the camera. For years I had assumed it was taken in Barcelona, but looking at it now I recognize the cottage in Louvie-Juzon. Benedicta recently removed the one of Amparo and found a dedication scrawled across the back:

To my Ramón, with the madness of madnesses,
with all my enthusiasm and more.
Always more!!
Your Frisky Little Goat.

Another photo Benedicta unearthed for me showed Amparo as a young girl seated in front of Miguel Sevilla, Casimira and Nati. The three older people are dressed in black (perhaps in mourning for a family member). Amparo looks as if she could soon be passing into adolescence. Sevilla and Casimira are staring into each others' eyes, Sevilla with a cigar in one hand, the camera case dangling from the other. Casimira wears a black veil over her hat, and glances up at Sevilla adoringly. Meanwhile, his pose expresses a condescending acceptance of her homage, as if he was thinking, 'You aren't really what I had in mind for someone as deserving as myself, but at least there's the café and the ice house.' His back is turned to Nati who stands frozen to the spot by some inner agony. Her eyelids droop, her hands are clenched, her mouth expressionless. Obviously, she is not a well person.

In the foreground, light bathes Amparo in contrast to the darkness that afflicts the others. She is dressed in white and holds what looks like a prayerbook. Rows of lace on the sleeves and a colored sash adorn her dress. Her Sunday best – they must have been on their way home from church. Her hair is done up in pigtails, one strand dangling over her forehead. The corners of her full lips form the first creases of a smile, mischief lurking just under the surface. 'I'm not going to laugh,' she is thinking.

Casimira and Sevilla pose as if they are the only ones having their picture taken. Sevilla has the self-satisfied expression of a man fixated on himself. The upper part of his profile is clean cut, but a self-indulgent puffiness distorts the area above the mouth and the lower lip curls disdainfully. Nati might not exist as far as he is concerned, although her right arm almost touches him.

Here were the people who destroyed Amparo and her family: Casimira with her blind adulation of Sevilla, Sevilla who would stop at nothing to take control of the inheritance, and poor, deaf Nati whose frail mind would crumble after the murders. Her medical needs compelled everyone except Casimira to renounce the family property.

In the midst of these shadowy forces poised over her, Amparo sat as fresh-faced and fragrant as a carnation. Her strength was in her softness, her vulnerability, her ability to love. Even if this book had never been written, Amparo's story would have outlived the sordidness of her betrayers' lives. Our immortality may exist only within the memories of the loved ones we leave behind.

*Standing L to R: Casamira Barayón (Amparo's oldest half-sister;*
*Miguel Sevilla (Casamira's future husband who would denounce*
*Amparo to the fascists); sister Nati Barayón.*
*Seated: Amparo, approximately 12 years old.*
*Estimated date: 1926*

Miguel and Casimira Sevilla moved away from Zamora and settled in Seville, perhaps to distance themselves from their guilt. What about the other villains? Viloria died insane in a state institution. Comes, the military governor, lived out his years in Zamora with only a grandson to question his actions. Perhaps an aged Catholic priest in a village named Paradinas occasionally fretted about the disposition of his soul. In one of the rare references my father ever made to Amparo, he wrote:

> I have discovered what the moralists call 'the feminine soul' (how I despise that term!) only in one woman: Amparo. She whom I loved was a physical being and yet, nevertheless, immortal. Physically immortal.

For once, my father and I can agree. Amparo had finally brought us, father and son, full circle.

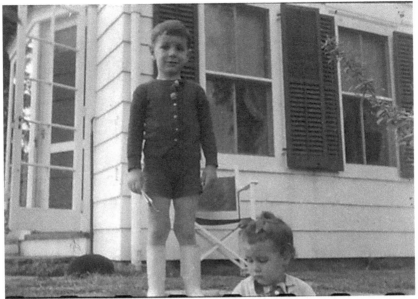

*Ramón and Andrea, Bedford Village, 1940.*

*Ramón and Andrea, in the brook, Bedford Village, 1940.*

*Photo of Amparo that Papá hid behind the one in an oval frame,
the only one that we had of her during our childhood.*

# Manitas de plata

El viernes último, tuvimos el gusto de oir por primera vez en la Radio Salamanca, a una pianista novel; pero que comienza a subir con firmes pasos la escala infinita del arte musical.

Amparito Barayón, bella y simpatiquísima señorita zamorana, nos ha sorprendido con un selecto recital de piano, en el que puso toda la vivacidad y exquisitez de su arte juvenil y depurado, como su alma de artistas.

Con la nerviosidad propia de todo "debut", pero también con la inconfundible certeza de los temperamentos elegidos, desarrolló brillantemente su escogido programa. Especialmente en la Marcha Fúnebre del genial y dolorido Chopín, supo arrancar al piano toda la grandeza patética de la emocionante y honda página; y en la Zambra Morisca, graciosa y típica obra del gran pianista y compositor salmantino, ya fallecido, don Felipe Espino, logró una interpretación irreprochable de gracia, sabor y estilo.

La señorita Barayón, Eva moderna y valiente por su ideología y cultura, no solo musical sino literaria, (tenemos sospechas de que también cultiva el jardín de las Musas) posée un gran temperamento artístico para el divino arte; tiene capacidad interpretativa, limpidez y dominio mecánico: todo lo necesario para ser una gran virtuosa del piano; una excelentísima artista.

La felicitamos fervorosamente por su triunfo y deseamos que no sea esta la única vez que nos haga el regalo apreciabilísimo de su arte y de su simpatía.

V. M.

*A review in Zamora's "La Opinión" of Amparo's piano recital in
Salamanca, November 29, 1927*

NOTE: My performance as a teenager of the same 'Marche Funebre' by Chopin (Prelude in C minor) was the reason that the concert pianist, George Copeland, decided to accept me as a student. At the time, I had no inkling that Amparo also played the same piece, although no doubt as an infant I had heard her play it.

Addendum to the Second Edition (2003)
An Usual Coincidence?

When *A Death in Zamora* was first published in 1989, my wife Judith and I flew East in July for a book party in Manhattan. Judith suggested that we also take the opportunity to try to connect with my daughter, Xaverie, from whose life I had been forcibly blocked by a sect known as 'the Bruderhof' where she had lived with her mother from the age of two. I had attempted a brief but serious sojourn with the group in the mid-1950s, but ultimately found their overly-strict total obedience requirements oppressive, not to mention my emotional inability to move back with Xaverie's mother (we had been separated for several years) without losing my sanity.

This time, whoever answered the telephone did not recognize my voice (and thus did not hang up as on previous attempts). Thus I was able to glean some information: Xavie had married two years earlier, and had just given birth to her second child, a little boy (the first was a girl). When I finally identified myself and asked to speak to my son-in-law, he reiterated for the umpteenth time, in what I have come to call "standard Bruderhofese," their refusal to allow me to visit my daughter. In reply to my questions, he agreed that I was considered "a runaway novice member" who had "broken my vow," not to mention having divorced Xavie's mom (the group priding itself on its public 'no-divorce-allowed' position)

Judy and I left the East Coast bitterly disappointed at the cultish behavior the Bruderhof continued to display. Two months later, I received a letter from my son-in-law informing me belatedly that Xavie had died a month earlier of a virulent melanoma within two weeks of her diagnosis. Well, I was absolutely flattened! Not that I ever expected anything different from this strangely hateful group, but somehow I had kept the hope alive in my heart of hearts that perhaps some day Xavie and I would see each other again.

But here's the strange part: she died almost at the same age as Amparo, leaving two children almost the same ages as my sister, Andrea, and I. Andrea at age four kept commenting about 'the woman in white' she kept seeing at the foot of her bed. Now I had never been much of a believer in reincarnation, but if there was such a thing, and Amparo had come back into the family at the first opportunity (Xaverie) what would she have come back to accomplish?

188 : A DEATH IN ZAMORA

Amparo died, unabsolved, outside the comfort of her religion, abandoned by family and far away from her husband.

Xavie died in the bosom of her faith, surrounded by fellow-believers and her loving husband.

Amparo died crying out for her children, not knowing what would happen to them.

Xavie gave her children over to the loving care of the community and her husband. She died knowing they would have the best lives possible, at least within the belief system of the group.

Amparo remained 'earthbound,' hovering near her children because of her concern for them, and also because in her belief system, her soul had not been 'released' by absolution.

Xavie was free to return to The Source, to the eternal peace that Amparo deserved.

Their characters were very similar. Xavie was very animated, full of chatter, always friendly with newcomers, and sought out by members who enjoyed her upbeat personality. She was also very musical. Make of these 'coincidences' what you want, but for me it's a comfort to believe that Amparo came back to another life to achieve closure and finally was able to go on. Perhaps the publication of my mother's story also brought a certain relief.

I should also mention that Xavie never knew the details of Amparo's life because I never did – nor had she read the original edition of this book, although no doubt she knew that her grandmother had been shot by the fascists. But one odd thing: in a memorial album I finally received full of stories about her, she once said to someone that "If I had grown up in Spain, my last name would be 'Barayón'" – not accurate, but it puzzled me that she knew my mother's last name because it was not something I knew until the mid-1970s. Xavie had had no contact with anyone who could have told her. Her mother had broken off all relations with my family when Xavie was very young.

Perhaps, it's just poetic to believe in these things, but it assuages my deep sense of loss from Xavie's passing, despite the fact that she had been lost to me these many years. However, as I mentioned, I always held onto the slim hope that some day we would have a chance to be together again.

One positive result of my attempts in 1989-90 to force the Bruderhof to allow me to interview members who had known Xavie was their suggestion that I "go ahead and find ex-members to talk to about her." Within three months I had located six, within a year thirty, and was publishing a monthly newsletter titled "KIT" of their stories and letters.

By the time another year had passed, I had formed a volunteer staff of four ex-members or children of the Bruderhof members who lived near me. We incorporated as The Peregrine Foundation, and started a lively network that published book-length life stories in a series titled 'Women from Utopia.' In 1999 I resigned as Executive Director to take another full-time position, with roughly three million words in print by KIT members and having been sued three times by the so-called 'pacifist' Bruderhof leadership.

Details of this particular ten-year chapter in my life can be found at:
http://www.perefound.org
Details of other chapters in my life can be found at
http://www.raysender.com

The ensuing years since the original publication of *A Death In Zamora* have brought translations of the book in Spanish and German. Also, further details have surfaced that not only throw some doubt on family members' avowed loyalty to Amparo, but also point to Generalissimo Franco as the alleged origin of the order for Amparo's assassination. It may not seem like much when Franco's scorecard of murders is totaled in some heavenly tribunal of the sort that my father imagined in *Los Cinco Libros De Ariadne*, but it does tend to place 'El Topolino' in the same category as other bestial types spawned with amazing frequency during recent times – or perhaps I should say throughout human history?

Recently I tried to estimate the number of violent deaths, both civilian and military, that occurred during the 20th Century. 'The First Measured Century Project' estimated more than one hundred million military and civilian deaths, but when I accessed various other sources that included conflicts other than the major wars involving the United States, I finally rounded off the figure to a very modest half-billion.

Recently, I was asked to write down my three best wishes, and I came up with the following:

1) That all beings enjoy peace and happiness forever, including me.

2) That the first to manifest out of The Unmanifest, The Alpha Love, or The Divine Mother if you will, come to earth and live amongst us.

3) That my family and children be safe, healthy, and perpetually surprised by elation – by 'eudaemony,' a word of which I've become enamored.

*Xaverie Sender, approximately 11 years old.*

## APPENDIX
### Amparo Barayón and the Impunity of Francoism
### Francisco Espinosa Maestre
### Translated by By Richard Barker

In mid-2004, with the social movement for the recovery of historical memory in full swing since the 1990s, and with the recent commitment of Rodriguez Zapatero's government to put into effect a law of historical memory, an event occurred which demonstrated the limits of reality. That summer, Anabel Almendral Opperman, the granddaughter of Pedro Almendral, who had worked as a doctor in the Zamora prison in 1936, used the opportunity of an interview with a journalist at the newspaper *La Opinión de Zamora* to declare that the twenty-nine-year-old wife of the novelist Ramón J. Sender, Amparo Barayón, murdered on October 11, 1936, had syphilis when she was treated in the Zamora prison by Anabel's grandfather. With this declaration, Anabel took revenge for a certain testimony which had stained the reputation of Pedro Almendral, a testimony that had appeared in the book *Muerte en Zamora* published in 1990 – fourteen years before! -- by Ramón Sender Barayón, son of the novelist and of Amparo, following extensive research into the death of his mother.

The testimony in question was that of Pilar Fidalgo Carasa who, in 1937, put into writing what she remembered about her stay at the Zamora prison. Neither she nor her newborn daughter had received any medical attention from Pedro Almendral, who also took the liberty of telling her that she should die for being the wife of a leftist. And since it was no longer possible to take her revenge on Pilar Fidalgo, and since it was Amparo's son who had made said testimony known in the Spain of the nineties, the doctor's granddaughter chose to do what she could to cause the most harm: spreading the false and malicious rumor that Amparo had contracted syphilis. To the crime of murder in 1936 was now added, almost seventy years later, the crime of defamation.

Although quite slowly, the rumor eventually made its way to the intended targets: to Magdalena Maes Barayón, Amparo's niece, who lived in Málaga; to Magdalena's daughter Mercedes Esteban Maes, who lived in England; and to Amparo's children, Ramón and Andrea, both of whom lived in the United States. And through Mercedes and her friend, the historian Helen Graham, the affair reached the historian Paul Preston and me. The attack was serious enough that the family tried to get the doctor's granddaughter to rectify her statement, reestablishing Amparo's dignity and that of her family members. The affair dragged on and the letters and articles sent to the newspaper occupied a good part of 2005.

In the midst of all this, Zamora's official chronicler, Miguel Ángel Mateos Rodríguez, intervened, playing several roles, among which it is worth emphasizing the following: detractor of Ramón Sender Barayón and Pilar Fidalgo; smokescreen for Anabel Almendral Opperman; self-promoter of his installments, which appeared in the same newspaper; propagandist for his own party and, above all else, defender of what happened in Zamora after the military coup. Without a doubt, his most colorful performance was to attribute the responsibility for the crime that ended Amparo's life to a minor character of third or fourth order.

Starting in mid-2005, the case began to grow cold. The doctor's granddaughter went on maintaining her silence, Zamora's chronicler went back to writing about his usual topics and *La Opinión de Zamora*, which had always acted on behalf of one side (that of the chronicler), was left without a topic that must have given the paper a certain vitality for a few months. As far as the family members were concerned, it was extremely troubling to see that they not only failed to get Anabel Almendral to rectify her declaration, but rather that the chronicler's articles cast even darker stains on Amparo's reputation and that of her family, and that at every opportunity the newspaper manipulated the affair on his behalf. Discouraged, they returned to their lives with the added sorrow of seeing how, in addition to having suffered the loss of Amparo, her memory was now stained by a dirty defamation that would go unpunished. Anabel Almendral's rectification had not occurred and to file a lawsuit would have been difficult given the geographical dispersion of the family. They were also burdened by the fact that the lawsuits that had succeeded since the transition to democracy were the lawsuits that the repressors' descendants had filed against people who had pointed out and implicated their relatives for criminal acts.

Today, thirteen years later, I reread the articles and emails generated by that affair with great disgust. It is hard to understand so much evil on the part of the doctor's granddaughter and her accomplices. Perhaps, beyond the fear of vengeance, it was influenced by the atmosphere created by the movement of historical memory which emerged in 1995-1996 and which was consolidated between 2000 and 2002. The right took it, and still takes it, very badly that the hidden past has come to light, especially in those provinces like Zamora where the terror came from only one side: the side of those who supported the military coup. They were unable to point out a single victim of their own and had to be satisfied with bringing forth minor conflicts that preceded the coup or by giving free rein to their imagination of what might have happened if the coup had not triumphed. What they absolutely did not want was that the truth of what happened in Zamora after the triumph of the military coup become known and, especially, the full names of those involved.

Ramón Sender Barayón's book, *Muerte en Zamora*, was both innovative and courageous. In the nineteen eighties, works devoted to the coup and the repression were very rare and we owe them all to the personal effort and political commitment of their authors. Consequently, the theory that anti-Francoism constituted an obstacle to the investigation of the repression is lamentable. Was one supposed to wait for the universities to decide that it was time to study that dark period? Fortunately, there were those who fulfilled the social function that the universities waited so long to take on. Ramón Sender was trying to find out what had happened to his mother and, in doing so, as was to be expected, he found out about many people who were close to his mother, some as witnesses of what happened and others who were implicated in the process that led to her murder. He told about it all in his book and that is why he could not be forgiven: he had broken the pact of silence.

Between 2001 and 2008 two initiatives developed that might have influenced this affair. On the one hand, there was the movement in favor of historical memory with numerous consequences across the nation, which would culminate in the judicial proceedings against Judge Baltasar Garzón. On the other hand, there was the inter-ministerial commission created by Rodríguez Zapatero's government with the goal of elaborating a law of memory. This law, which would betray all expectations, was eventually passed in December, 2007, after many difficulties, but became meaningless only months later when Judge Garzón's initiative became known, an initiative which sought, for the first time, to bring some justice to the victims of the July 1936 military coup. The law would have opened the door for cases like that of Amparo to emerge from the legal vacuum where they had languished until then and come to be considered for what they were: crimes against humanity.

But the hope did not last long. Neither the political nor the judicial world could agree to open this pathway, so the judge was immediately besieged and, shortly thereafter, expelled from the fifth court of Spain's highest judicial body, the *Audiencia Nacional*. Once again, the right emerged victorious and its historical memory, which is nothing else than the one created by Francoist propaganda, could continue undisturbed. For the associations of historical memory, very much committed to Judge Garzón's proposal, the outcome was especially disappointing because they had been convinced that it was the only way to channel and elevate their social mobilization. It was also disappointing for the small group of jurists, historians (including me), and forensic experts who were supposed to advise Judge Garzón. We all, judge, associates and advisers, were convinced, as Elizabeth Jelin, a specialist in human rights, had written, that "justice is, without doubt, the most basic part of memory."

With the maneuver that brought down the judicial order of the *Audiencia Nacional*'s fifth court, the law in question became, once more, a watered-down law of memory, in response to which the right employed an old practice with which it had a great deal of experience: accept but do not comply. This vacuum was reinforced in 2011 when the conservative Partido Popular came to power and decided to withhold all funding from anything related to historical memory. We therefore find ourselves in an absurd situation in which the judicial initiative is exercised from Argentina, as in the case of Ascensión Mendieta, and in which the funds for the exhumation of cadavers are generally provided by individual citizens and even by other countries.

At the same time, the boasting of the right and the shameless displays of Francoist paraphernalia have increased. In the forty-three years that have transpired since the transition to democracy, we have seen the restrained right of the eighties evolve into an ever larger and more emboldened right, consisting of those who, nostalgic for the past, were catered to by José María Aznar's legislation and, since then, have become more and more aware that they can say and do things that had previously been unthinkable. At the same time, it becomes more and more apparent that during the fourteen years that the *Partido Socialista de Obreros Españoles* governed, in a decision that was as lacking in morality as it was full of pragmatic self-interest, they chose to act as if the past did not exist, thereby missing the opportunity to relate historical truth, as it was emerging, with juridical truth.

After what we have revealed above, after this journey from the exaggerated declaration by the granddaughter of the doctor at the Zamora prison in 1936 to the impunity of Francoism established by the 1977 Amnesty Law and confirmed by the two-party system also known as the "1978 regime," all that remains is to applaud the decision to re-edit Ramón Sender Barayón's book along with the additional information contained in the above account. On their part, the doctor's granddaughter and her accomplices can sleep tranquilly, but their names and actions will forever be tied to the story of a criminal defamation.

AMPARO BARAYÓN:
THE HISTORY OF A SLANDER[1]
By Francisco Espinosa Maestre
Translated by By Richard Barker
Excerpted from *Shoot the Messenger: Spanish Democracy and the Crimes of Francoism: From the Pact of Silence to the Trial of Baltasar Garzon*
(Canada Blanch / Sussex Academic Studies on Contemporary Spain)

In the city of Zamora, at eleven o'clock on the eleventh day of October, nineteen thirty six, in the presence of D. Agustín Pérez Piorna, Municipal Judge, and D. Mario Aparicio de Santiago, Secretary, the death of Dª Amparo Barayón Miguel, 29 years of age, native of Zamora, is registered [...]. SHE PASSED AWAY _____, on _____, eleventh day of the present month at _____ and _____ minutes, as a result of _____ as determined by _____ and medical examination, and her cadaver will be buried in the Municipal cemetery of this city. (From the Death Certificate).

In May 1982, only months after the death of the novelist Ramón J. Sender, who had died in January of that year, the magazine *"INTERVIU"* published an article entitled "This is how they killed Ramón J. Sender's wife," signed by Heriberto Quesada. Without a doubt, it is one of the best articles in the series that the magazine published on the fascist repression, as much for the quality of the writing as for the meticulous research that

---

1 Chapter from the book by Francisco Espinosa Maestre, *Shoot the Messenger? Spanish Democracy and the Crimes of Francoism*, translation by Richard Barker, Sussex Academic Press, (2013) pp. 43-69

went into its three pages, a fine example of investigative journalism, as opposed to other cases where the most absolute sensationalism prevailed.

Shortly thereafter, in July, Ramón Sender Barayón, son of Ramón J. Sender and Amparo Barayón Miguel, decided to travel to Spain in search of traces of his mother, murdered in Zamora in October 1936. Ramón's, as well as his sister Andrea's, peculiar relationship with their father precluded satisfactory answers to their many questions and doubts. The trip resulted in the 1990 publication, by Plaza & Janés, of a book entitled *Muerte en Zamora*. On the cover, there was a photograph of Sender in the foreground and another of Amparo in the background, along with the question "What were the circumstances of the death by firing squad of Ramón J. Sender's wife?" The book had been published a year earlier by the University of New Mexico Press, with the title *A Death in Zamora* and was translated into Spanish by Mercedes Esteban Maes Kemp, a resident of Cornwallis (England) and cousin of the book's author. In it, Ramón Sender Barayón related, almost in the style of a travel journal, the story of his quest and its results. It is likely that Ramón and Amparo's son came across Quesada's article during his trip, since some of the people he contacted must certainly have brought it to his attention. But although he made liberal use of it for his book, he mentions it only once, without naming the author nor including it in his bibliography.

The book reads like a novel, but the terrible part is that the story he tells, his mother's murder, was real. After the military coup, Ramón J. Sender thought his wife and their two children would be safer in Zamora, where she was born, than in Madrid, but Zamora fell immediately into the hands of the rebels with nightmarish results. Although their origin is somewhat murky, Amparo Barayón's problems began the day she came to an appointment related to her application for a passport. With her daughter in her arms, she made a complaint, directed at the new governor imposed by the rebels, about the death of her brother Antonio, assassinated that very day. Shortly thereafter she was arrested and incarcerated. She would remain in prison until she was taken out and shot.

One of the testimonies cited by Ramón Sender in his book was from Pilar Fidalgo Carasa, the author of a text entitled "A Young Mother in Franco's Prisons," published in the newspaper "*El Socialista*" in May 1937, and in London and Paris after the Spanish civil war. The quote from Fidalgo, who had also just given birth to a daughter, is the origin of the defamation that concerns us here:

> Because I continued hemorrhaging, I constantly begged
> the warden for help. Finally she brought the prison doc-
> tor Pedro Almendral who merely came as a matter of
> form. Upon seeing my suffering, he commented that "the
> best cure for the wife of that scoundrel Almoína is death."
> He prescribed nothing – neither for myself or my baby.[2]

What we know is that Amparo Barayón, arrested on August 28, 1936, was killed on October 11 in one of those dark and dirty intrigues made possible by the military coup. Amparo was a catholic and tried to confess, but the priest, as he would later tell one of her sisters, refused to absolve her because she was not married in the Church. Besides Amparo and her brother Antonio, another brother, Saturnino, council-man for the Republican Left party, would also be killed. Both brothers used to run the Café Iberia, which was regarded as something like the unofficial Republican meeting hall in Zamora. The family always believed that Amparo's killer was the lawyer Segundo Viloria, an ex suitor of hers who, it seems, ended his life in a lunatic asylum and about whom we have evidence of his participation in the death squads operating in Zamora after the coup (see Appendix II).

The Spanish edition of *A Death in Zamora*, translated by one of the author's cousins, had a striking peculiarity: a series of "E. N."'s, Editor's Notes, which could more accurately have been called "Notes against the Author." They are corrections and commentaries, mostly absurd, a good sample of which would be the one that corrects a quote from Pilar Fidalgo that states: "In the province of Zamora more than six thousand people were killed, six hundred of whom were women" (p. 164). The footnote says:

> The Nationalist historian – but one of the most impartial
> – Ramón Salas Larrazábal, in his book *Pérdidas de
> la Guerra* (Barcelona: December, 1977), referring to
> Zamora writes...

In 1990, when the Spanish edition of *A Death in Zamora* was pub-lished, it was already well known that Salas Larrazábal's work, edited by Planeta in 1977 and whose "exact figures" were endorsed by Hugh Thomas in his monumental edition the same year of *La Guerra Civil*

---

[2] Sender Barayón, Ramón, *Muerte En Zamora*, Plaza y Janés, Barcelona 1990, p. 160

*Española,* published by Urbión, represented the last Francoist operation to whitewash the regime's great foundational massacre. Nevertheless, the key to our story lies elsewhere. *A Death in Zamora,* which exposed the maliciousness of Zamora's conservative middle class and told part of what it had done, did not sit well in those circles, unaccustomed as they were to hearing the truth. No one responded openly, thinking perhaps that it would have made things worse, since there were still people alive who had provided their testimonies to Ramón Sender Barayón. They decided to bide their time. For example, someone who knew of Sender's book and had seen Pilar Fidalgo's reference to Dr. Almendral, swore vengeance, but would wait fourteen years for the opportune moment.

On July 13, 2004, *"La Opinión de Zamora"* included an interview by Begoña Galache with Ana Isabel Almendral Oppermann on the occasion of her donation of an oil painting and a photograph to the Provincial Government – called "works of art" by the newspaper – with portraits of her father and grandfather, doctors associated with that institution. The following was the second question:

> "He was a doctor at the jail. What was that experience like for him?"
>
> "That's right. He worked in the jail. In fact, it was my grandfather who took care of Ramón J. Sender's wife in the prison. The writer's son, in a book he wrote while in the United States, says that his mother was ill in the jail, that nobody attended to her, and that a doctor who stopped by said that, in the final analysis, with what little remained of her life it was better to leave her where she was. But it was not like that. My grandfather did not let her die on her own. On the contrary, he helped her. She was terribly ill from syphilis and my grandfather said that with what little remained of her life it was better to take her to the infirmary. This was many years ago, but there is a lot of confusion in the book *Muerte en Zamora* and I want to dot the i's and cross the t's. It really struck me the way some of the facts are distorted."

Someone at the newspaper, probably conscious of the implications of the declaration and aware of what he was doing, gave the article the strange headline "My Grandfather Did Not Let Sender's Wife Die

When She Was in Jail." Consequently, the motive for the interview, the donated "works of art," was relegated to the background. What mattered was the defamation: Amparo Barayón, according to the prison doctor's granddaughter, had syphilis. The journalist and the newspaper saw no problem in backing her up.

But Almendral, intentionally or not, was confused. In his book, Ramón Sender Barayón never once alluded to the treatment his mother received from the doctor. What he did do, among other things, was transcribe Pilar Fidalgo Carasa's testimony, and those of other people, and present the Right in Zamora with a mirror image of the reality of the "Glorious National Uprising" in a small provincial capital where not a single right-winger had suffered any harm before the military coup. What Almendral could not forgive was that Sender had identified the role her grandfather played after the 1936 coup and, albeit quoting someone else, had placed in his mouth the words "the best cure for the wife [Pilar Fidalgo] of that scoundrel Almoína [her husband, a prominent socialist militant from Benavente] is death." And she found no better way to attack the guilty party, Amparo Barayón's son, than to come out with the statement that his mother was suffering from syphilis, as if she had died in the infirmary. It is even possible that Almendral's granddaughter knew, as Ramón Sender had been told by many people he interviewed, that Amparo went insane and that, to torment her, her captors convinced her that the person responsible for her suffering was none other than her husband.

A few months later, the news of the interview reached Amparo Barayón's family. Perhaps the first to hear of it was her niece Magdalena Maes Barayón, living in Málaga who, years after the war and still quite young, transferred her aunt's remains from the common grave where she was buried to the Maes family pantheon. Magdalena must have contacted her daughter Mercedes Esteban Maes, the translator of *A Death in Zamora*, who was living in England, and from there the news reached Ramón Sender in the United States. It was the historian Helen Graham, a friend of Mercedes, who passed the story on to Paul Preston and to me, enabling us to be participants in and witnesses to a story that would go on for another year.

The family took up the challenge and, toward the end of January 2005, composed a letter that would be published in *La Opinión de Zamora* on February 14:

To the Editor,

On Tuesday, July 13, 2004, your newspaper published an interview with Anabel Almendral, granddaughter of the Zamora doctor Pedro Almendral, on the occasion of her donation of some family portraits to the Zamora Provincial Government. During the interview, Anabel Almendral makes several statements about Amparo Barayón Miguel, wife of the writer Ramón J. Sender. The following statements are inaccurate:

•That Ramón Sender Barayón wrote a book about his mother "when he was in the United States." Ramón has lived in the United States most of his life because of his mother's assassination and his father's exile, but when he wrote *A Death in Zamora,* he spent many months in Spain interviewing his parents' families, as well as a great number of people who knew of his mother's death.

•That in his book *A Death in Zamora,* Ramón Sender Barayón had written "that his mother was ill in the jail, that nobody attended to her, and that a doctor who passed by there saw her and said that in the final analysis, with what little remained of her life, it was better to leave her where she was." The quote in the book is not from Amparo Barayón, but from Pilar Fidalgo Carasa, Amparo's fellow prisoner who, in her testimony "A Young Mother in Franco's Prisons" (London: United Editorial Limited, 1939, p. 6), affirmed that "… the prison doctor Pedro Almendral merely came as a matter of form. Upon seeing my suffering, he commented that "the best cure for the wife of that scoundrel Almoína is death. He prescribed nothing for me." (quoted by Ramón Sender Barayón in *Muerte en Zamora*, Plaza & Janés, 1990, p. 160). Let us clarify here that Pilar Fidalgo Carasa was an eyewitness to these events.

•That Amparo Barayón Miguel "was terribly ill with syphilis." According to the testimonies of her surviving family members, Amparo Barayón was in good health when she entered the prison. She had a daughter only months old and a boy just a few years old, both of them healthy. Her husband, Ramón J. Sender, died in his eighties of old age and a lifetime of heavy smoking. Her children, Ramón and Andrea, are now both in their seventies and, naturally, free of syphilis.

We are aware that it has taken us seven months to respond to the many errors contained in the aforementioned interview. Among many other misfortunes, Amparo Barayón Miguel's assassination was the cause of the family's dispersal. We all live far from each other and news takes time getting around. Nevertheless, and in spite of the intervening months, it seems to us we have a right to refute the declarations published in your newspaper.

We await your prompt reply and publication in your newspaper of the text of this letter in its entirety.

Our attentive greetings,[3]

The response took only three days to appear, but it was not from the granddaughter of the prison doctor, but from Miguel Ángel Mateos Rodríguez, secondary school teacher, councilman representing ADEIZA (Association of Zamora Independents), and Zamora's official chronicler. He called on Ana Isabel Almendral, "esteemed academic professional" (professor of Philology at the University of Castilla La Mancha), to prove the part about syphilis or admit her mistake; he defended her grandfather with the story of his difficulties during the Popular Front government, in addition to describing him as a man concerned, shortly thereafter, for the lives of his companions; and, in passing, he attacked Ramón Sender's book, calling it historical fiction. Naturally, he did not mention Pilar Fidalgo. Nor did he concern himself with the obstacles Sender Barayón faced in the 1980s while investigating his mother's death. The attack against Ramón Sender's book was echoed by other habitual contributors to "*La Opinión de Zamora*," who followed the same line, defending Dr. Almendral. The book had attacked "one of their own, and the decent people of Zamora," who had not forgiven Sender, came to the doctor's defense. The "esteemed academic professional" and her slanderous swipe at the memory of Amparo Barayón had faded into the background or, at most, was interpreted as an understandable overreaction given the harm Amparo's son

---

[3] letter signed by Ramón and Andrea Sender Barayón, Magdalena Maes Barayón, Mercedes Esteban Maes-Kemp, Ignacio and Monica Esteban-Maes, and Ana Marín Esteban,

had done to her family as well as to other well-known Zamora families whose members appear throughout the book, some as assassins, others as accomplices or instigators and, finally, others as mere passive spectators.

On March 14, a new letter from the family, signed by Mercedes Esteban Maes, was published in *"La Opinión de Zamora:"*

> I have not reacted immediately to the two articles expressing opinions of our response to Anabel Almendral's declarations published in July 2004 in *"La Opinión de Zamora."* I was waiting for Dr. Almendral to retract her statement and apologize for tarnishing the memory of my great aunt, Amparo Barayón Miguel, as the Zamora historian Miguel Ángel Mateos had requested (*"La Opinión de Zamora,"* February 17, 2005). This has not happened. Obviously, silence implies confirmation.
>
> Let me start from the beginning and refresh the reader's memory. On July 13, 2004, *"La Opinión de Zamora"* published an interview with Anabel Almendral in which she asserted that her grandfather, Dr. Pedro Almendral, "treated Ramón J. Sender's wife in prison because she was terribly ill from syphilis." She also attacked Ramón Sender Barayón's book, *Muerte en Zamora*, in which the son of Ramón J. Sender and Amparo Barayón investigates his mother's death in October 1936, alleging that "there is a lot of confusion in the book." At the same time, she displays her own confusion when she says that: "In his book, the writer's son says that his mother was ill in the jail, that nobody attended to her, and that a doctor who stopped by said that, in the final analysis, with what little remained of her life, it was better to leave her where she was." As is made clear in *A Death in Zamora,* this incident comes from Pilar Fidalgo Carasa's testimony, a historical document published in London in 1939, which contains the declarations of a woman who was Amparo Barayón's fellow prisoner and an eyewitness to the events she narrates. The protagonist of the incident is not Amparo Barayón, but Pilar Fidalgo Carasa, who affirmed that … "Dr. Pedro Almendral came purely for form's sake. When he saw how I was suffering, he commented that

'the best cure for the wife of that scoundrel Almoína is death' and he did not prescribe me anything."
"A Young Mother in Franco's Prisons" (London: United Editorial Limited, 1939), p. 6. Quoted by Ramón Sender Barayón in *Muerte en Zamora* (Plaza & Janés, 1990), p. 160. In our letter of February 14, 2005, we offered irrefutable evidence against Almendral's declaration that Amparo Barayón was ill from syphilis. We also corrected other errors in Almendral's interview.

On February 17, 2005, an article by the Zamora historian Miguel Ángel Mateos appeared in which he provided documentary evidence that confirmed the baseless nature of Almendral's insulting declaration regarding the state of Amparo Barayón's health. He also asked Anabel Almendral to admit her mistake, since an "esteemed academic professional should not lower herself to fueling false rumors worthy of gossip circles." Although his article had no effect on Anabel Almendral, whose silence continues to imply confirmation, we are grateful for his support.

That said, I need to respond to the second part of Mateos' article, where he attacks Ramón Sender Barayón's book *Muerte en Zamora*, alleging that it is a work of "historical fiction" based on "unsupported, imagined and erratic information from dubious and weak oral sources." *Muerte en Zamora* is not a historical novel: it is a second-generation testimony comparable to works published by and about the children of survivors and victims of the Holocaust. In many cases, the testimonies collected by Ramón in his book are first hand accounts. My mother, Magdalena Maes Barayón, Amparo's niece, assures me that her memory of those events is as clear today as they were almost seventy years ago. I would not call her a "dubious source." There is also Pilar Fidalgo Carasa's testimony in "A Young Mother in Franco's Prisons," a very important historical document from the perspective of any historian worthy of the name. Let us give an example: Mateos says in his article that Ramón Sender Barayón makes accusations against his own uncle Miguel Sevilla (among many others) "based on unsupported, imagined and erratic information from dubious and weak oral sources, far removed from the events being narrated." In "A Young Mother in Franco's Prisons," Pilar Fidalgo Carasa testifies that when Amparo Barayón knew they were going to kill her because they had wrested her daughter Andrea from her arms, "she wrote a farewell letter to Sender which I kept for a long time but had to tear into pieces and eat because of the continual searches to which we were subjected. In this letter, she delivered her children to his care and held Sevilla responsible for her death." My mother, Magdalena Maes Barayón, clearly remembers Miguel Sevilla arriving at the Barayón's café, where the family was gathered, saying, "Tonight they are going to kill Amparo." It seems to me neither fair nor rigorous for Mateos to call these sources weak or dubious.

Because of Mateos' allusions to the need for a "trained and, of course, impartial historian," I think it appropriate to make clear that the letter we wrote to "*La Opinión de Zamora*" in response to Almendral's statements, and to which Mateos responded in his article, was not only signed by Amparo Barayón and Ramón J. Sender's children, Ramón and Andrea, and by me, her niece, with a degree in History and twenty years experience as a university professor in Great Britain, but by nine other signatories whose names were not published, I imagine for lack of space. Besides various family members, including Magdalena Maes Barayón, the letter was signed by Francisco Espinosa Maestre, a historian specializing in the repression; Helen Graham, Professor of Contemporary History at Royal Holloway, University of London, United Kingdom, a specialist on the Spanish Civil War and the early Franco regime; and Paul Preston, Professor of History at the London School of Economics and author of some of the most important works on the Spanish Civil War. We are all in agreement about the importance of *A Death in Zamora* as a historical document containing testimonies by survivors of the war, as well as the experiences and quest of a man from whom the war stole not only his mother but his homeland.

And here it is fitting to include a plea to Miguel Ángel Mateos: the documents he cites in his article were not accessible when Ramón carried out his research in 1983. We beg you to inform us where we can obtain those sources, of incalculable value to the Barayón family.

I also feel obliged to comment on the final paragraphs of Mateos' article. With the intention of exonerating Dr. Almendral, if he had indeed been the original source of the insulting rumor about Amparo's syphilis, Mateos affirms that Almendral's life "had been placed in serious danger" following an incident that occurred in May 1936. In another article, published on February 21, 2005, R. Gamazo repeats this defense of Dr. Almendral. Gamazo, after commenting about "testimonies that only a trained and, of course, impartial historian can evaluate and interpret" (see our credentials above), relates an anecdote, referring no doubt to the same incident in which Dr. Almendral's life may have been in danger in May 1936. It is regrettable that Dr. Almendral was in some sort of danger, just as the excesses committed in the province of Zamora before the war are regrettable. But it is more important to remember that what is in play here is not what could have happened to Dr. Almendral, but what in fact did happen to Amparo Barayón Miguel, whose memory has been attacked by Dr. Almendral's granddaughter. It is not surprising that Dr. Almendral survived. According to the Francoist historian Ramón Salas Larrazábal in his book *Pérdidas de la Guerra*, the leftist repression was non-existent in the province of Zamora while there were one thousand two hundred and forty six victims of the right wing repression. We will have to wait for the results of a more serious investigation. The truth, as Mateos says, citing Ricardo de la Cierva, is unlikely or impossible to achieve, but what is certain is that Amparo Barayón was assassinated in Zamora and the responsible parties are those who were brought to power by the military coup in July 1936.

Mercedes Esteban Maes

The debate goes on when, on March 29, *"La Opinión de Zamora's"* correspondent in Benavente, Isabel Reguillón, writes an interesting article entitled "Chronicle from a Jail in 1936." Her point of reference is the testimony of Pilar Fidalgo, Benavente's schoolteacher arrested on October 6 and transported to Zamora because she was married to José Almoína, secretary of the Socialist Organization. Reguillón narrates the fate of some of the residents of Benavente in October, 1936, and repeats Pilar's allusions to Amparo Barayón and other women.

When Reguillón's article appeared, there was another curious phenomenon under way. During March and April, the local chronicler Miguel Ángel Mateos was writing a series of seven long articles entitled "Death in Zamora, the Tragedy of Amparo Barayón." It is obvious that the newspaper was on the chronicler's side. His articles were published on the best days and printed on the most favorable pages, while the writings of the Barayón family and others were relegated to the letters section and appeared on less important days. Mateos rails against Pilar Fidalgo and Ramón Sender, and devotes many sections to justifying and whitewashing the conduct of priests, fascists and others who supported the military coup, all the while employing a liberal discourse which, nonetheless, does not conceal the author's ideology. He even attempts to dismiss certain charges against Amparo Barayón's ex-suitor, the lawyer Segundo Viloria: "I do not claim to justify what can in no way be justified: the irresponsible attitude and activities of Viloria throughout the Civil War. I am not yet ready to reveal who was responsible for Amparo Barayón's death by firing squad. I will do that in the part of this series to be published by *"La Opinión de Zamora"* at the appropriate time. I do not want to be so explicit nor reopen old wounds [...] What I can affirm is that Viloria neither took charge of, nor directed, nor participated in the assassination of Amparo Barayón. There is irrefutable evidence of other executions he carried out., but not this one. I realize that stories require suspense as well as action" (*"La Opinión de Zamora,"* April 6, 2005). Here we can see how the newspaper exploits the sensationalism of the "Amparo Barayón affair" and how the chronicler takes advantage of the pulpit provided him by the newspaper to advertise the forthcoming episodes of his series. He has achieved his objective: center stage no longer belongs to Amparo Barayón, but to the chronicler himself and the revelations he promises to mete out in small doses.

On occasion, for example April 8, the newspaper simultaneously publishes a letter from Mercedes Esteban Maes and an article, the sixth, by Mateos in which he alludes to the same letter. First, Mercedes Esteban's letter:

To Mr. Mateos:
I have read with surprise, even astonishment, M. A. Mateos' dismissals of Pilar Fidalgo's testimony and Ramón Sender Barayón's book. He dismisses Pilar Fidalgo's memories by citing documents that she was unable to consult for obvious reasons. What a great mistake it was on the part of Pilar Fidalgo to speak of six thousand victims of the fascist repression in Zamora when there were only four thousand! Besides the fact that this type of cheap attack is unworthy of someone who thinks of himself as an impartial historian, Mr. Mateos seems to forget that if a person living in exile misstates someone's second surname, it does not in any way disqualify what she says about the brutality she observed while imprisoned. Mr. Mateos' certainty in denying the possibility that a female prisoner was raped displays not only a lack of imagination, but complete ignorance of how things were in the prisons run by the so called Nationalists.
With regard to Ramón Sender Barayón's book, Mr. Mateos dismisses the author because his sources were oral testimonies and yet, when it comes to secrets he himself has been told, oral sources seem perfectly acceptable. Mr. Mateos boasts of his vast knowledge, but one must ask why he did not help Ramón Sender when he was carrying out his research for *A Death in Zamora*. If that was impossible for some reason, why did he not speak up when the book was published? Instead of "holding those cartridges in reserve," as he said, it is high time for him to stop showing his superiority over his victims (Pilar Fidalgo and Ramón Sender) and tell us once and for all who were responsible for the assassinations of Amparo Barayón, her brothers, and several thousand more people in the province of Zamora. And he ought to apply the same rigor to the documents generated by those who carried out the military coup and see if he can

convince us of the legality of so many "courts martial," "death sentences," and "executions." Ah, and one more thing. He should not forget to give us the exact number of people assassinated since he has demonstrated his superiority to Pilar Fidalgo regarding that question.

Mercedes Esteban Maes

In April 2005, given the direction the affair was taking, Amparo Barayón's family looked into the possibility of taking legal action against Almendral's granddaughter. They were told that, according to article 18 of the Constitution, it would be considered in the context of the right to honor, either as a criminal lawsuit after taking legal action for the crime of libel, or as a civil lawsuit seeking protection of the right to honor through a Grand Jury, which is the normal procedure, initiated by filing a suit signed by a barrister and a solicitor. But in spite of the fact that this would be the ideal solution and what they wanted, the family did not feel they were capable of going through with it: their geographical dispersion – especially in the case of Amparo's children who were thousands of miles away – and the fact that they could not rely on a single family member in Zamora – dissuaded them from pursuing this course.

What Amparo's children did do, thinking it might have some effect, was to send a letter to Dalmiro Gavilán, editor-in-chief of the newspaper's opinion section, in which they asked him to act as intermediary between them and Almendral Opperman, whom they asked for a retraction. They even sent her a sample that she could use:

To Srta. Anabel Almendral:
It seems to us that there should be a civilized way to resolve this matter without having to take some sort of legal action. We understand, of course, that it may be possible you heard this story about syphilis from your grandfather or some other family member and are simply repeating what they told you.
Nevertheless, since there is no truth to this defamation and since it a serious offense to the memory of our mother, who died guiltless at the hands of hired assassins, we must ask you with all sincerity to make a public retraction. This retraction should consist of the following text and be published in "*La Opinión de Zamora*:"

*"After further reflection and having become aware of
new information about Amparo Barayón Miguel's sit-
uation during her incarceration in Zamora in 1936,
I have decided to reconsider my words published in
"La Opinión de Zamora" in July 2004, regarding any
possible illness suffered by Amparo Barayón Miguel.
Given the harsh conditions under which the incarcerated
women were living, it is possible that my grandfather,
Dr. Almendral, may have either misdiagnosed Amparo
Barayón or confused her with someone else.
I understand that Amparo could in no way have been
suffering from the last stages of a disease as infectious
as syphilis without her children manifesting some sort of
symptoms. Bearing in mind that they never showed said
symptoms at that time, nor during the entire course of
their lives (according to their own testimonies and those
of acquaintances), and having looked through the testimonies of several women who were incarcerated with
their mother – cited in her son's book – I realize that
my information was incorrect. I pass on my sincerest
apologies to the Barayón and Sender families for
allowing such a declaration to appear in a public
newspaper, and I hope that, with this correction, the
matter can be considered resolved."
Signed: Anabel Almendral*

This declaration will serve to satisfy Amparo's family,
which honors a brave woman who was illegally arrested,
incarcerated under terrible conditions and assassinated
simply for being the wife of a well known radical writer.
Her children hope you can publish this retraction so they
will not be compelled to take other public measures that
will only serve to revive memories that are painful for all
of us. Peace and justice is our primary objective.

Signed by Ramón and Benedicta
[Andrea Sender Barayón] as direct descendants

Naturally, nothing came of it. Ana Isabel Almendral had said what
she wanted to say, disappeared from Zamora and did not make any more
public statements on the matter. It is the newspaper and the chronicler

who exploit the situation, each for their own interests, while Amparo Barayón's family and their friends seek compensation and the restoration of Amparo's honor. All to no avail. On the contrary: the chronicler Mateos takes advantage of the situation to attack Ramón Sender's book and those who told him what had happened in Zamora. Each of Mateos' articles constitutes a warning that he is the one who knows the most about the matter and the only one with the right to speak out. His message, confused but smooth-spoken, is aimed at the same social sector portrayed in Sender's book: do not worry, they cannot prove anything, I have the documents and I will not share them; besides, I will be the one who provides the definitive version in my articles and books. Later, during a conference held in 2006, Miguel Ángel Mateos will disclose "the party materially responsible for Amparo Barayón's assassination." His talk, reported in the press, is not to be missed.

Basically, what was said by the "expert," as the journalist Jesús Hernández defined him in his article in *La Opinión de Zamora* on December 23, was that Amparo Barayón was free to leave Zamora but did not do so, and that she may have "spread rumors," which "perhaps weighed heavily against her." He denied that she was a "dangerous communist," as she was called in a report from the military governor (a document that underscores the governor's character and the style of those who carried out the coup and which allows the chronicler to present himself as the victim's defendant); she was thought to be a "spy" and "in the service of the government in Madrid," which Mateos also denies in a show of clairvoyance; "her assassination was due to decisions that went beyond what was strictly determinative (sic) by the civil governor himself" (?); and finally, the great secret: Amparo Barayón's killer was a certain Martín Mariscal, a sergeant in the Falangist militia. It turns out that Mateos has discovered the document recording Amparo's removal from prison on the night of her assassination with the signature of Mariscal as the one in charge of taking her to the cemetery.

What Miguel Ángel Mateos seems to have forgotten is that the Falangists were merely carrying out the orders of their superiors. What does it matter whether it was Mariscal or anyone else who fired the shot? Besides, Mariscal surely did not operate all by himself. Who told the chronicler that Viloria was not in the group? Maybe Mr. Mateos has the names of the members of the firing squads operating in Zamora in those days. But the story does not end here. Having rescued the family honor of those he wanted to protect, the local chronicler describes the killer's fate. "He had problems in Zamora because of his behavior," we are told. The problem was that he began to charge money in exchange for saving people from the firing squads. Then he fled Zamora and enlisted in the Legion in Toledo where, according to Mateos, another Zamora native heard him recount his activities in Zamora. "It is a fact," Mateos adds, "that he shot most of Zamora's prominent victims," including Amparo Barayón. Word of Mariscal's boasts reached the Legion lieutenant and the Legion imposed justice on him. So the killer paid for his crime and the Zamora bourgeoisie was off the hook. The problem of the repression in Zamora was solved.

And what an evil person Amparo's killer was! According to Mateos, this Mariscal was strong, violent, gruff, profane, bloodthirsty, lacking any ideology – although he adds that "he was in the hard right wing of the Falange" – and had an itchy trigger finger, in other word, "a bloodthirsty psychopath" and "a pervert of limited intelligence" who "used his strength and his Falangist blue shirt to commit outrageous abuses."

Evidently, it is easier to divert attention toward an individual like Mariscal than to point a finger directly at those who were actually responsible for the great massacre carried out in Zamora. Finally, Mateos used the conference to refute a claim that, until then, no one had made: in Dr. Almendral's report "there is nothing about Amparo suffering from any type of disease." This refutation demonstrates that the Zamora chronicler had forgotten that it was not the prison doctor who had defamed Amparo Barayón; it was his granddaughter, in revenge for the book by Amparo's son Ramón.

Afterwards, silence reigned again: Ana Isabel Almendral Oppermann with the affront to her honor avenged, and the Barayón family without hope of restoring theirs. In the middle, *La Opinión de Zamora* and the city's chronicler, undoubtedly satisfied, not so much for having carried out their duty to keep the public informed as for having rescued the Zamora right wing and its sacred legacy.[4]

---

[4] According to Candice Ruiz, investigator of the Republic and of the military coup in Zamora, last year the city government, from a proposal of the Republican Circle, dedicated various streets to people related to the republican experience who were assassinated as a consequence of the uprising, among those the 'Hermanos Barayón.' Nevertheless the local press did not inform who these people were, or what happened to them.

**22**

## COMARCAS
Miércoles, 22 de mayo de 2013

**La Opinión**

El destino de uno de los mayores represores de la Guerra Civil en Zamora

**De republicano a falangista**

El sargento de Milicias, Martín Mariscal, Aragonés de origen, donde fue líder del Partido Republicano Radical, en enero de 1935 llegó a Zamora transformado en un destacado falangista que durante la Guerra Civil exhibió abusos, excesos y violencia. La fotografía pertenece a la colección de Caja España, hoy depositada en la Filmoteca Regional de Castilla y León. Su autor es Pedro Gutiérrez Somoza (Foto Duero).

# Ni un tiro ni una venganza

El acta de defunción demuestra que Martín Mariscal, asesino de Amparo Barayón, no falleció de muerte violenta, como se creía, sino de un cáncer en 1951 y en su casa

**Irene Gómez**

Ni una venganza ni el acatamiento de la orden de un superior militar para liquidarlo. Fue un cáncer de estómago lo que acabó con la vida del falangista Martín Mariscal, autor material de la muerte de Amparo Barayón, la mujer del escritor Ramón J. Sender, y de otros muchos notables de izquierda zamoranos en los primeros meses de la Guerra Civil española. A las 16.00 horas del 31 de julio de 1951, en su casa del número 8 de la calle Eloy Gonzalo de Madrid, acompañado de su mujer, Encarnación, quien le asistió en los últimos momentos de su vida pese a estar separados desde años atrás y a la edad de 65 años, terminaba la vida del funcionario de Correos que tan macabra huella dejó en Zamora.

La partida de defunción desvelada por Manuel González Hernández, un estudioso de El Piñero apasionado por la historia e investigador de la represión en Zamora durante la Guerra Civil, descarta ese final de leyenda de quien fuera uno de los más violentos protagonistas de la represión.

El documento, rescatado del Registro Civil de Madrid en el distrito de Chamberí, desmiente la teoría sostenida por el historiador Miguel Ángel Mateos, según la cual Martín Mariscal habría muerto después de que José Palacios, hijo de Ramón Palacios, de Morales del Vino y una de las víctimas del conocido como «sargento veneno», coincidiera con él en Toledo. Orgulloso de sus crímenes no habría tenido empacho en jactarse de la muerte de Ramón Palacios, así que el hijo habría hablado con el

**El certificado y una carta al ministro de Comunicaciones**

El Registro Civil de Madrid guarda el acta de defunción (izquierda), escrita a mano. Arriba, carta manuscrita de Martín Mariscal en octubre de 34 al ministro de Comunicaciones, César Jalón, recordándole la promesa sobre su traslado. A la derecha, censo de Zamora, donde aparece domiciliado en la calle la Estación número 14.

teniente de la Legión, «quien le garantizó que arreglaría el asunto». Según Mateos caben dos opciones, o que el propio hijo se deshiciera de él, o que unos legionarios lo mataran por orden de su jefe.

Ninguna de las dos teorías se llevaría a término. Martín Mariscal acabó sus días postrado en una cama. «después de una larga y dolorosa enfermedad», precisa Manuel González, doce años después del final de la Guerra Civil.

¿De dónde había llegado semejante personaje tan bronco y sanguinario? Manuel González quería saber quién era ese falangista, protagonista en primer término de los asesinatos de El Piñero, y a quien el historiador Miguel Ángel Mateos adjudicó en 2006 la autoría material del asesinato de Amparo Barayón.

Gregorio Martín Mariscal Hernando había nacido el 12 de marzo de 1886 en la localidad de Bijuesca (Zaragoza) «en el seno de una familia acomodada, religiosa y conservadora». Hijo de Clemente, médico, y Encarnación, ese mismo día es bautizado en la iglesia de San Miguel Arcángel, para trasladarse después con su familia a El Frasno, donde su padre ejercería su profesión médica; allí nace Federico, el segundo hijo, en el año 1887. Dos años después la familia se instala en Morata de Jalón, siempre en la provincia zaragozana, donde la residencia se prolongaría durante 21 años. Mientras Gregorio Martín va creciendo, la familia aumenta con la llegada de Graciano (1889), José Vicente (1891), Laureano (1893), Domingo Jesús (1895) y María del Carmen (1897).

De acuerdo con la investigación de Manuel González, «los Mariscal Hernando intentan dar a sus hijos una extraordinaria formación en el campo de la medicina». Pero Gregorio Martín opta por sacar una plaza como funcionario de Correos, ejerciendo en Calatayud, Ateca y Ricla, «a la vez que hace política local integrado en el ala dura del Partido Republicano Radical, donde ya apunta maneras» y se le relaciona con «las masonerías locales y provinciales».

A la edad de 29 años contrae matrimonio con Pascuala Manuela Lajusticia, de 26, en Calatayud, fijando después su residencia en Ricla, «hasta bien entrados los 30 años». Martín Mariscal prosigue su carrera política alcanzando la presidencia del Partido Republicano Radical en Ateca «sus excesos son bien conocidos en la zona», precisa Manuel González. Pero de 1933 a 1935 el partido presidido por Alejandro Lerroux «sufre la pérdida de muchos afiliados por la corrupción que tienen en sus filas a nivel nacional». Y este declive se deja notar en los dominios del político local que, «sabedor de sus excesos, se siente desprotegido y tiene miedo».

Es entonces cuando, «para sentirse seguro, consigue su traslado a Zamora», donde aparece a principios de 1936 «vistiendo ya uniforme de la Falange con el grado de sargento de milicias». Una metamorfosis a priori inexplicable. Lo cierto es que Martín Mariscal funcionario aparece empadronado a principios de 1936 como vecino de Zamora en la calle de la Estación y después en Víctor Gallego, junto a su mujer y dos sobrinos de esta.

Pasa a la página siguiente

Photo of the assassin Mariscal, from an article by Irene Gomez in Zamora's "La Opinión de Zamora," May 22, 2013.

ANNEX I
DOCUMENTS
*Death in Zamora*: The Tragedy of Amparo Barayón[5]
by Miguel Ángel Mateos
(*"La Opinión de Zamora,"* February 17, 2005)

In *"La Opinión de Zamora"* (February 14, 2005), with understandable delay and bluntness, Amparo Barayón's children responded to Anabel Almendral, that "Amparo was not suffering from syphilis," providing personal information and evidence that deserve the utmost respect and consideration.

Almendral's claim (July 13, 2004) surprised me, although I took it with a grain of salt. Having gone through the relevant documents, which are abundant, I had not read anything to support her claim. In the various reports about Amparo that came to light, all of them hostile since they were intended to justify her assassination (October 11, 1936), not a word is said, nor any comment made, about syphilis. If there had been any truth to Almendral's claim, the chief commissioner of investigation and surveillance – M. P. – who did not mince his words when it came to describing the conduct, affiliations and suspicious activities of political detainees, would, I think, have reported it to the commanding military judge – Juan Losada. For example, in a report referring to Amparo Barayón on March 4, 1937, M. P. writes "that said individual female (sic) was considered a dangerous communist, [...] that her husband Ramón Sender (he should have written Ramón J. Sender), a journalist with the *"El Sol"* company (it was a newspaper) [...] traveled from San Rafael to Madrid on July 18 to cash some checks, [...] that Amparo, along with her children and a servant, came to Zamora and lodged with her brothers, who were also considered dangerous extremists [...]," etc., etc. It is no small feat to commit so many errors in so few words. War propaganda.

In other reports he calls her "an anarchist, a red, a dangerous revolutionary and extremist, a spy, an agent of Moscow and of the International Red Aid Society," and other anathemas in vogue at the time to disqualify the accused.

---

[5] Miguel Angel Mateos published eight articles about this affair between February and April, 2005. Here only the first one will be published. Those interested can find the others in the "La Opinión de Zamora's" library..

But neither in the records of the provincial jail – see her prison file – in which the military governor Hernández Comes writes: "Be so kind as to admit and hold at the disposition of my authority in the establishment under your supervision Amparo Barayón Miguel, twenty nine years of age, single (obviously only in the eyes of the church in the nationalist zone where civil marriages were not recognized), black hair, also black eyebrows, regular nose and mouth, round face, healthy in appearance and coloration, tall of stature, by profession: employee of the Ministry of Agriculture residing in Madrid, Menéndez Pelayo St., 41..."

Nor in the report from the jail's infirmary, where files were kept, nor in the chaplain's report have we found the faintest clue. Amparo Barayón was so degradingly slandered and vilified that I think if they had been aware of the alleged illness, it would have been reflected in the reports in order to further tarnish the memory of this poor and unhappy woman, who was known to be an enthusiastic catechist at the church of San Juan. Anabel Almendral's allegation could be considered a slanderous rumor but would never, in the eyes of the law, rise to the level of libel, as Amparo Barayón's children write in their response. Anabel's information must have come from oral sources connected to the Almendral family and professional circles, but it does not seem to be backed up by any clinical, official or unofficial documents.

If there is any proof, let us see it and, if not, it seems only fair to retract the statement. Even if it were true, no harm would be done by such a retraction. The worst part is that it is not true. Idle chatter over drinks at a bar or the confessions of a repentant Mary Magdalene need to be examined carefully and fact checked. If not, an esteemed academic professional should not lower herself to fueling false rumors worthy of gossip circles. Otherwise, she lowers herself to the same level as Ramón J. Sender Barayón when he makes accusations against his own uncle Miguel Sevilla, against Hernández Comes – whom he repeatedly and erroneously calls Claomarchirant (sic) on several occasions – against Segundo Viloria, against many members of the Barayón family, against his own father, and against many others, based on unsupported, imagined and erratic information from dubious and weak oral sources far removed from the events he is narrating, even if it is unreasonable to doubt the good intentions of those he interviewed.

Consequently, if *Muerte en Zamora* is intended as historical fiction, the product of the author's fantasies and inventiveness, he is quite at liberty to write it. Its merit would depend upon his eloquence. But if what is intended is to narrate and preserve for posterity real events involving specific people to whom he attributes explicit responsibility for certain actions, and especially in relation to such a complex, subjective and contentious matter as the Spanish Civil War, the most exhaustive, contextualized and profoundly analyzed information possible is required.

I understand Ramón J. Sender Barayón. He needs an explanation and cannot understand the tragic and, from any perspective, unjust death of his innocent and grief-stricken mother. But I cannot approve most of what is written in his book, because it does not conform to the events as known and documented, either orally or in writing.

I also understand Dr. Pedro Almendral, if in fact it was he who passed on the unfounded rumor – he could not have been the source– that Amparo Barayón "was terribly ill from syphilis." Anabel's grandfather was an old style liberal and a follower of Santiago Alba Bonifaz. He was almost lynched outside the San Martín Workers' Center when he was falsely accused of negligence in the death of "El Pelao" in May 1936. They had forgotten that "El Pelao" had been treated, with due diligence and competence, by Dacio Crespo, according to the medical report. Almendral was also accused of carelessness in his treatment of a worker affiliated with the Socialist Party at the Zamora Clinic.

If Dr. Félix Valbuena Artolozábal had not hastened to protect him, Almendral's life would have been in serious danger. There are documents to prove it. After the coup, Almendral advised the famous humanitarian doctor Felipe Anciones to flee Zamora and go into hiding because he was about to be arrested. Later, Almendral begged the governor to spare Anciones's life. Given the outcome, Pedro Almendral did not seem to have much influence with those brought to power by the coup. Being an old style Albist liberal, he did not have the best of credentials for interceding on behalf of anyone.

Nevertheless, until Anabel Almendral provides evidence, I cannot approve her unfortunate and highly debatable assertions about something that happened almost seventy years ago, assertions that do not rise above the level of idle gossip.

The best way to understand and comprehend our controversial un-civil war today is to study it rigorously until the existent documentation is exhausted. Hiding one's head in the sand, refusing to speak or write about it, as some would prefer, only serves to encourage rumors,

slander and errors which, in my opinion, are harmful to many families' reputations. As Ricardo de la Cierva said, "To think we can arrive at the truth strikes us as unlikely, and the whole truth, impossible."
Miguel Ángel Mateos
(*La Opinión de Zamora,* February 17, 2005)

Truths Large and Small
by Paul Preston
(*La Opinión de Zamora,* April 10, 2005)
I have read with great interest the seven articles written by Miguel Ángel Mateos about the repression in Zamora in general and about the cases of Amparo Barayón and Pilar Fidalgo in particular. As might be expected of the city's official chronicler, the articles contain many details that would otherwise never have seen the light of day. For that, we owe him our thanks.

Nevertheless, there are aspects of his articles that seem to me unworthy of both Miguel Ángel Mateos and of "*La Opinión de Zamora.*" I am referring to the venom with which he tries to discredit the book by Ramón Sender Barayón and the sarcasm he uses to diminish the value of Pilar Fidalgo's testimony, which he does by mocking her ignorance of documents that have become available only half a century after the events she describes. With regard to the book by Ramón Sender Barayón, and referring to a previous letter published in "*La Opinión,*" he writes "I imagine that its signatories, the historians who have written in favor of the book, especially Professor Preston, have not read it. I am sure they have signed like those who used to sign manifestos without having read them.

Well, I have read the book. I am not in the habit of signing in the dark. I also happen to know that the historians Helen Graham and Francisco Espinosa Maestre have read it. I know because I have discussed it in detail with both of them. It is possible, even probable, that the book by Sender Barayón might contain minor errors of detail. The nuances and corrections made by Señor Mateos in this regard are certainly valuable. However, this does not detract from the reality that, by placing on the agenda his mother's death, Pilar Fidalgo's imprisonment and mistreatment, and the many assassinations that took place during the repression in Zamora, Sender Barayón has done a great service to the history of the period. There are truths large and small. In other words, it is possible to recount a big overarching truth without necessarily having all the minute details correct. In fact, the valuable information being published by Señor Mateos is appearing only now because he has decided to reply to Sender Barayón's book, and has done so only after a delay of nearly fifteen years. It is almost as if Señor Mateos feels offended that Sender Barayón had dared to trespass onto what, as the official chronicler, he regards as his private reserve.

Throughout his articles, *Señor* Mateos has manifested a commitment to precision, even to the point of demanding it of those who have not had the same opportunities he has had to examine more recently available sources. Given this obsession with exactitude, it is difficult not to be startled by the sheer anti historical nature of Señor Mateos' statement that "If the military coup had not failed and there had not been a war, there would certainly have been no repression and no firing squads. Thus, it is only after July 25, when the armed conflict started, that there are the first executions, committed either by uncontrollable elements or elements remotely controlled from afar."

Can this possibly mean that *Señor* Mateos is unaware of the secret instructions issued in April 1936 by the director of the military conspiracy, General Emilio Mola, and which were published in 1939? Mola stated "It has to be born in mind that the action has to be violent in the extreme so as to subdue as soon as possible the enemy which is strong and well organized. It goes without saying that all leaders of political parties, societies and trade unions not part of the movement will be imprisoned and exemplary punishment carried out on them in order to choke off any rebellion or strikes." Is it possible that Señor Mateos does not know that there was a fierce repression in Valladolid, in Seville, in Huelva, in Cádiz and many other provinces before July 25? Is it possible that *Señor* Mateos is unaware of what happened in Ceuta and Melilla on July 17, immediately after the coup?

I said earlier that there are truths large and small and, by the same token, there are errors large and small. So let us overlook the fact that *Señor* Mateos refers to Señora Mercedes Esteban Maes as "*el Señor* Esteban Maes Barayón" or that he refers to the "book" by Pilar Fidalgo when no such book exists, but only fewer than twenty pages based on statements by her, published in the French press and in a short English pamphlet. It is necessary to show some understanding when reading things and to judge them with sensitivity, recognizing what is of value in each book or article. For that reason, it is possible to see beyond his mistakes and the gratuitous sarcasm of his tone and recognize the merit in his work.

Paul Preston

(*La Opinión de Zamora*, April 10, 2005)

Extrajudicial Deaths

by Ramón Sender Barayón

(*La Opinión de Zamora*, April 10, 2005)

Here in the United States, writers who receive negative reviews are told: "Count the number of words they write about you and thank them." Bearing this in mind, I ought to thank Mr. M. A. Mateos profusely for his series of long articles. Regarding the historical errors he points out, I sincerely wish he had been able to help me during the two trips I took to Zamora in the 1980s to investigate the events that led to my mother's assassination.

I am not a historian, and when I traveled to Zamora, I hardly understood Spanish, although I could rely on the help of my wife Judith, who did speak it. The only documents I had access to were my mother's birth certificate and baptismal record, and a fraudulent death certificate. Since the only sources at my disposal were the interviews I conducted with people who, during almost forty years, had been unable to talk for fear of losing their own freedom – or even their lives – I think my attempt to tell my mother's story deserves some recognition. If it has served no other purpose, my book is at least a reminder to the citizens of Zamora that they ought to acknowledge the thousands of extrajudicial deaths that took place, tacitly approved by those in power. In his attempt to correct my errors, it is possible that Mr. Mateos has done us all a favor by drawing our attention to the documents now available for consultation, and by awakening the public's conscience to the fact that, to date, nothing has been done in Zamora to commemorate publicly the many women who were brutally incarcerated and dragged out in the darkness of night to be shot in such a cruel fashion that it would be inappropriate to describe it here. Although Mr. Mateos alludes to similar assassinations that took place in the Republican zone, I do not believe that excuses the enormity of the extrajudicial deaths that took place in the areas occupied by those who carried out the coup, especially in Zamora.

Personally, I always feel grateful whenever Amparo's story is told with ever greater truth. I will always be grateful to Pilar Fidalgo Carasa for her testimony. Any errors to be found in her declarations to the Spanish Consul should be attributed to the brutal treatment from which she had just escaped.

Ramón Sender Barayón
(*La Opinión de Zamora*, April 10, 2005)

About Amparo Barayón's Assassination
by Francisco Espinosa Maestre
(*La Opinión de Zamora*, April 13, 2005)

For the past several weeks I have been following what M. A. Mateos is doing with his articles. It is worth recalling the beginning of the affair: last summer Dr. Almendral's granddaughter took advantage of an interview in this newspaper to launch an inappropriate attack on the memory of Amparo Barayón, assassinated along with two of her brothers in 1936. In order to spread the false rumor that Amparo was suffering from syphilis, the doctor's granddaughter had to distort and misrepresent Pilar Fidalgo's recollections of her imprisonment. And it was when Amparo Barayón's family reacted to this slander that Mateos entered the fray. At first he pretended he was not taking sides and, to prove his impartiality, proposed that if Anabel Almendral could not back up her claim, she should make a retraction. But from the person in question, not a word.

Then, as if he were on the same relay team as Almendral, he takes up the baton and begins ridiculing Pilar Fidalgo's testimony and Ramón Sender Barayón's book. With the crudest devices as his only recourse, Mateos attacks them both. The trick he employs consists of presenting their testimonies as if they were works of history. For Mateos, Pilar Fidalgo's personal recollections of her passage through the Zamora prison are worthless and the same goes for Ramón Sender's inquiries into his mother's final days. They are a series of errors and falsehoods. He is the one who knows, his sources are all valid and, furthermore, he has all the information. For several weeks now, article after article, he goes on utilizing memory in the service of righteousness, unlike everyone else.

The last thing he has told us is that the guilty party in Amparo Barayón's death is Ramón J. Sender for sending her to the slaughterhouse. This was to be expected. But he takes it even further. However often he calls her that "exquisite, unhappy woman," that "innocent, suffering mother," or that "good and worthy lady," as if writing a melodrama, he is not at all credible and the suspicion floats through his writing that she herself was responsible for her tragedy when she insulted the civil governor brought to power by the coup. After all, what did she have to complain about? All they had done was murder her brother. In fact, other than attacking Fidalgo and Sender's writings, the only thing Mateos has accomplished since he entered the fray, despite his obfuscations and dissimulations, is to blame Ramón J. Sender for his wife's assassination and exonerate fascists, paramilitary forces, hired killers and priests at the service of the military coup. His conclusion is that if the coup had triumphed everywhere, there would not have been a repression. That must be why, wherever it succeeded, the top priority was respect for life. Like in Zamora. As someone has said, history, conveniently utilized, can become the most powerful narcotic of our times.

Francisco Espinosa Maestre
(*La Opinión de Zamora*, April 13, 2005)

To the Historian Mateos
by Antonio Viloria
(*La Opinión de Zamora*, April 16, 2005)

We must recognize the importance of stressing the time period during which the action of a drama takes place. This is true for all types of dramas, but especially for the crimes committed during our Civil War. As if following a serialized novel, I have anxiously awaited each of your articles in this newspaper, which would bring me closer to the *dénouement*, no less tragic for being known beforehand. These are legitimate strategies used by schoolteachers to hold their students' attention. But here such devices were not necessary, because "our war" has marked us with fiery scars and, when evoked, summons images, situations and characters vaguely remembered that form a part of our collective memory. We even share last names with some of them. The whole drama is cloaked in a panicky vertigo where one perceives the horror of the hunted prey and the snuffing out of lives as hidden hatreds are unleashed and scores are settled in the shadow of cemetery walls. It is praiseworthy that there are professionals who deal with the spoils of death. For that reason, we owe them our admiration. But, oh, the investigation of death at close quarters demands the utmost respect!

That is why I have taken it upon myself to write this note because, in my opinion, Mr. Mateos' history of Zamora reveals a lack of historical rigor when he makes assertions, that are not supported by facts as they should be and are written in a style of devastating certainty, about the direct participation of one of my relatives in Consuelo [sic] Barayón's death. Since the work was published, I have held my tongue for years, in spite of the convictions and opinions of some historians that such a condemnation does not conform to the truth. Now, with the publication of Miguel Ángel Mateos' articles in "*La Opinión de Zamora*," my suspicion that the blunt assertions in his history of Zamora are untrue is confirmed. It is the typical plotting of a drama, with good guys and bad guys, and roles assigned by the new demiurge, who interprets events to suit his purposes. Is it not frivolous to issue blunt assertions that fall apart under the first serious scrutiny? It makes one doubt his scientific rigor. Because how can events be reinterpreted in this way without providing the necessary evidence?

He skims superficially over reality, picking the characters he needs and assigning each of them a role. Is it not arrogant, and an attack on public harmony, to air controversial issues and emit verdicts of guilt to third parties who had nothing to do with that tragedy? But, as has been pointed out by other readers of this newspaper, we can expect no less from someone who continually disparages the assertions of those who do not share his opinions. As if that were not enough, M. A. Mateos takes the liberty of interpreting the behavior of a person close to me with apparent benevolence, along the line of "good lad who kept bad counsel, etc." Leave it alone and stop stirring up dirt.

Antonio Viloria
(*La Opinión de Zamora*, April 16, 2005)

A Family's Sensibilities (Reflections for Don Miguel Ángel Mateos)
by Fernando Maes Arjona Barayón,
Castellanos de Moriscos, Salamanca
(*La Opinión de Zamora*, April 19, 2005)
I am sitting at my word processor with a book in my hand, *Muerte en Zamora*. I have opened it to the central pages and gaze at the photograph of the Maes Barayón family. I am the little one to the left, the one who looks like he wants to put his finger up his nose. I am looking at my grandmother Magdalena and, now that I have reread the book, I understand why she was always so sad. Mr. Mateos, as Mr. Preston put it so well, there are truths large and small.

I am going to tell you how I became aware of the existence of the writer Ramón J. Sender. It was at my school run by missionaries of the Claretan order on the day we studied this author in our literature class. *Srta.* Lourdes, who knew my family, called on me to tell my classmates about him. I could not say anything because I knew nothing about him. With this anecdote I want to tell you that there are families that have suffered so much that they do not want to involve even their closest relatives in that suffering. They only want to forget.

*Muerte en Zamora* is a book of great sensibility, a son's homage to the mother he barely knew. It is a book that does not deserve your detailed clarifications. I do not know History but I see my father's eyes in the photograph and, this morning, I do not like the way they look. We all know that in any war, people who lose their sons, daughters, brothers, sisters, or spouses suffer, and suffering does not differentiate between winners and losers but, if such a thing is possible, the suffering of the losers is greater. Believe me Mr. Mateos when I say that the history in seven installments that you have published in this newspaper has done nothing but reawaken memories in people with no desire to remember. I ask you, please, save this harsh and objective history, with its detailed clarification, told – pardon the expression – in such a pedantic fashion, for your classroom. Without a doubt, your pupils will be the winners.

Fernando Maes Arjona Barayón,
Castellanos de Moriscos, Salamanca
(*La Opinión de Zamora*, April 19, 2005)

A Little Seriousness, Mr. Mateos
by Saturnina Lorenzo García,
Toro (*La Opinión de Zamora*, April 20, 2005)

I have read with great interest the controversy provoked by the inopportune declarations about Amparo Barayón by one of Dr. Almendral's descendants. Since Amparo Barayón is dead and could not defend herself, her family has come forward to defend her from the attacks on her personal dignity, a totally proper response. We all know, even you, that Amparo Barayón was assassinated. She did not die from an illness. The proper thing would have been for Dr. Almendral's descendant to retract what she said and apologize; she did not do so and we are not going to oblige her to. Let her be. The regrettable part is that you, a sensible person, are determined to find errors in the book that Sender

Barayón wrote about his mother and, day after day, turn out articles on the same subject so incessantly that it has become tiresome.

You say that Sender Barayón got information for his book *Muerte en Zamora* by interviewing people whose responses may have been somewhat influenced by the personal situation of someone interviewed in your book *La República in Zamora*, volume I, page 695, section 4, Oral Sources, where you list a series of people you interviewed. If you use interviews as a source of information, why is it that Sender Barayón is not allowed to do the same? You are not being serious don Miguel Ángel. You have other sources of information which, by the way, are less reliable than personal interviews. You know as well as I do that a good part of the documentation related to the Civil War is falsified. Besides, perhaps –I do not know– Sender Barayón did not have access to documentary sources and therefore got his information from people. It is wrong to censure him for that.

I do not doubt your merits as a historian and I admire your capacity for work, but I advise you to be humble enough to accept the opinions of other historians, some of whom are specialists in the Spanish Civil War, like those who signed one of the letters from the Sender Barayón family. Take my word for it, don Miguel Ángel Mateos Rodríguez, only God is omniscient. We poor mortals only possess some part of the truth. We will only arrive at the whole truth if each of us contributes that small part we possess. To claim that my truth alone is valid and disqualify others' share of the truth is pride, and I remind you that God rejects the proud.

Saturnina Lorenzo García,

Toro (*La Opinión de Zamora*, April 20, 2005)

## ANNEX II

Toward the end of August 1936, while Lieutenant Colonel José Redondo, Commander Gervasio Fernández Noaín and Captain Juan Rodríguez Guillén were at the Civil Guard barracks in Zamora, a delegation arrived from Villalpando consisting of, among others, the mayor (Maximiliano Peláez Blanco), the doctor, Tonanzos, and the judge, Juan Esteban Romera. The purpose of their visit was to request that the Civil Guard corporal, whose last name was San Román, be relieved of duty "because he was afraid and, according to them, did not dare to operate energetically in the events unfolding in the town." According to the captain's declarations months later, the judge was the principal spokesman during the meeting. Besides reminding them that the corporal could not be held responsible since there was a line officer there, Lieutenant Colonel Redondo asked them to submit their complaint in writing, which the members of the delegation refused to do.

What we know is that a few days later the Zamora civil governor ordered the governmental delegate to pay a visit to Villalpando with his patrol. This delegate was Sergeant Luis Valera Nieves, better known as "Sergeant Poison," whose duties since July 18 until mid October 1936, were "to arrest individuals who had stood out for their opposition to the aforementioned Movement and for their extremist ideas, and to adopt and carry out with respect to those individuals whatever measures he deemed advisable and fitting."

The day "Sergeant Poison" approached Villalpando, his patrol consisted of the lawyer Segundo Viloria, Julio Gómez, Carlos Gómez and the *requeté* Domingo Gómez. The objective, since according to the aforementioned complaint, "there were leftist elements in said town who were considered undesirables and that it was necessary to remove them from the town," was the following:

To arrest the individuals of said town who had stood out as extremists and opponents of the Movement, with orders to the effect that all those who had taken up arms against the Civil Guard or armed forces be left dead in the cemetery of the aforementioned town.

The patrol arrived that morning in the town, where it was met by the mayor, the judge and the other members of the delegation, who put themselves at the patrol's disposal and proceeded to draw up a list of those who should be arrested. Those on the list were taken to the barracks that afternoon, in the presence of Corporal San Román and the line officer. As they were arriving, "Sergeant Poison" made inquiries to find out if they should be taken to Zamora or directly to the cemetery wall. It was precisely when the two groups of prisoners were halfway formed that the judge, Esteban, who was standing guard at the barracks door, came in and said "that he could not consent to any of those arrested being taken to Zamora or executed because that would lead to an uprising of all the townsfolk against said judge and the other local authorities, who would be blamed for said arrests and executions."

Then, Sergeant Valera telephoned the civil governor, who, apprised of the situation, ordered that "only the most rebellious be taken and that the rest be set free." Meanwhile, Judge Esteban, somewhat out of control, called Corporal San Román a coward and a liar in the presence of the mayor, Valera, the line officer, and Viloria. In his report, Valera maintained that the judge's behavior "was not due to the judge's anti-patriotic sentiments or directed at the National Movement but, on the contrary, due only to said gentleman's kindness, his desire to avoid bloodshed in the town, and the fact that he and other members of the town's authorities would be blamed for what happened because it was they who went to the provincial government to report on those who were under arrest." Valera also recalled that, during that day, the judge "was very adamant about carrying out the aforementioned arrests and executions of persons who deserved it." For which reason he says it is possible that the judge's change of mind was influenced by the fact that, when the moment arrived to take the prisoners away, the area around the barracks was so crowded with people that the Civil Guard had to clear the nearest stretch of highway.

These statements about the incident in Villalpando are from the investigation to remove Judge Juan Esteban Romera from his post. They are statements by Captain Rodriguez Guillén and Sergeant Juan Valera Nieves, both taken the 16th of November, 1936.

## Acknowledgments

I wish to thank the National Endowment for the Arts for making possible the completion of this book. Also I wish to give my heartfelt thanks to the following: Kim Chernin for her warm encouragement and editorial advice; my American mother Julia Davis for a line-by-line edit of the first draft; Peter N. Carroll for his help on a final restructuring; above all, my wife Judith Levy-Sender whose fluency in the language and personal warmth made contacts with my Spanish family easy and understandable.

I wish to acknowledge the collaboration of Fernando Primo Martínez in Zamora in conducting interviews and researching addresses of informants. Also, I would like to thank friends of my mother and my Spanish relatives who gave unstintingly of their time, especially my aunt Concha Sender Garcés whose detailed recollections did so much to make this book possible, my cousins Magdalena and Melchora Maes Barayón for their unswerving loyalty to Amparo's memory, and cousin Mercedes Esteban Maes-Kemp who corrected some translations – and subsequently translated the book for both Spanish editions. My first stepmother, Elizabeth Sauzon, my aunt Marcelle, my mother's sister, Eugenia, contributed vital details.

Dionisia Diaz Cortes' children and her cousin María, my childhood friends Maruchi and Pepi Rivera, all added important information as well as Amparo's piano student María Uria. For details of prison conditions in Zamora, I am indebted to Palmira Sanjuan, Leonor Martínez Robles and to Pilar Fidalgo Carasa as well as Dionisio Heredero. So many of my Spanish family assisted us that it is impossible to name them all here. All I can do is offer my sincere thanks for their collaboration and their warm inclusion of me once more into their lives.

All royalties from this edition will be donated to The Association for the Recovery of Historical Memory – *Asociación para la Recuperación de la Memoria Histórica* (ARMH), a Spanish organization that collects oral and written testimonies about the White Terror of Francisco Franco, and excavates and identifies the bodies often dumped in mass graves.

## Bibliography

Julia Davis. *The Sun Climbs Slow*, E. P. Dutton & Co. Inc., New York, 1942. A fictional treatment of our arrival in Julia's life, although many of the scenes with the children are accurate portrayals.

Pilar Fidalgo. "A Young Mother In Franco's Prisons," United Editorial Ltd., London, 1939. A major source of information on the conditions in the women's cell in Zamora. The Southworth Collection at the University of California, San Diego, has a copy.

Pilar Fidalgo. "Nine Months In The Hands Of The Fascists, A Personal Testimony," *"El Socialista,"* May 20, 21, 22, 1937, Madrid. Testimony Pilar Fidalgo gave before the Spanish consul in Bayonne shortly after she was repatriated from Zamora.

Enrique Lister. *Nuestra Guerra*, Colección Ebro, Editions de la Librairie du Globe, Paris, 1966. Lister's colorful autobiography as the communist ironworker who evolved into one of the Republic's top military leaders during the civil war. I quote his opinion of Ramón J. Sender.

Joaquín Maurín. Letter to Ramón J. Sender, from the large collection of Maurín/Sender correspondence in the Archives of The Hoover Institute, Palo Alto.

Ramón J. Sender. "Letters to Joaquín Maurín," Archives of The Hoover Institute, Palo Alto.

Ramón J. Sender. *Los Cinco Libros De Ariadne*, Ediciones Destino, Barcelona, 1977. My father always referred to this novel when I asked him for details of Amparo's childhood. I have translated selections that seemed appropriate. Also it contained important information about their last hours together in San Rafael.

Ramón J. Sender. *Selecciones De Poesia Lirica Y Aforistica*, bilingual edition with translations by Florence Talamantes, El Sol de California, San Diego, 1979. His sonnet to Amparo is quoted.

Ramón J. Sender. *Seven Red Sundays*, Liveright Publishing Co., New York, 1936. An early novel set during a proletarian uprising in Madrid. It recounts the tale of Amparo's placing of a bomb in the telephone building.

Ramón J. Sender. *The War In Spain*, Faber & Faber Ltd. London, 1937 *Counterattack In Spain* in the American edition, Houghton Mifflin Company, Boston, 1937. An autobiographical account of the author's activities during the first six months of the civil war. I have utilized it as a source for the chapter on my father.

## Suggested Readings on The Spanish Civil War

Arturo Barea. *The Forging Of A Rebel*, David-Poynter Ltd., London, 1972.

Frederick Benson. *Writers In Arms*, New York University Press, New York, 1967.

Claude G. Bowers. *My Mission To Spain*, Simon & Schuster, New York, 1954.

Ronald Fraser. *The Blood Of Spain, An Oral History Of The Spanish Civil War*, Pantheon Books, New York, 1979.

Helen Graham. *The Spanish Republic at War 1936-1939*, Cambridge University Press; 2003

Helen Graham. *A Very Short History of The Spanish Civil War,* Oxford University Press; 2005

George Hills. *The Battle For Madrid*, St. Martin's Press, New York, 1977

Gabriel Jackson. *The Spanish Republic & The Civil War*, Princeton University Press, 1965.

Dan Kurzman. *Miracle Of November, Madrid's Epic Stand*, G. T. Putnam's Sons, New York, 1980.

Francisco Espinosa Maestre, Richard Barker, translator. *Shoot the Messenger?: Spanish Democracy and the Crimes of Francoism: From the Pact of Silence to the Trial of Baltasar Garzon* (Canada Blanch / Sussex Academic Studies on Contemporary Spain) 2013

Soledad Fox Maura. *Connie:* Biografía de Constancia de la Mora, 2017

Constancia de la Mora. *In Place of Splendor: The Autobiography of a Spanish Woman, 1939*

Paul Preston. *The Spanish Holocaust: Inquisition and Extermination in Twentieth-Century Spain*, 2013

Robert A. Rosenstone. *Crusade On The Left*, Pegasus, New York, 1969.

Hugh Thomas. *The Spanish Civil War*, Harper & Row, Revised & Enlarged Edition, New York, 1977.